# CHANGING THE SUBJECT

# CHANGING THE SUBJECT

*Philosophy from Socrates to Adorno*

RAYMOND GEUSS

Harvard University Press

CAMBRIDGE, MASSACHUSETTS
LONDON, ENGLAND | 2017

*Library of Congress Cataloging-in-Publication Data*
Names: Geuss, Raymond, author.
Title: Changing the subject : philosophy from Socrates to Adorno / Raymond Geuss.
Description: Cambridge, Massachusetts : Harvard University Press, 2017. |
Includes bibliographical references and index.
Identifiers: LCCN 2017010499 | ISBN 9780674545724 (alk. paper)
Subjects: LCSH: Reasoning. | Questioning. | Philosophy—History.
Classification: LCC BC177 .G48 2017 | DDC 100—dc23
LC record available at https://lccn.loc.gov/2017010499

*hilaritatis causa*

*Endlich!*
*Die Freiheit!*
*Die Harpunen fliegen.*

*Der Regenbogen lagert in den Straßen*
*Nur noch vom fernen Summen der Riesenbienen unterhöhlt.*

*Alle verlieren alles, das sie, ach wie oft,*
*vergeblich überflogen hatte. . . .*


At last!
Freedom!
The harpoons fly.

The rainbow is stockpiled
In the streets
Only hollowed out from below
By the distant humming of huge bees

Anything that had ever flown,
oh how often, in vain, over anyone:
everyone loses all of that.

—MERET OPPENHEIM, *Husch, husch, der schönste Vokal entleert sich* (1933)

# CONTENTS

*Preface*                        *xi*

*Note on Sources*                *xix*

Introduction                     1

*One:*    Socrates              13

*Two:*    Plato                 46

*Three:*  Lucretius             72

*Four:*   Augustine             93

*Five:*   Montaigne             115

*Six:*    Hobbes                138

*Seven:*  Hegel                 157

CONTENTS

*Eight:* Nietzsche 181

*Nine:* Lukács 200

*Ten:* Heidegger 226

*Eleven:* Wittgenstein 250

*Twelve:* Adorno 274

Conclusion 294

*Notes* 305

*Further Reading* 317

*Index* 325

# PREFACE

One of the most striking images in all of literature, including all philosophical literature, is to be found in book VII of Plato's *Republic*. In an underground cave, prisoners are chained up with their backs to a source of light. They have been this way all their lives from birth, and they pass the time looking at the shadows that are cast on the walls in front of their eyes. These shadows appear, flicker, coalesce, dissolve and melt away, and (sometimes) reappear, and (from time to time) they form certain more or less regular patterns; they sometimes succeed one another at random, but at other times they seem to exhibit some kind of order. Some prisoners become adept at mapping the sequences of shadows, to the limited extent to which any regularity at all is discernible in their appearances and disappearances; common sense is the name given to the skill they have learned to develop in studying this play of shadows.

Suppose, Plato suggests, someone were to free some of these prisoners, turn them around, force them to face the light, and show them the objects that threw the shadows which they had spent their lives watching. Plato says they would be dazzled, blinded, and distressed. Yet the pain and disorientation of this reversal, which destroys their hard-acquired common sense, is a necessary concomitant of the process of coming to a real understanding of the world in which they live. Eventually—but that 'eventually' could designate a very considerable amount of time—the liberated prisoners might learn to understand the play of shadows even better than those who had never been freed, because they might be able to acquire some knowledge of the real objects themselves that threw the shadows. If they then continued to take the shadows seriously at all, it would be as the effects of something else, not as substantive entities important and causally efficacious in their own right—except in so far as their deluded flickering might move the prisoners who always had been and still were in chains to one form of belief or speech rather than another.

To take an example from our political life, the 'shadows' are a bit like modern rights discourse. Saddam Hussein gasses his own population in the 1980s and the United States pats him on the back and gives him weapons: he is an important ally. Suddenly in the 1990s he makes himself a nuisance, and people 'discover' that he has been violating the human rights of his own citizens, and so his country is invaded. After the second invasion of what is, after all, a purportedly 'sovereign' state and recognised member of various international organisations, carried out against the will of the UN Security Council, the US commander in charge of the forces occupying Iraq sternly warns Iran not to violate international law by interfering in the 'internal affairs' of Iraq because it is a sovereign country. 'Human rights' are *presented* by those who appeal to them as if they were a powerful and coherent body of principles that are to govern what happens. However, if one simply studies the way they function in real political contexts, one will never get anywhere;

trying to find any continuing, reliable rhyme, reason, consistency, or substance in appeals to 'human rights' *at this level of analysis* is clearly a mug's game. Some people think that behind these shadows there stands the normative reality of Law or an ideal budget of Human Rights which it is the philosopher's task to reveal. Blessed are they who, even though they have not seen, yet do they believe. Others think that, to change the image, the philosophers' Natural Law, or Human Rights, are, as it were, shadows of shadows—that they are not substantive reality but a hallucination of people who have spent too much of their time watching shadows, and that understanding, if not exactly 'reality', is to be found elsewhere. In either case, no one thinks that understanding is to be gained by simply cultivating our skill at classifying and mapping these shadows. One way or the other one has to change the subject to make any progress. Either one needs an ideal theory of Human Rights/Natural Law etc. or one needs another kind of theory of how humans act and speak, which also does not take their mere professions completely at face value. It might not be clear which of the proposed new mappings deserves to be taken most seriously, but all of them are, each in its own way, attempts to construct something that is the opposite of common sense: in any case one is in some sense changing the subject. That is what—or, at any rate, that is one thing that—philosophy has been.

This book arose as a result of the accidental conjunction of two very different things. First, in 2010 one of the managers of Heffers Bookshop in Cambridge, England, asked some academics from different disciplines at Cambridge University to put together a list of the ten most interesting books in their respective areas, not the ten that had historically been most influential or the ten currently most generally popular or most highly regarded by current advanced practitioners or the ten that showed the highest degree of literary polish or were pedagogically most useful, but the ten that would, simply, most repay serious study because they had something inherently important to say. As a particularly good customer of the shop, I was asked to put together such a list for 'philosophy'. One further requirement Heffers imposed was that there should be only one work by any given author, which turned out to be a very helpful practical limitation, if only because it prevented me from even being tempted simply to list five or six dialogues by Plato. The limitation to ten items also turned out to be a useful intellectual discipline in a number of ways: my first few trials at putting together a list were complete failures because, I eventually realised, I was still allowing myself to be influenced by exactly the kinds of considerations that I was being asked to ignore. I was still being guided by the general reputation of the philosopher in question, by questions of historical influence and of centrality to the existing discipline or even to the usual curriculum. Only after several go-rounds did I feel I had freed myself from these concerns, which it would be perfectly appropriate to take into account in a different kind of enquiry, but which ought really to be irrelevant to deciding which works were powerful, engaging, enlightening, and worth the attention of the easily distractible members of early twenty-first-century populations.

The second factor in the genesis of this book is that I had always been embarrassed by the mistakes, lack of syntactic and lexical variety, and general clumsiness of my written French but never seemed to have the time to undertake any kind of serious improvement. So after my retirement in January 2014, I made an arrangement with the Cambridge Alliance Française. I had a routine: I would write two or three 800- to 1,000-word essays in French every week, and then have them discussed and corrected by one or the other of the three excellent teachers I was fortunate enough to find there (Anne-

Laure Brevet, Isabelle Geisler, and Aline Guillermet). After a year or so of this regime, I did think I noticed a slight improvement in my written French, but a problem emerged: I had written over a hundred of these mini-essays and I needed more material, that is more topics. I had started by going through my usual resources of personal recollections from my life, scurrilous stories about people I knew, invented narratives, dreams, political commentary, mock epistolary exchanges, translations of short texts from Greek, Latin, or German, and brief comments on favourite works of literature, but I felt I was beginning to repeat myself. I needed some fresh ideas and subjects, ideally topics that would require very different and more complex forms of syntax and lexis, without excessively taxing my own limited imaginative powers. While clearing out some old files in the summer of 2015, I happened to come across the list of especially worthwhile philosophical books I had made for Heffers in 2010, which had since lain unnoticed, and I thought I had found what I needed. I could write French essays of a very different kind from those I had been doing: introductory essays of 5,000 to 7,000 words on each of these ten philosophical works written at a speed of 1,000 words for each session. This, mixed in with a continuing flow of other essays on topics from my usual sources, would certainly keep me in material for a year at least. My excellent editor at Harvard University Press, Ian Malcolm, very generously judged that I might write these essays in English rather than French and that the result might be publishable. I abandoned the original specification by Heffers; external constraints are often useful, but there is no need to fetishize them. Raising the number of works treated from ten to twelve and then eventually adding a further introductory first chapter and a brief conclusion gave me a bit more scope than the original dispensation would have allowed.

While I was writing this book I happened to read Paul Veyne's autobiography, in which he describes how at the École normale in the 1950s all the students were obsessed with the issue of whether they should become *scientifiques* or *essayistes*.[1] Fortunately, I have come to the conclusion that 'essayistic' treatment is a fully appropriate way to approach the material in this book—not necessarily the only way, but one that should be in every way perfectly acceptable, given the nature of philosophy as it has been commonly understood for the past 2,000 years.

The history of philosophy is a dignified and important object of study which deserves to be pursued with all the philological exactitude, historical rigor, hermeneutic skill, and analytic acumen we can muster, but this book is not intended as a contribution to historical (or any other subarea of) scholarship. It is not addressed to scholars at all. Rather it is intended as an intellectually relaxed, essayistic introduction to some issues that I take to be of interest, by way of a discussion of some historical texts, and its ideal reader would be the intelligent person with no special training in academic philosophy who thinks that philosophers have sometimes raised some interesting questions and who wishes to try to get clear about whether this is the case and what some of these questions might have been, in the interest of thinking about them further.

Although the book presupposes no prior knowledge of philosophy and I have tried to make my presentation in each chapter as clear and as simple as I can, the book does, I think, have a cumulative structure, so most readers will find it most useful to start at the beginning and read the chapters in the order presented here rather than treating them as separate essays each of which can be read on its own.

In a work of this kind errors, in particular, I must say, historical and interpretative errors, are inevitable; of course, I try to get the reading of these texts right—otherwise what would be the point?—but since my real concern is with the issues, in principle the text could retain the value I hope it might have despite being full of mistakes in historical interpretation. A certain amount of distortion is also introduced precisely by my attempt to focus on those aspects of these texts that seem to me most likely to reward sustained consideration, which means that a certain amount of what I take to be less interesting is undertreated or completely ignored. 'Worth considering' obviously does not mean 'true'. I realise that this may be thought by many readers to display rather too relaxed an attitude to an important aspect of this material, but those for whom that is true will find no dearth of works to cater to their taste. With respect to a number of other aspects of this work that might seem unfamiliar to readers, I am also inclined to reply as the early nineteenth-century writer Jean Paul did with reference to his *Vorschule der Ästhetik*:

> *Es wird doch jeder mehr als eine—meine—Ästhetik in der Studierstube haben. Gut, was also in meiner fehlt, das ergänz' er sich aus der ersten besten; warum soll ich eine erste beste schreiben, da sie ohnehin schon oft genug da ist.*[2]

> Anyone who reads this book at all will be likely to have more than one 'Aesthetics' on his shelf in addition to mine. So then he can easily supplement what is missing in mine from any of these standard treatments; why should I write another standard treatment, given that there are so many of them around already.

Because of my attempt to keep this text as uncluttered and elementary as possible, and also my own failing memory, I know that I have pinched any number of points in what follows from others—sometimes from their conversations, sometimes from their written work, sometimes from their publications—but failed to document this. I apologise unreservedly to the persons concerned.

I am also especially grateful to Alex Englander, Lorna Finlayson, Peter Garnsey, Gérald Garutti, Alexis Papazoglu, Richard Raatzsch,

Tom Stern, and Eva von Raedecker for discussions, during the past five or six years, of the topics treated in this book. I wish also to thank the two readers of the manuscript for Harvard University Press whose helpful reports allowed me to avoid or correct a number of errors, misleading statements, and infelicities in the penultimate draft. My greatest debt of gratitude is to Hilary Gaskin, whose comments improved every page, and who, in any case, is the sine qua non of the work.

# NOTE ON SOURCES

At the end of this note, I give a list of the works on which the individual chapters of the book focus and also bibliographical information about an English translation (of all the works except Hobbes' *Leviathan,* which was written in English). The existing translations into English of the various works discussed here are of highly variable quality, ranging from the more or less reliable to the downright absurd, passing through cases of truly heroic failure to render superlatively rebarbative texts into comprehensible English prose and fanciful creations of the imagination that have some value in the diagnosis of widespread social pathologies, but are otherwise without interest. I have not been able to consult and compare all the hundreds of existing translations of various of the works discussed here, so I have settled on translations that are widely available and moderately readable and that do not present a text that is mind-bogglingly at odds with the sense of the original, as I have been able to construe that. Since I work from the originals, the translations I give in the text may deviate slightly from those in the listed translations, but I don't propose to discuss those deviations, except where I think it is necessary to make a specific point.

I have intentionally tried to avoid giving specific page references to works discussed because in my experience that tends to reinforce the idea that one can extract juicy bits from the corpus without concern for the context from which they are taken. In all cases in which it has been possible, I have tried to use standard systems of reference that are independent of the pagination of particular editions and also, as just mentioned, to refer to larger sections of text (e.g., chapters) rather than to individual pages. Thus, references to Plato are to the invariant Stephanus pages; to Lucretius by the line number (which is actually so specific as to violate the general principle I just enunciated); to Montaigne by volume and essay number (i.e., I.1 = volume I, essay 1); to Adorno's *Minima Moralia* by section number; to Heidegger's *Being and Time* by the apparatus of sections and subsections into which that work is divided, etc.

In an attempt to keep what is intended basically as a pedagogical text uncluttered so that the main line of argument remains as visible as possible, I have tried to keep notes to a minimum, and in particular to eschew completely any discussion of the secondary literature on the texts.

At the very end of the book is a list of works that some readers may find useful for further study of the topics raised in each chapter. Some (but not all) of these 'further readings' look like 'interpretations' of the works treated in each main chapter, but many of them are not in any sense interpretations but *alternative* treatments of the same subjects discussed in the main work under consideration. I should note that I have listed them because of their intrinsic interest and not, for instance, because I necessarily endorse them either as correct interpretations of the works they treat or as 'better' discussions of the same topics.

Here is a list of the texts on which each chapter tries to focus:

Chapter 1: Plato. *Apologia Socratis*. In *Opera: Volume I*. Edited by E. A. Duke, W. F. Hicken, W. S. M. Nicholl, D. B. Robinson, and J. C. G. Strachan. Oxford Classical Texts. Clarendon Press, 1995. / *The Apology of Socrates*. In *The Trial and Death of Socrates*. Translated by G. M. A. Grube. Hackett, 1975.

Chapter 2: Plato. *Platonis Respublica*. Edited by S. R. Slings. Oxford Classical Texts. Oxford University Press, 2003. / *The Republic*. Edited by G. R. F. Ferrari. Translated by Tom Griffith. Cambridge Texts in the History of Political Thought. Cambridge University Press, 2009. / *Complete Works*. Edited by John Cooper. Translated by various hands. Hackett, 1997.

Chapter 3: Lucretius. *Lucreti de rerum natura libri sex*. Edited by Cyril Bailey. Oxford Classical Texts. Oxford University Press, 1921. / *The Nature of Things*. Translated by Alicia Stallings. Introduction by Richard Jenkyns. Penguin, 2007.

Chapter 4: Augustine. *S. Aureli Augustini Confessionum, libri XIII*. Edited by Martin Skutella. Bibliotheca Teubneriana. Teubner, 1996. / *Confessions*. Translated by Henry Chadwick. Oxford World's Classics. Oxford University Press, 2009. / *S. Aurelii Augustini Episcopi De Civitate Dei, libri XXII*. Edited by Bernhard Dombart and Alfons Kalb. Bibliotheca Teubneriana. Teubner, 1993. / *The City of God against the Pagans*. Edited and translated by R. W. Dyson. Cambridge Texts in the History of Political Thought. Cambridge University Press, 1998.

Chapter 5: Montaigne, Michel de. *Les essais*. Edited by Jean Balsamo, Catherine Magnien-Simonin, and Michel Magnien. Bibliothèque de la Pléiade. Gallimard, 2007. / *The Complete*

*Essays of Montaigne.* Translated by Donald M. Frame. Stanford
University Press, 1958.

Chapter 6: Hobbes, Thomas. *Leviathan.* Edited by Noel Malcolm.
Clarendon Press, 2012.

Chapter 7: The two works by Hegel which I cite most frequently,
his *Phänomenologie des Geistes* and *Grundlinien zur Philosophie des Rechts,* have been translated into English as: *Phenomenology of Spirit,* translated by A. V. Miller, Oxford University
Press, 1977 and *Elements of the Philosophy of Right,* edited by
Allen Wood, translated by H. B. Nisbet, *Cambridge Texts in the
History of Political Thought,* Cambridge University Press, 1991.
References to these works will appear in the text in the following form: (3.100/75) which is to be read as: volume 3, p. 100
of *Hegel: Werke in zwanzig Bänden,* edited by Eva Moldenhauer and Karl Markus Michel. Suhrkamp, 1970, which
corresponds to p. 75 of the translation by Miller listed above.
Similarly (7.20/23) means: volume 7, page 20 of the *Werke* to
which corresponds p. 23 of the translation by Nisbet. References to other works by Hegel will appear in footnotes as
appropriate.

Chapter 8: Nietzsche, Friedrich. *Zur Genealogie der Moral.* In
*Friedrich Nietzsche: Kritische Studienausgabe.* Edited by Giorgio
Colli and Mazzino Montinari. Walter de Gruyter, 1967. / *On the
Genealogy of Morality.* Edited by Keith Ansell-Pearson. Trans-
lated by Carol Diethe. Cambridge Texts in the History of
Political Thought. Cambridge University Press, 2011.

Chapter 9: Lukács, György. *Geschichte und Klassenbewußtsein:
Studien über marxistische Dialektik.* 1923. Lucherhand,
1970. / *History and Class Consciousness: Studies in Marxist
Dialectics.* Translated by Rodney Livingstone. Merlin Press,
1971.

Chapter 10: Heidegger, Martin. *Sein und Zeit.* Niemeyer,
1927. / *Being and Time: A Revised Edition of the Stambaugh*

*Translation.* Contemporary Continental Philosophy. SUNY
Press, 2010.

Chapter 11: Wittgenstein, Ludwig. *Philosophische Untersuch-*
*ungen / Philosophical Investigations.* Translated by G. E. M.
Anscombe. Blackwell, 1953.

Chapter 12: Adorno, Theodor W. *Minima Moralia: Reflexionen aus*
*dem beschädigten Leben.* Suhrkamp, 1951. / *Minima Moralia:*
*Reflections from Damaged Life.* Translated by E. F. N. Jephcott.
Verso, 2006.

# CHANGING THE SUBJECT

# INTRODUCTION

## A Game of Chess in Times of Plague

What is philosophy? In what kinds of human situations does it arise? What is it intended to do? It is my basic contention that one of the characteristics of philosophy, perhaps exactly what distinguishes it from science, is that it generally avoids giving a direct answer to a direct question. Rather it changes the question, and what is most interesting to observe and most enlightening is to look carefully at *why* and *how* the question changes, for what reason and with what result.

In this spirit, then, rather than answering the question of what philosophy is directly, let me invite the reader to think about Ingmar Bergman's 1957 film *The Seventh Seal*. In the late fourteenth century a knight returns from the Crusades to a Sweden in the grip of the Black Death. He sits on a beach, sets up a game of chess, and waits for Death, who duly arrives to take him. The Crusader, however, says he knows that Death likes to play chess, so why don't they have a game? The Crusader is not going to be able finally to escape Death in any case, so what does Death have to lose by a short stay of execution while they play? If the Crusader wins, he gets a reprieve (for the moment, at any rate); if Death wins, he takes the Crusader with him immediately. While the game is played, the Crusader can continue to live. The game is played, following the usual rules of the game of chess, in a series of short rounds, a few moves at a time, over the course of several days. The Crusader thinks he has a strategy that will allow him to win, but his religious conscience trips him up. He feels that, after the mayhem of the Crusade, he needs confession and absolution. Death pretends to be a priest and, while hearing the Crusader's confession, he gets him to reveal his intended strategy. A strategy revealed, however, is not of much use, and Death rubs this in by commenting that he will remember what the Crusader has said. Eventually a situation arises in which the Crusader sees clearly that Death will soon be able to force checkmate on him. While making his next move, the Crusader 'accidently' allows his robe to sweep across the board, throwing the pieces to the ground, then claims he cannot remember where they were on the board. This does not work, of course, because Death has a good memory; he replaces the figures on the board in their previous positions, makes the move which brings about checkmate, and wins the match.

The Crusader has been on an utterly pointless journey, trying, while in the grip of religious mania, to wrest military control of a fly-blown speck of useless desert from the members of another human group who are demonised because they happen to have a set of religious beliefs that are actually only microscopically different from his own. He returns home to find the plague raging. So he is faced with a complex situation which one would call intolerable (except that he has no choice but to bear it) in two respects. First, he suffers from a lack of orientation and a sense of emptiness in his life; he feels he has accomplished nothing and does not know how even to begin to act so as to remedy that. This is a very general feature of his situation and one for which there is unlikely to be any quick and easy solution—or indeed perhaps any real 'solution' whatever. Second, he is immediately threatened by the plague; there is reason to believe that at the start of the film he knows he is already infected and thus about to die.

As the film opens, the Crusader is focused on the more immediate and pressing of these two concerns and is looking for a way out of a situation of imminent death from the plague. He tries three approaches to finding a way out, each of these approaches instantiated in one moment of the story. First of all, he suggests to Death that they play a game of chess. Doing this requires, for obvious reasons, a great deal of intellectual and moral initiative and imagination, but the approach works at least to the extent that it does stave off the inevitable and gains the Crusader time. His second approach consists in elaborating a strategy for winning the game of Chess by following the rules to bring about a configuration on the board which is recognised as a checkmate of his opponent. He tries this, but it does not work. Death thwarts him in a way that actually has nothing to do with chess strategy per se. External observers might, to be sure, judge that Death's action has not been not totally above board, but so what?

We do not know, of course, whether the Crusader's strategy would have worked if he had been able to spring it on Death in the unexpected way he intended. It might not have been an especially clever strategy, and the Crusader might have lost anyway. This, however, is all speculation. Again, it seems pointless to 'object' to what Death does here. What would it even mean to say that Death was not being sporting or honourable or acting in a way that was proper? Death does not violate the rules of chess, which nowhere, as far as I know, contain a provision to the effect that one of the players may not induce the other to reveal his or her intended strategy. That is enough, and more than the Crusader has reason to expect. Even if Death did cheat, and admitted it, what recourse would the Crusader have?

This brings us to the third approach. Just as Death secured an advantage to himself not by playing an especially brilliant move on the chessboard but by doing something else completely (sitting with his cowl over his face in a church until the Crusader came in to confess), so the Crusader tried to secure an advantage to himself by knocking over the pieces. This was a way of trying to escape from a situation that seemed hopeless. He was not acquiring an advantage *in* the game of chess. The rules of chess specify how pieces are initially positioned, what counts as a permissible move, when a game is over and who has won, etc., but just as the rules of chess contain no provision against dressing up like a priest, so they also do not forbid knocking the pieces over. The Crusader was trying to find a way out of his difficult situation not by making a recognized move *in* the situation but by changing the definition of the situation itself. They are no longer making moves in chess; the Crusader is struggling for his life. This is, at the very least, a different kind of game altogether, and what he does is probably not best construed as part of a 'game' at all.

I have distinguished three moments: first, deciding to play a game, and this specific game; second, making various recognised moves in that game; third, redefining the situation by reference to a wider situation in which it is embedded. The suggestion that motivates this book is that the moment of 'philosophy' is definitely not the second of these three moments. It is *not*, that is, the moment when either the Crusader or Death analyses the board and thinks up and executes an especially brilliant move. Rather I wish to suggest that to understand what philosophy is, it makes more sense to consider the third moment, the moment when the Crusader tries to find a different way out by *changing the situation*—in this case by knocking over the pieces and thus putting an end, he hopes, to the chess game. He does not actually succeed, but that is a separate matter. Knocking the pieces over is not making a move in chess; it is thinking of the world as not exclusively defined by the rules of chess but as set in a wider context. Philosophy takes place when someone, an individual or a group, begins to try to look for a way out which might include transforming the framework of some situation, changing the rules, asking different questions. The moment of philosophy occurs when the Crusader shifts from asking 'Which of the possible moves on the board should I now make?' to 'How can I avoid having Death take me?' He may originally have thought that answering the first was a way of answering the second, but he now recognises that that is not the case. Philosophy arises when one first realises that these are two different questions. The fact that one is never *finally* going to 'win' against Death is also a possible object of reflection, but it is neither here nor there in *this* discussion.

The most characteristic feature of philosophy is its connection with a moment when the gears shift, the code breaks down and changes or is changed, the definition of the situation is thrown into question, and we need to reflect on the wider context within which a course of action (including possibly a discussion) has been proceeding, when expectations change and terms need to be redefined. Let me give a few more examples of the kind of phenomenon I have in mind. If I am a barrister and I hide my opponent's wig so that he cannot speak in court, I am not by doing that making any argument that has any legal standing. I am doing something quite different, which may or may not work (and which may or may not have certain *other* consequences for me). Or imagine the case of an operatic tenor who is 'killed' but must remain on stage as a visible corpse for the rest of the act and who uses the time to have a nap.

5

Or suppose I am a member of Parliament. The Government and Opposition benches are on opposite sides of the House, 'two sword-lengths' apart, in order to discourage duelling. Now suppose that, when I am recognised by the speaker, I stand up and, instead of asking a question, pull out a gun and shoot a government minister; I have certainly done something which will most likely be reported in the newspapers, but it is in a clear sense not really a contribution to the parliamentary debate in the narrow sense of the term. Here I have rather clearly taken a step outside a given framework of rules and expectations, redefined the situation, and acted in such a way as to impose that new definition of the system on others. No member of the opposing front bench will be likely to respond to my firing a pistol at someone in the chamber with a rebuttal, an argument, an answer, or a long rambling speech; other kinds of things will happen. When Haydn transmitted the message to his employer Count Esterházy that the musicians of the Court orchestra were tired of the summer residence and wanted to return to Vienna, he did so by writing a symphony in whose final movement the players one by one stop playing, put away their instruments, extinguish their candles, and leave the room, until only two are left.[1] He had, in the late eighteenth century, musical means for annotating any note a flute was called upon to play, and even for annotating silence, but there is no notation for 'flautist extinguishes his candle'. Nevertheless Count Esterházy apparently got the message. Finally, suppose some of the passengers on an airplane decide to make a gesture of political protest at US policy in the Middle East by reconstruing the airplane in which they are travelling as a flying bomb and, deviating from the regular flight path, crashing it into a building.

These examples show a number of things. First, the role of cognition in the examples is very different. In Haydn's case, he had to plan and calculate carefully, violate expectations sufficiently to keep the Count's attention, but do so in such a way that the Count was not completely disoriented and yet did not fail to get the message. In the case of the MP who shoots the minister, the example is not described in enough detail for us to know whether this was a considered act—an attempt, for instance, to change the political situation from parliamentary rule to civil war—or simply an unreflective action taken in the heat of the moment, or even another move in a completely different game we are unaware of. Different kinds of cognitive skills, such as observation, strategic planning, hermeneutic acumen, analytic and argumentative skills, play a particularly important role in philosophy, although the specific form these take in different contexts can well differ.

A second point is that it is by no means clear that changing the situation through reconfiguration represents either moral (or cognitive) progress. Whether the examples above represent moral progress will depend on one's judgement about whether or not it was a good idea for the musicians of Esterházy's Court orchestra to return to Vienna, whether one thinks it was on the whole a good thing or a bad thing for the minister to be assassinated or the building to be toppled by an airplane with the resulting death of most of those inside, or whether hiding the barrister's wig did or did not contribute to advancing justice, the common good, or various other possible values. Usually there will be some understanding of the fact that simply observing that the usual rules, procedures, meanings of terms, habits of behaviour, expectations, and so on have been violated does not *in itself* answer the question of whether what has happened was or was not a good idea; that will in general have to be (finally) evaluated relative to some wider context, and it will not always be clear or uncontroversial what that context should be. Thinking that the systematicity, comprehensiveness, and consistency of a set of rules and procedures *in itself* is the final word on the practical good is a possible position, but it should be considered an extreme and extremely implausible one. Most people will have existing views—some will even have strong views—on some of these cases, although at least one strand of philosophy proposes open-mindedness as a special virtue of the philosopher.

A third point is that routinization probably cannot be avoided and can very easily set in; probably some routinization will always occur in our responses to the situations that gave rise to philosophy. Haydn had no form of musical notation at his disposal to express that the musicians at this point were not merely to remain silent but to extinguish their candles, get up, and leave the room. He could, to be sure, have used another existing symbolic system, namely language, to write under the oboe part something like 'Oboist löscht seine Kerze aus und tritt ab', and eventually, if the need for such a symbol became recurrent, he might just write 'Obab' or invent a grapheme such as √ or ⇓ to put directly into the score. Similarly, presumably at some point it was a surprising novelty that the musicians of the Vienna Philharmonic shouted out 'Prost Neujahr' to the audience at the New Year's Concert—it was not usual for musicians to address the audience rather than simply playing the notes of their music—but now this has become part of the traditional practice, and the audience would be disappointed if the orchestra members did not wish them a happy new year from the stage.

If one is looking for what is distinctive in philosophy, then, it is not primarily the attempt to deal with the sorts of question that arise in the context of what I called the second approach. On the other hand, it is probably a mistake to think that there is anything like a single transhistorical nature or essence of 'philosophy'; there are only related historical practices, and some of these practices will be associated with mastery of certain forms of rule-guided behaviour: correct Latin, *disputatio* according to fixed rules, formal abilities of various kinds such as those needed to do mathematics. However, it is also the case that philosophy was rarely *simply* identified with skill in one of these activities. Many early philosophers were shamans (Empedokles), highbrow circus performers (Hippias), partisan political leaders (Solon), founders of religious orders (Pythagoras, if he existed at all), or language reformers (Prodikus).[2] Nevertheless, philosophers have repeatedly succumbed to the particular illusion that they have *all* been engaged in (essentially) the 'same' activity over the millennia and that this activity is the explanation and defence of a set of rules of correct thinking and acting. This view is obviously very deeply rooted at least in modern ways of thinking—so deeply rooted, in fact, as to be almost (but not quite) irresistible. Humans are like many other animal species in having an inclination toward predictability, routines, and habits; having these gives us a sense of security for perfectly understandable reasons, as societies get more complex and predictable coordination becomes a pressing issue. The introduction of systems of rules and procedures is an obvious way of attaining this valuable goal. To be sure, no one is foolish enough to think that any system of rules we might now have actively and explicitly available to us is the best one possible, but the general idea of an aspiration toward a closed system of rules remains. This aspiration often takes the following form: Like the system of rules for chess, we might have, or eventually come to have, a full system of rules for nature ('metaphysics' in one sense of that term) or for all of our knowledge of the world (epistemology) or for how to act (ethics). If this goal were to be reached, philosophy could stop being a way of shifting gears and become the internal analysis of closed structures.[3]

Some of the cases discussed earlier might be thought to add credibility to this approach. We start out, like Haydn, with the 'usual' musical notation but imagine adding to it, so that 'flautist blows out his candle and leaves' has its own specific, dedicated sign, and that means, as it were, that the concept of specifically musical performance gets extended, because now it is not a correct or authentic performance unless there are candles to blow out (whereas before forms of illumination were not at all marked in the score and played no role in what we are tempted to call 'the music itself'). Or perhaps knocking over the chessboard is reconstrued as part of a bigger 'game' (either Existential Chess or maybe Human Survival in the Face of Death), which can be construed as having something like rules and in which knocking over the board is a recognised move (perhaps with its own sign in chess notation). One can see these developments as part of a process of 'internalisation' taking place: what *was* a stepping outside the boundaries of the game to its larger context becomes one move in the new, overarching game. Surely, one might claim, this process could go on indefinitely, and at the end we would have a Final Framework or Supergame or Context-not-Relative-to-Any-Further-Context. Philosophy would have the task of internally describing these rules (which would be one which philosophy itself, as a human activity, would have to abide by) and showing how as yet unregularised parts of the natural and human world could be shown to fit into the Final Framework. Some forms of theology think that God plays the Supergame; if he does, did he or did he not also invent the game he plays? Perhaps philosophy is the notation of the rules he follows. Knowledge of philosophy might even increase one's skill in playing that game based on internal game rules one could formulate.

Just to repeat this important line of argument in slightly different words: At some point I may move out from thinking about the next move in chess, the next argument in Parliament or the Court (moment 2), to thinking about how to make my way in the world in a wider sense: how to escape Death, remove an objectionable person from the political landscape, or prevent the opposing party from putting their case. If I do make this move in one of these cases, in one sense I have put aside the rules of chess, of parliamentary debate, or of legal procedure. Now the question is whether by doing that I am always merely entering a *new* context which is itself governed by a set of rules which can be explicitly formulated and studied (and which could have been formulated antecedently if I as an individual, or we as a species, had been clever enough and interested enough to do this). It is the assumption of this book that views like this, that human life is like a chess game with rules, have shown themselves to be untenable and thus that looking for a way out of problematic situations won't always mean looking for another system of rules like any of the ones we know.

I have spoken of the second and the third of the three 'moments' in the story of the encounters between the Crusader and Death. But what of the first? One might well think that it required more imagination to propose to Death a game of chess than it does to try to knock over the board when one is about to lose, and that is probably true. It would be good to be able to think of philosophy as potentially having a genuinely originative and constructive rather than a merely analytic or reproductive function, and perhaps some philosophers—I am thinking especially of Hobbes and his idea of 'the state'—are best understood in these terms. Certainly some philosophers, such as Dewey and the French philosopher Foucault, were keen to promote a new kind of philosophy, which would be an activity of constructing new conceptual tools for human life.[4] However, one will note that the Crusader does not propose to invent a new game but to play an existing, well-known one: chess.

What would it take to convince Death, who we have every reason to believe is a hypertraditionalist, to play a newly invented game and, what is more, one invented by one of his subjects? Perhaps what is first required is to disabuse ourselves of the (theologically based) idea that Death is anything like a person. I invite all interested readers to try to pursue this thought further.

*Chapter One*

# SOCRATES

The nineteenth-century moralist J. S. Mill thought that it was better to be Socrates dissatisfied than a pig satisfied; how did he know? After all, he was neither Socrates nor a pig. For that matter, how could even Socrates himself have known whether he would prefer to be a pig (satisfied or unsatisfied) rather than himself (satisfied or unsatisfied)? Although Mill did not seriously consider the possibility that anyone might prefer to be the pig, he did, nevertheless, think it worthwhile to try to give something like a reason for the claim he makes, as is indicated by the exact words he uses in his 'Utilitarianism': 'It is better to be a human being dissatisfied than a pig satisfied; better to be Socrates dissatisfied than a fool satisfied. And if the fool, or the pig, is of a different opinion, it is only because they only know their own side of the question'.

This quotation puts together in a concentrated way two of the main issues that have obsessed philosophers since Socrates. First, some distinction is being made between being 'satisfied' (or 'dissatisfied') and being 'better' (or 'less good'). This refers to possible states of persons (or person-like animals), but there is a parallel distinction between the things or states that make a person satisfied: Socrates is satisfied; knowing the answer to a riddle or having correct change in one's pocket when one needs it is satisfying. What is the difference between something being satisfying and something being 'good'? It would be natural to think *grosso modo* that when we speak of some state as being satisfying rather than (necessarily) good, we mean to call attention to some distinction between someone's subjective state, their state of mind as they immediately experience it, and some more detached, external, or 'objective' judgement that could be made on that state. You may think that last glass of wine was satisfying, but wait until you wake up tomorrow (or in the middle of the night tonight). It may be highly satisfying for you to have pinched my wallet, but it is still possible to judge (from my perspective, from that of the common law, etc.) that it would have been better that you not have done that.

The second issue this passage raises is that of difference of opinion. People have differences of opinions about what is better and what is worse, and, if one takes Mill's account seriously, so, it seems, do pigs. Has anyone, however, ever canvassed the view of the pig? In fact, someone has, at least in imagination. One of the moral essays of the ancient philosopher Plutarch is a dialogue between the wise Odysseus and a talking pig named Gryllos. Gryllos had at one time been a human being, and so he could actually, if one takes the story seriously, compare the two states, human and porcine, by virtue of having had direct experience of living each of the two kinds of life. He had been turned into a pig by the goddess/witch Circe, who gives him back his speech so that he can talk with Odysseus. Gryllos defends the opinion that pigs are not only morally superior to humans but also that being a pig is more satisfying than being a human; so being a pig is in every way 'better'.[1] Let us, then, imagine

14

a discussion between Gryllos and Socrates. One of them, presumably, has made a mistake and is wrong, but which one? We can imagine at least three kinds of reasons for making a mistake in a case like this. First, there could be a 'simple' mistake of the kind with which we are almost universally familiar. I am not paying attention properly, am distracted, impatient, careless, and I read the word 'down' in the manuscript as 'clown' or add up the column of figures incorrectly. Similarly, I might make a simple snap judgement about the theft of the wallet without paying adequate attention to some of its relevant consequences (public shame, prison perhaps). A second way I could be thought to make a mistake would be not in mistakenly applying the 'correct' universally accepted criteria to the case but in evaluating the case with reference to a deviant or even to the *wrong* set of criteria. Thus, I might be thought to have made a mistake if I judge that it is better for you to have picked my pocket (than not to have done so), basing that judgement on my observation that you are an especially dexterous and graceful pickpocket whose work is elegant. Perhaps the exercise of your gift for larceny really is attractive, a delight to watch, but, as we might say, that is not the point; the 'right' criteria to use for deciding what is 'better' are moral and perhaps legal, not aesthetic. A third way I could be thought to make a mistake is that there could be something about me as a judge, apart from momentary bouts of inattention or a tendency to use completely wrong criteria, that disqualifies me. So Mill asserts very firmly that if one is dealing with a disagreement of this kind about the relative merits of two states, one should disqualify the opinion of a judge who has direct experience of only one of the states in question, in favour of the judgement of someone who has direct experience of both. So either Socrates and the pig are both disqualified, if neither of them knows both of the states being compared, or, in Plutarch's version—in which Odysseus is substituted for Socrates as the model human sage and philosophers—the sage is disqualified and the pig wins.

It is not hard to see that Mill's argument is completely implausible, or rather that it is not even an argument at all, but just a relatively unreflective expression of his own prejudices. To revert to Mill's original formulation, first of all, how does Mill know that Socrates would himself agree that it is better to be himself dissatisfied than a pig satisfied? Second, how does Mill know that the pig 'knew only one side of the question', whereas, presumably, Socrates knew both sides?

On the first of these two issues, Mill's mid-Victorian bluster stands in stark contrast to the great circumspection which the Socrates whom we get to know in Plato's dialogues uses in approaching these matters.* Socrates repeats again and again that he

---

*There was a historical Athenian named Socrates who was condemned to death and executed in 399 BCE. He wrote nothing himself, but he occurs as a character in a contemporary comedy by Aristophanes and also as a character in Plato's dialogues, and we have some other, scattered, more or less contemporary *testimonia* about him. There is considerable controversy about the extent to which the character 'Socrates' in Plato's dialogues does or does not represent correctly the real historical personage, his opinions and methods. A further complication is that the character 'Socrates' in Plato's dialogues seems himself to change as Plato's own views develop. Finally, later philosophers have a tendency to treat earlier philosophers as if they were not real concrete individuals but as if their proper names stood for a characteristic set of doctrines or methods or even a general style of philosophising. When this tendency gets the upper hand, 'Socrates/Socratic' and 'Plato/Platonic' can come to be detached from any close connection with the actual doctrines of these two figures and be used as general terms to designate kinds of approaches. Eventually 'Socratic' can come to designate something very significantly different from anything the historical Socrates (or any of the characters named 'Socrates' in any of Plato's dialogues) could conceivably have envisaged. There is nothing inherently wrong with this—it is one way human language usage develops and can lead to an enrichment of one's conceptual possibilities—but it does make it exceedingly diffi-

knows nothing, except that he knows he does not know various things which others think they know (*Apology* 21d).[2] This claim is intended to be shocking because Socrates is visibly and demonstrably so clever—his accusers warn the jury against being taken in by his cleverness (17a–b)—and one can, and should, immediately wonder what the point of administering this shock is. One consequence of Socrates' claim, though, would seem to be that he does not claim to know that it was better to be himself than a pig. This immediately raises what has been one of the obsessive concerns of philosophy: What do we mean when we say we 'know' something, and under what circumstances should a claim to knowledge be allowed to stand? In English the word 'know' takes three different grammatical constructions, and it means something slightly different in each.[3] First, there is 'know' with a direct object, as in 'I know Martin; he is a good friend who lives three doors down from us and always takes very good care of our cat when we are away'; 'He knows Cambridge; he has lived here all his life'; 'She knows the sound of an oboe, having played the oboe herself for twenty years'. In these cases 'I know' means 'I am acquainted or familiar with', usually because I have had direct experience of'. Some philosophers have called this 'knowledge by acquaintance'. This sense of 'know' is distinguished from that of the 'know' that takes a subordinate clause beginning with the word 'that'. I may know *that* Ulan Bator is in Asia without 'knowing' Ulan Bator (in the way in which I know Cambridge, that is, by having lived here). Similarly, I may know

cult to distinguish different 'Socrateses': the 'real' Athenian, the various figures who populate different Platonic dialogues, and the 'Socrateses' of later conception. The question of the relation of these to each other is important and interesting, but this question will not be treated in this book. 'Socrates' will be used as a mere ambiguous place-holder.

Cambridge well and yet not know some fact about it (such as that it contains so-and-so many traffic lights). This is called 'propositional knowledge'. Finally, I may use 'know' with a complement consisting of a clause beginning 'how to', as in 'I know how to ride a bicycle' or 'I know how to get you to Mitcham's Corner' or 'She knows how to keep a secret, if necessary'; 'She surely knows how to make a usable pot from that lump of clay; she is, after all, a trained potter'; 'He knows how to throw a dried pea through an opening five centimetres in diameter at a distance of two metres'. Here 'know' refers to a practical ability or skill. Having this kind of skill, though, is something different from possessing any particular kind or amount of purely propositional knowledge. I can reliably get you to Mitcham's Corner without necessarily being able to tell you in so many words exactly how to do that, that is, without giving you a set of correctly formulated directions. And reading and cognitively mastering the contents of a book on playing the oboe won't make you an oboist. In addition, if she is a good potter she will be able to make a pot out of a lump of clay she has never seen before, that is, with which she has had no previous direct acquaintance. Equally, just 'directly experiencing' the clay, say by smearing it thickly on your face, will not make you a potter.

Some philosophers have had a further obsession, however, in addition to trying to sort out exactly what was meant by 'know' in any given context. They have wished to devalue much of what we think we know—it is not really 'knowledge' but something less than that, such as 'mere opinion'—and to discover (or perhaps promote or even invent) a kind of propositional 'knowledge' that has a privileged status, particularly as a reliable guide to action. Plato was instrumental in establishing a usage which distinguished very sharply between '(real) knowledge' and '(mere) opinion/belief'.[4] Thus, under normal circumstances I would unproblematically claim I know that since privatisation of the railways, the government subsidy for rail transport has increased, ticket prices have also increased, and the service is still significantly less good than that on comparable parts of the French or German (or even Italian) national networks. However, one can also see why someone might say that I don't really 'know' this. I think I know that the government subsidy has increased, but that is just because I have read that in various newspapers which might all be unintentionally in error, or they might be trying to mislead me; my direct experience of ticket prices is very limited; and comparison of my trips on the train here in Britain with trips in France, Germany, and Italy is at best anecdotal. So I don't really 'know' (especially if one is keen on connecting 'knowledge' as closely as possible with certainty or complete reliability); I simply have beliefs or opinions about it. Beliefs and opinions may not necessarily be wrong, but then a random guess may not be wrong, and yet we will be loath to call it an instance of 'knowledge'.

If a mere opinion may be true, what is it that pushes a true belief into the charmed and privileged circle in which it counts as 'knowledge'? This is a matter of great controversy, but in general one can say that philosophers have wanted to reserve the honorific 'knowledge' for true opinions that have two further properties. First, they are *especially* well supported (often this means they are supported by one of the pet methods the philosopher in question prefers), and second, they are particularly reliable as guides to action, or perhaps even 'certain'. One can already notice one way of developing this that makes Socrates' claim to ignorance less shocking than it might initially seem to be. Maybe he is merely denying that he has this especially high-octane 'knowledge'—which is a special status assigned only to something that satisfies especially stringent demands—about anything. This might, of course, depending on what conditions are imposed on (real) 'knowledge', be compatible with admitting that he has 'knowledge' in the everyday sense; namely he has opinions and beliefs that are better or worse supported and that generally guide him in acting.

So perhaps Socrates does not 'know' it is better to be him than a pig, but he has a belief to that effect, perhaps even one for which he can muster some support, although not enough for him to be comfortable speaking of 'knowledge'. Even if, though, one puts aside what might be a special philosopher's use of 'know' in some highly technical sense, Socrates seems reluctant to express any beliefs about what states are comparatively better than others. In *Apology* he even says that he does not know how to evaluate death (40c–41e). Is it the passage to another world? Is it annihilation? Is it like dreamless sleep? In any of these cases, he thinks being dead would probably be better than being alive. So at the end of his speech, Socrates tells the jury at his trial that they go now to life, he to death, and he has no idea which is better. Furthermore, this does not seem like some kind of hyperbolic 'philosophical doubt', a doubt that arises because some belief that we accept in everyday life without much questioning fails to attain the stratospherically high standards of certainty which some philosophers wish to impose in order to speak of 'real knowledge'; rather it seems to be like our ordinary garden-variety uncertainty: the kind that actually affects our action. I know (in the everyday sense) that I am sitting in my loft typing, but I could have some kind of philosophical doubt about whether I am not really dreaming or hallucinating or making some mistake about my surroundings, so I don't 'really' know. Nothing about this is going to make me actually stop typing. In contrast, I know I don't know which horse is going to win a certain race tomorrow at Newmarket. Not having any interest at all in games of chance or competitive sports, I am also uninterested in this, but even if I were interested, the fact that I don't have any idea which horse has the best chance of winning would make me likely to hesitate to bet. Socrates' attitude toward an afterlife is more like my attitude toward the race at Newmarket than like my attitude toward whether or not I am sitting in my loft. His uncertainty affects his action, making him unwilling to do various things it might be appropriate for him to do, if he had reason to think that death was something bad, such as escaping from prison and running off to Thessaly, as various of his friends propose that he do.

Socrates spent his life seeking this kind of gold-plated philosophical knowledge, in particular knowledge of how to lead a good life, but he did not think he had attained it in any area of life; that is what he means first of all when he says he does not know anything except that he does not know anything,[5] but in addition, he is unsure about whether he 'knows' much of anything in the usual low-powered everyday sense of 'know'. Socrates doesn't think he knows whether death is better than life. Why, then, should he think he *knows* that Gryllos, the talking pig who was formerly a man, is mistaken in his praise of the swinish life? Gryllos waxes lyrical about the life of pigs: pigs have access to a whole world of complex, infinitely pleasurable and sophisticated smells that are completely inaccessible to humans; humans, in contrast, have only a rudimentary olfactory apparatus and very primitive discriminatory powers. How can Socrates be so sure that Gryllos is wrong to claim that being deprived of this whole world of sensation is a disaster? How can Socrates reject Gryllos' assertion that no one could fully appreciate the magnitude of this loss who had not himself been a pig?

This brings us to the second part of Mill's original claim, that one can discount the testimony of the pig because it knows 'only one side of the question' (i.e., only what it is like to be a [satisfied] pig), whereas Socrates is to be presumed to know both sides of the question, because he was acquainted with both states, the human and the porcine, and therefore to be a better judge of the issue. Note here the shift from the second sense of 'know' (=Socrates, or the pig, 'know' which state is better; that is, one or the other of them 'has an opinion'=has purported propositional knowledge) to the first sense of 'know' (=Socrates, or the pig, have direct acquaintance with what it is to be Socrates dissatisfied or the pig satisfied). Recall, though, that in Plutarch's dialogue it is the pig, who had been both a man and a pig, who has the advantage of direct experience of both states over Odysseus (who has only been a man), and the pig's considered judgement must be held to have more weight. Plutarch's dialogue is an invention, of course, but it does point out what, it seems, would have to be true for Mill's comparison to be convincing: Socrates would have to be able to become (or be transformed into) a pig and thereafter to remember what it was like to be a man and also judge that being a man was better.

'Socrates' opinion is to be given more weight because he knows both sides of the question' can mean two different things:

1. Socrates is directly acquainted with the state of *being Socrates* lying blissfully and lethargically in a pool of mud, with the sun beating down, having gorged himself on a huge pile of acorns.
2. Socrates is directly acquainted with the state of *being a pig* lying in a pool of mud, etc.

Now the first case may or may not actually be true. In fact, it is most unlikely literally to have been true, because what would Socrates have been doing in the pool of mud? Trying to chill out? Trying to discover what it is like to be a pig?[6] Still, it is in principle possible that he had such a mudbath, and we might think that even if he did not have this direct experience, he could easily extrapolate from experiences he did have and 'imagine' what it would be like to have such a mudbath. On the other hand, Socrates has no direct experience of *being* a pig in any state (lying satisfied in the mud or not). He may, of course, again 'imagine' what this would be like and compare the imagined state of being a pig satisfied with that of being himself dissatisfied, but then how do we know that the pig could not imagine being Socrates? The question here is who is the better *judge*, but if one excludes from the beginning the very possibility that the pig has or could articulate any preferences or opinions, then by that very fact one has excluded the possibility that the pig can be *any kind* of judge. Perhaps that is a reasonable view, but if that is the case, what is the point of the whole comparison? Then one might as well have said directly: Socrates dissatisfied is better because he at least can judge, whereas a pig—elated, somnolent, debauched, or depressed—cannot be a judge at all. Of course, in doing this one will simply have begged the question: How do we know it is better to be a creature capable of articulating judgements rather than to be one who is incapable of doing so? Perhaps one wants to say we 'just know that'. No need, then, to bother with philosophy.

To put this point in a slightly different way: conceivably Socrates had had the experience of being in the same, externally specified circumstances as those which a pig would find highly satisfactory: big cooling pool of mud; lots of nice acorns and slop; rich, pig-friendly smells filling the air. This does not mean he has had a direct experience of *being a pig*—only of living (as a man) in circumstances that a pig would find pleasant. Even if he did have direct experience of bathing in lovely mud, the only conclusion he could have definitively drawn was that he, as Socrates, preferred to be dissatisfied rather than to be (as Socrates) in conditions which a pig would find highly agreeable. That in itself does not show that Socrates' opinion about whether it is better to be himself or a pig has any special standing.

23

Mill, in a way that seems clearly to be incorrect, treats the comparison between *being* Socrates and *being* a pig as if it were a matter of choice between two possible states, that is, as if it were like the choice that might confront Socrates one night between having sex with Alcibiades or having sex with Xanthippe. But the comparison does not have this structure at all. Socrates can choose to act in external ways that resemble those in which a pig behaves, for example to sleep in a pool of mud, or he can choose not to do this, but he cannot choose to *be* a pig (unless he can find a Circe with an appropriate magic wand; Alcibiades' magic wand shows itself to be inappropriate and inadequate).

Furthermore, in considering Mill's original choice between the pig satisfied and Socrates dissatisfied, it is unclear what the basic unit of comparison actually is. Is it the detached momentary state of a pig in a field in Suffolk wallowing happily on one particular afternoon, as compared with the momentary state of Socrates, scratching his head in perplexity and frustration because he still does not understand what Protagoras is saying? Or is it the life of a pig who has what is, for a pig (as far as we can tell), a highly satisfactory life, taken as a whole, with all its pleasures and pains, compared to the whole life of Socrates, even if that life is one of great dissatisfaction? Mill's general approach gives priority to the first of these two interpretations, which amounts to the claim that a human life, for these purposes of evaluation, can be analysed into a series of episodes (lying in the sun in a field in Suffolk, sleeping undisturbed in the sty, eating slops in the rain, etc. for the pig; arguing with Xanthippe, walking to the agora, standing and talking with Euthyphro, etc. for Socrates). Mill assumes that there is one clear sense of 'satisfied/dissatisfied' that can be used of both Socrates and the pig, and that is highly dubious. Whatever is true of Mill, it is rather clear that for Socrates the appropriate unit of analysis, discussion,

and evaluation is not primarily the individual action or some individual momentary state, but a type of life as a whole.[7] If you wish to
think about how it is best to be or to live, you do that not by considering successively individual actions that you might perform but by
looking at the shape of a human life as a whole. After all, one of the
ways in which the *Apology* may seem slightly strange, if one compares it with speeches for the defence with which we are familiar in
more modern legal contexts, is precisely that Socrates acts as if what
is on trial is not any *specific* individual or datable act or acts he performed, but his general mode of life, and his accusers and the jury, as
far as we can tell, seem to think he has got that right and is giving a
defence of the right kind (although one they do not accept). It is his
'philosophical' manner of life that is on trial, not any particular
thing he did.

It is perfectly understandable that people who live in an unpredictable, unsteady, and potentially dangerous world, that is, in any
world we know of, should be deeply concerned to make the 'right'
practical decision in the individual emergencies that sometimes confront them: Is this a venomous or a nonvenomous snake? Is the
water drinkable—I am very thirsty—or not? Is the only path out of
these mountains the one to the left or the right? Do I step out of the
way of this oncoming car or not? It is then not a wholly unnatural
assumption to think further that as human beings we should be focused on trying to decide whether to act in such pressing situations
and, if so, how exactly to act. Emergencies, though, present themselves to us as detached episodes, so that it makes sense for us to
think that what we really need to do in life is simply be able to decide what to do and react appropriately in each such episode as it
arises. Human life, however, as a whole is not like this; a series of
emergencies, or rather those that are like that tend to be very short
indeed, because who could survive the press of constant necessity?

Humans have the ability to refrain from acting immediately and to step back from some immediate situations and reflect beyond any immediate context of action. Sometimes this is highly disadvantageous or even fatal—if you spend too much time trying to determine whether *this* snake is venomous, it may be too late for you—but if the inhibition of immediate action was never possible, human life would be radically different from what we know it to be. Even a philosopher who was as keen to connect thought directly to action as Marx was asserts that one characteristic property of human action is that it does not react merely to the immediate given properties of the situation but acts according to a predetermined plan elaborated in the imagination. I don't merely step under a tree when it rains; I commission an architect to imagine how natural materials could be shaped and joined together so that in future I don't need to look for a tree.[8] Even if philosophical reflection aims to improve real life, the appropriate conditions for conducting it include being to some extent insulated from the demands of immediate action. As the ancients would have said, philosophy requires leisure.[9]

If Mill tends automatically to think first about individual cases, Socrates starts from the idea of a kind of human life considered as a whole. To consider a given human life as a whole, however, is to see its unity, and to give priority to whatever makes that unity possible. He takes for granted that a human life is not just a sequence of individual actions. Individual actions don't generally stand by themselves but fit together into larger patterns that are connected with more long-lasting goals that humans pursue, moral views to which they subscribe, and lasting dispositions they have. Thus, to take a case much cited in the ancient world, a man may at some point intentionally decide to follow a diet heavy in meat *because*, for instance, he wants to be a wrestler. It is not exactly right to say that this decision could make no sense except as a means to this goal—he might find he simply had a taste for meat, or he might wish to flaunt his prosperity in a society in which meat is a rarity—but in general he will have one goal or another in mind, or the action will be of the kind we call 'habitual' or 'traditional'.[10] When one acts in the way everyone (in one's society or social group) has 'always' acted, one is not usually making a conscious decision, as the would-be wrestler does. Often, too, there will be some traditional reasons that are given for acting *comme tout le monde*. There may be actions that do not fit into this pattern, acts that are not instrumentally directed at the attainment of some further state of affairs: I eat meat now in order, in six months, to be able to wrestle better. They may also not exactly be 'habitual' or 'traditional', at least if one takes such actions to be essentially routine, automatic, or unthinking. I may mount my high horse and say, like Luther, 'Here I stand; I can do no other' in the face of something I find morally outrageous and am not willing to tolerate, regardless of the consequences. Here, too, though, this decision will be very unlikely to stand in isolated magnificence without any connection to a panoply, not so much of further goals but of further reasons for acting. In Luther's case the reasons are given by a complex theology and a set of religious experiences. One of the bizarre aspects of Socrates' inner voice (31c–32, 40) is precisely that, whenever it does speak it always says 'no', preventing him from doing something he is about to do; it never says 'yes' or endorses any course of action, and it never gives a reason for its judgement. These features are so unusual that they astonished and perplexed even Socrates himself. They are one of the reasons Nietzsche thinks Socrates is a pervert.[11]

As many have come to realise, a truly gratuitous action, one fully outside the human web of goals and reasons, is rare indeed.[12] Just as an individual act makes sense only relative to a goal or a reason, so, too, the goal (or the reason) itself will be significant and comprehensible in the context of a person's other and further desires, beliefs, reasons, attitudes, dispositions, and values. One man wants to become a wrestler to gain glory; Luther wants to be pleasing to God. Since individual actions have their sense in such a context, it would be right to evaluate them not on their own but in their appropriate larger whole. One final reflection is that this 'larger whole' has no natural limit before one comes to the whole of a person's life with all its goals, reasons, values, desires, and commitments. Some later philosophers might say that even an individual's life is too small a unit to study if one wishes seriously to understand human life—one needs to consider a whole human society or the life of the whole human species or all sentient life in the universe—but Socrates does not seem to take that step. Still this instantiates a form of argument that one frequently finds in philosophical writings: an individual action makes sense only relative to goals and reasons; those goals and reasons make sense only relative to further goals, reasons, desires, etc. One can continue to argue in this way indefinitely; therefore the appropriate unit for analysis is the whole human life. I merely point out that 'I can go on and see no natural place to stop' does not automatically imply 'I must grasp "the whole"—as if it were obvious that such a thing even existed as something determinate—before I study any individual case'.

The contrast between Mill and Socrates can be seen with particular clarity if one looks at a case like that of Euthyphro, a priest who is on his way to indict his father for having unintentionally caused the death of one of his slaves.[13] Mill would presumably have focused on the details of this particular case and the consequences of acting in this way: Was it better or not for Euthyphro to indict his father? Socrates operates in a completely different way. He doesn't actually discuss the case in hand at all—the death of the slave and Euthyphro's plan to indict his father for murder. Rather he shifts the discussion to the concept of 'piety'. What is piety and what kind of human life instantiates it? The one thing that is clear to Socrates is that a pious human life does not consist in performing a string, no matter how long a string, of individual pious acts. Piety is some kind of structural property of a life as a whole; it is the coherence and unity which a life of a certain kind exhibits overall.

To say that a human life exhibits an overall coherence, is, however, to make a statement that has an odd and slightly ambiguous status. On the one hand, it looks like a report of a quasi-empirical fact, but on the other it can look more like a methodological principle that we adopt in trying to understand others (and ourselves). Finally, it is clearly intended to have more aspirational power than the normal report of a fact has, and it seems to propose and recommend to each individual a substantive end rather than being a mere heuristic principle.

Perhaps the 'recommendation' is so strong as almost to amount to a demand. Clearly the 'coherence' which a human life does (and should?) exhibit is not a form of mere logical consistency, but beyond that it is hard to say exactly what it is supposed to be. In any case, it must be a strange kind of coherence, because it must be one that is compatible with a certain kind of *in*coherence. If not, what space would there be for criticism or self-improvement? Or can the pious person never fail to be pious, feel regret for this, strive to do better? In addition, there are distinct *types* of lives which have what look very much like different forms of coherence: a life devoted to the attainment of public honour (through politics, athletic competition, war); a life organised around the pursuit of money and possessions; a life in which one aspires to be a fit companion for one or the other of the gods (Hippolytus and Artemis);[14] a life devoted to

CHANGING THE SUBJECT

contemplation. Can one say anything about which of these types of coherence (and types of life) is better?

Socrates, despite claiming to know nothing, actually has quite a lot to say on this subject. In particular he has two answers to the question of which life is better, as we can discover by seeing how he actually acts and argues and what he explicitly says. First, human life, he thinks, is a practical activity, and thus it should be possible for us to understand it in the way we understand other, more limited, practical activities. These activities include such things as cooking, sewing, carpentry, pottery, singing, nowadays perhaps driving a car, gambling, setting up a company, filling out an income tax return. We observe that these practical activities can be done better or worse, that some specific people are able reliably to do them better than others can, and that those who can do them reliably better than others are generally said to be 'excellent' because they 'know what they are doing'; that is, they have a kind of knowledge which guides them. Human life, Socrates assumes, can also be seen in this way. It is an activity that can be performed in a better or less good, a more or a less excellent, way. A person who performs the activity of singing is an excellent singer who knows what she is doing. A human who performs the activity of living (or perhaps living a properly human life) is a good human or a person who has the virtue or excellence of 'wisdom'. As the singer's song is guided by her knowledge of how to sing, the good human's life is guided by the knowledge of how to live (called 'wisdom'). What we moderns would call the question of 'motivation' also has a clear and simple answer: Just as all singers want to be excellent singers—otherwise why would they sing?—and all potters want to make good pots, so all humans want to be living a good life, that is, to be excellent human beings. Differences are the result of the presence or absence of knowledge about how to attain this goal. Socrates is

30

looking for this form of knowledge. But is it actually true that *all* singers want to be excellent singers? Might I not want to sing for all sorts of other good reasons? If that seems implausible, is it also obvious that all humans want to be excellent humans? This simply attributes to everyone without much argumentation the specific agonistic code of ancient freemen (and ancient aristocrats). What about the possibility, developed later by Hobbes, that what people want is not to be excellent but to survive, which is a completely different thing? Or what about the idea, proposed in different and variant forms by different people, that what humans want is relief from care or release from striving or quietude or 'pure vegetating like a plant'?[15]

The term used in Greek for 'excellence' (ἀρετή) is also sometimes translated 'virtue'. This can be very confusing because 'excellence' and 'virtue' have very different connotations in English. Unfortunately, both terms are used in a very wide sense to cover virtually any kind of human goodness, that is, being good at something. Although Socrates is keen on linguistic and conceptual exactness and in distinguishing the different meanings of different terms, the distinction of different meanings is a *goal* of enquiry, something not simply given at the start but to be worked toward; fully clear distinctions emerge only gradually. There is no reason to think Socrates attained this goal even at the end of his life. So 'good man', 'virtuous man', 'man of excellence', at least at this point in the discussion, are not to be systematically distinguished, and one can move inferentially from one of them to the other.

The second thing Socrates says specifically that he knows is that humans must 'examine' their lives (38). Once again, he does not say you must think before you act or that you must reflect on each individual action before you perform it. This is connected with his view that the basic unit for evaluation is a (kind of) life (as a whole), not the individual items such as particular dispositions, values, and performances. We know what Socrates means by 'examine' because he gives us rather full examples of it. To examine means to subject to the kind of dialectical investigation we see Socrates conducting in the dialogues. It means being able to give a correctly formulated account of what you are doing and exactly why you are doing it (if you are, for instance, a craftsman such as a potter), or it means giving a correctly formulated account (λόγος) of what you believe and why you believe it (if you are any human being). Furthermore this account must stand up to verbal cross-examination by Socrates, who will demand the greatest possible clarity and precision in the account and will investigate its internal consistency, the consequences of holding it, and its compatibility with various other beliefs that most people are tacitly agreed to hold.

The usual translation of this Socratic thesis is 'The unexamined life is not worth living for man' (ὁ δὲ ἀνεξέταστος βίος οὐ βιωτὸς ἀνθρώπῳ [38a]), but this seems to me slightly misleading. The phrase 'not worth living' appeals to (differential) values, as if to say that some lives are more, and some less, 'worth living'. The fool lives a life that is less worth living and the philosopher one that is more or most worth living, but both are in a sense full human lives. However, the meaning of verbal adjectives like βιωτός is to designate not (differential) value so much as possibility; so it means 'liveable', not 'worth living', and in the negative it is sometimes used to mean something like 'intolerable'. So the unexamined life is not one that a human *could live* or could bear to live or could tolerate living. It isn't that the fool can fail to investigate his own life and that this will mean his life is lacking in something; rather it is that, hard as he might try, not even the fool can fully avoid reflecting on his life. A person with a concussion can ignore Socrates, and perhaps certain people with dementia or who live in a persistent vegetative state (like the one recommended by Schlegel[16]) can also do so, but they are not fully human. One may find this view ridiculous or repellent, but it is, I think, a key to understanding what many philosophers in the past have thought. A fool may make a mess of his discussion with Socrates, but even he, as long as he is not concussed, completely demented, or in a merely vegetative state, that is, as long as he lives anything like a full human life, cannot simply and completely ignore the questions Socrates asks. To the extent to which he is a human being at all, albeit a fool, he will (eventually) see the point and then will have no alternative but to engage. So many of Socrates' interlocutors get angry with him rather than performing the ancient Athenian equivalent of shrugging their shoulders, because they cannot bring themselves really to see what he is doing as irrelevant to them. His discussions touch them, whether they like it or not.

To start with the first of the two things Socrates implies that he knows—that there can be a form of knowledge about how to live one's life which is in some sense parallel to the knowledge the good potter or the excellent singer had, respectively, of how to make a good pot and how to sing well—one might point out that this seems prima facie very implausible. Potting is a relatively well-defined activity with a clear beginning and clear end and with (more or less) agreed standards of quality in any given society. Human life as a whole does not seem to have any such properties; it is not well-defined in the same way. A potter works in his studio from 8 a.m. to 6 p.m., but then he goes to the pub to play darts. What he does in the pub is not, of course, without *any* relation to his potting; playing darts may help increase his manual dexterity and hand-eye coordination, skills very useful in potting. Nevertheless excellence in darts is not excellence in potting. At some point the potter will take a holiday and go rock climbing in Scotland or lie in the sun on a beach in the Mediterranean. What would human life 'after hours'

33

or 'on holiday' even look like? 'Being a human being' is not a role one can adopt or put aside like 'being a potter'. One is never, as a human being, 'off duty' in the way a soldier or police officer might be 'off duty'. Or, if this is possible, it requires a more serious reconfiguration of our ways of thinking about human life than any of the philosophers treated in this book envisaged. Similarly, what is most striking about human life is precisely the absence of any clear universally recognised goal, or rather any clear universally recognised goal that is not a merely and utterly vacuous formula ('happiness', 'utility', 'goodness', etc.). Furthermore, in living we are making up the standards for evaluating life as we go on. Or, if one finds that formulation too harsh, at any rate we are continually trying to discover what standards there are, criticising proposals about how we should evaluate life, and worrying whether our own ways of judging and evaluating things are well-grounded. That is part of the reason people would have given for thinking that philosophy exists at all.

To put this point in a slightly different way, Socrates construes being a potter on the model of being in a race, either in a race with all other existing potters for excellence or in some kind of more depersonalised race, that is, a race to attain the highest level of proficiency on some abstract scale. This 'agonistic' conception is deeply rooted in Greek culture (and in ours).[17] Is it the right way to think about human life as a whole? Of course, this is not the only way to organise a race. In addition to the agonistic, first-past-the-post race, there is the 'Maoist' kind of race, in which the runners are grouped and race together; after each heat the members of each group are changed until all the groups cross the finish line at about the same time. Then there is the 'Caucus race' from *Alice in Wonderland*, in which wet people run around in a circle until they get dry, and at that point the race ends.[18] One might argue that these other races are not 'really' races at all. Why not? Thinking about the Caucus race is

salutary in some other respects, too. The first is that everyone wins
this race (or perhaps, equivalently, everyone loses because we all
die eventually); the second is that, as one of the organisers (the
Dodo) says, the best way to explain it is to do it. This would be
absolutely intolerable to Socrates; it is an affront to everything he
most deeply believes. He certainly did *not* think that the best way
to 'explain' how to make a good pot or what 'justice' is was to
make one or to act in a just way. The thought that just doing was a
sufficient manifestation of knowing, however, was perfectly available to Greeks of Socrates' time. Herodotus, who lived a generation before Socrates and wrote a history of the Persian Wars, has
the Persian king Darius say to one of his associates, 'πολλά ἐστι τὰ
λόγῳ μὲν οὐκ οἷά τε δηλῶσαι, ἔργῳ δέ'. [There are lots of things that
cannot be made clear in words/argument (λόγος), but that can be
made clear by doing them (III.72).] If the potters and wheelwrights
whom Socrates investigated had responded to him resolutely in
this fashion, perhaps we would have been spared the great *malheur*
of 2,000 years of philosophy. One can, of course, point out various
ways in which human life is not really exactly like a Caucus race,
but that is not the point. The question rather is whether human
life is *more* like Olympic sprinting than it is like a Caucus race. It
is not self-evidently ludicrous to think this an open question.

This brings us to the question of the unexamined life. The atten-
tive reader will have noticed that Socrates thinks that if I am a skilful
agent/producer in some area ('knowing' in the third sense discussed
earlier), this is because I 'know' something (in the second sense analysed earlier); that is, I have some propositional knowledge.[19] However, I can know how to ride a bicycle without being able even to
describe what I am doing, much less being able to give an account
of *why* I do what I do. So even if there was a kind of 'knowledge' of
how to lead a good life, it would not necessarily have propositional

35

form, and the person who had it would not necessarily be able to stand up to Socrates' questions and give him good answers. A further question here is whether 'examination' *must* take the form of Socratic dialectic, defence of a position in the argumentatively free flow of question and answer. Even if we think that some kind of scrutiny is an integral part of human life, does it have to be the dialectic? Couldn't we imagine other ways of examining or scrutinising our lives?

'Unexamined' has an odd structure when used by Socrates. We generally think of an examination as something with a definite beginning and an end, something that comes to some kind of conclusion. Examining is usually a matter of standing back and asking questions; then, when I have come to some conclusion, I may continue to act. However, for Socrates the examined life is not a life that is examined but a life spent in examining. What would an unending examination be? Socrates' unclarity about the exact relation of thought and action, of which this is an instance, has dogged the history of philosophy ever since.

Socrates' views about 'the unexamined life' might also easily give rise to two further misconceptions. First, one might mistakenly think that since no one can say Socrates' questions are irrelevant— if he is given a chance to put them with his usual pungency— therefore Socrates himself is irrelevant or superfluous because even a fool will eventually ask the questions for herself. However, it is one thing not to be able to avoid seeing the relevance of a question and responding, and another altogether to be motivated (and able) to begin to ask the questions oneself. Socrates analyses this failure to ask questions as a form of 'laziness', and he sees his job as that of a gadfly sent by god to sting the torpid into motion (30d–31). The second misconception is that if people 'see Reason' (as it emerges from dialectical discussion), they will act accordingly. This would be a comforting thought if it weren't so palpably and almost insultingly false.

*Apology* is infinitely fascinating because it announces both the beginning and the end of Western philosophy with a crack of complete failure which resounds down the centuries. Whatever the 'historical' Socrates might or might not have thought, the Platonic 'Socrates' who became the patron saint of Western philosophy puts the case for rationalism in very strong terms. Reason (λόγος) is supreme; it is in itself so clear and so attractive to humans that they cannot fail (eventually) to see and understand it and, once they have seen it, to *act* on it. That is what the little treatise *asserts,* but what it *shows* is the complete failure of this dogma. The jurors are not convinced (or they fail to act on their conviction, which amounts to much the same thing). Many of those who did see what Socrates was about didn't approve of his activity or of him at all and thought he was an exceedingly dangerous individual. Socrates suggests that this is because he didn't have enough time to convince them of the reasonableness of his views and actions. In retrospect it is hard to find this claim at all plausible. Did he fail to convert Alcibiades to the life of philosophy because he did not spend enough time with him? How about Critias, a student of Socrates who was one of the major players in the coup against the Athenian democracy which has come to be known as the regime of the Thirty Tyrants?

Hegel pointed out long ago that an Athenian jury in a legal case is not in general called on to make some kind of philosophical judgement about human life nor, for that matter, to judge cases relative to the kind of highly procedural and formalist criteria of conformity to 'the law' which we have inherited from later Roman practice. An Athenian jury was not intended to be 'apolitical'; the jury system is almost always specifically cited as an essential component of the 'democracy'. Serving as a member of a jury and giving a judgement was an integral part of what it meant to be an Athenian citizen and was an archetypically 'political' act. There was, of course, some notion of 'law', although it must be pointed out that the distinction between what we would consider to be 'proper' law and something more vague, such as customary morality, was not nearly as sharp as it was later to become.[20] So the jury was called on to make a decision about whether or not the accused was guilty as charged. Of course, they would make this decision according to their best lights of what custom and 'law' required and permitted and what was best for the democracy as an ongoing enterprise. We can, of course, look back at them and say they ought to have used completely different criteria, imagined a very different kind of society, been very different people, but it is not clear what the point of such an anachronistic exercise would be. Since Socrates was guilty as charged, it is not at all surprising that a majority, if a slim majority, of the jury condemned him.[21] He could perhaps quibble sufficiently about the nature of his religious beliefs to get off on that count, but he pretty clearly did have a 'new god', namely the inner voice that sometimes told him to desist from doing something he proposed to do. As far as 'corrupting the youth' is concerned, Hegel seems to have got it right to hold that a fundamentally traditionalist society like late fifth-century Athens could not have survived as the society it was if it had a population of young people who systematically subjected it to the kind of 'rational' scrutiny that Socrates had invented and directed at it. If 'trying to corrupt the youth' meant making them fundamentally unfit to reproduce anything like existing society, then it was right for that charge to stick.

I have discussed two of the things Socrates seems to have claimed to know. There is perhaps a third thing which he does not claim strictly to know but which structures his behaviour in the way in which firm knowledge structures the behaviour of those who believe they possess it. Socrates says that he does not fear death because nothing bad can befall a good man. He does not strictly say he knows this but that it is the content of a 'good hope' he has (39–42). This does, however, finally point to a deep incoherence in Socrates' beliefs and way of life. His deepest beliefs, those which structure his life, are not couched in terms of ratiocination but appeal to what he 'hopes' for, what 'the daimonion' tells him (not) to do (without giving any reasons), and pious obedience to the god of Delphi. Just to repeat, on the one hand, he is completely committed to the idea of 'giving a rational account' (*logos*) of oneself. The shoemaker can be said to know only if she can say, describe, and explain what she is doing and why she is doing it. And in principle there seem to be no limits to the extent to which she would need to be able to continue that 'explanation'. On the other hand, Socrates admits that his own life is oriented not around a 'logos'(reason) in the sense of an argument or a way of being for which he can give a logos, but around a whole series of other, non-logos-based phenomena: enquiry at the oracle of Delphi and, following what he takes to be the implications of that, an internal voice that never gives reasons, and finally his own 'good hope' that no evil can befall a good man. A 'hope' is, however, not a reasoned reason.

Thinking about how humans should live has (at least) two dimensions, not just one, and Socrates recognizes both. There is the question of 'the good' or of 'how things must be to be for the best'. This question is complex enough because of the different ways in which something can be 'for the best': how exactly the bread must be cut in order to be 'for the best' depends on the bread (baguette, round loaf, *petit pain,* brioche, pumpernickel) and also on what you want to do with it (make sandwiches, feed the birds, produce canapés). Still, more or less everyone in more or less any society that one can imagine has *some* grasp on the general idea that some objects are better for some purposes than others are and that some states of affairs and ways of acting are better than others. The second dimension is not so much that of better and worse, of excellence and its opposite, as that of human concern or care, of relevance or importance to humans. Of course, there is a 'best' way of dealing with a particular kind of bread so as to make it easiest to cut, transport, and throw to the birds, and easiest for the birds to find, eat, and digest, but frankly I could not possibly be bothered to discover what that way is. I simply don't care. Just as I simply do not care who wins the UEFA Cup (although I know in principle that some football teams are better at playing the game than others are), who produces the best computers (although I know in principle that some must be better than others), or which breed of dog has the keenest sense of smell (although I know that the various breeds differ in this regard). Socrates combines these two dimensions when he says that he asks any citizen of Athens he meets, 'Why are you not taking care that your soul be the best it can be?' ([πῶς] οὐκ ἐπιμελεῖ τῆς ψυχῆς, ὅπως ὡς βελτίστη ἔσται [29d].)

If *some* rough and ready distinction between more and less excellent, better and worse is the bread and butter of human life, the specific cocktail which Socrates proposes is an unusual mixture containing four principal components. The philosopher is to:

1. Have a special concern for the unity of whole human life as the expression of the unity of the human soul
2. Be concerned not just to act well, but to attain a particular kind of knowledge of 'the good', the better, and the best kind of human life
3. Pursue self-knowledge

where 'knowledge' is taken to be instantiated in a dialectical process of discussion in which one can 'give an account of oneself' and of what one claims to know by answering fully and adequately Socratic questioning (where this is the fourth component).

As far as the unity of human life and the human soul is concerned, it is useful to look at a passage from another Platonic dialogue. In *Phaidros* Socrates is walking outside the walls of Athens with a young friend named Phaidros. They come to a place where legend has it that the daughter of one of the early kings of Attica was abducted by Boreas, the god of the North Wind. Phaidros wonders whether the story is true. Did anything like that ever happen? If something did happen, is it to be given a 'mythological' interpretation (was it really a god who took the girl off to be his plaything) or a debunking, naturalist explanation (was she just blown off the top of some rocks by the north wind and killed)? Socrates says:

> I have no time at all [for this sort of thing, i.e., for explanations of natural phenomena or of particular events]. The reason is, you know, that I am not yet able to do what the oracle at Delphi tells us to do, namely to know myself. It would seem to me ridiculous while I am still in ignorance about myself even to consider anything else. So I basically ignore all the tricky explanations people propose of natural phenomena and simply accept whatever the generally accepted view is and instead focus on considering myself, asking whether I happen to be a wild beast composed of more diverse, independent strands and more incandescent than Typhon or a tamer and simpler animal, which has a part in a divine and modest nature. (*Phaidros*, 229e4–230a6)

The details of Plato's formulation here are not unimportant. 'Typhon' was a mythical monster whose exact appearance and nature are not completely clear, perhaps because those who spoke of him were not clear or because different people had different views. In some accounts he seems to have been an amorphous creature or one capable of swiftly changing his shape, and in others a creature with a body composed of combined shapes drawn from different animals. Sometimes he is represented as having a human torso ending in serpents' tails.[22] One standard early description by Hesiod is as follows:

> and from his shoulders there were a hundred heads of snakes, of terrible dragons flickering with dark tongues, and under their brows [? snake-brows?] in those awful heads his eyes darted fire, and from all the heads fire blazed when he looked at you. And there were voices in all those terrible heads, producing all sorts of different unholy sounds; sometimes a sound for the gods to understand; then again at other times the sound of a load-roaring bull, uncheckable in his power, proud of aspect; sometimes again they produced the sound of a lion who had an untiring spirit: sometimes again a sound like that of a pack of whelps, a wonder to hear; and again sometimes he hissed and the huge mountains echoed with the noise. (*Theogonia*, 824.35)

Typhon's snake-like tentacles seem in one form or another to have been common to most of the accounts that were given of him. This is the reason Plato's Socrates describes him as a 'many-plaited' entity composed of 'many different strands'. In Hesiod, Typhon is the last prehistoric monster who seriously contests control of the world with Zeus. After defeating him, Zeus cast Typhon down 'into Tartarus'—some later authors claim he was buried under Mount Etna[23]—where he is held responsible for irregular, unpredictable, and violent storm winds and for volcanic eruptions, hence the reference to incandescence.

This ambiguity, variability, or even indeterminacy makes it particularly appropriate for Socrates to appeal to him in this context, where the issue is precisely whether or not Socrates himself has a single determinate nature, and, if so, what that nature is, whether or not his 'soul' is unified. In Hesiod each of Typhon's limbs has its own voice, or rather each has a voice capable of producing different sounds. It is possible to imagine that each head made its own noise at any given time; that is, if they all spoke together, each had, as it were, a 'mind (and soul) of its own'.

There seem to be two slightly different things about Typhon that represent states of affairs that Socrates fears. First, he is afraid that he might have a complex and convoluted (or indeterminate) 'nature' like that of Typhon rather than a simple and unitary soul. If Typhon speaks with a number of different voices out of his various snake heads at any particular time, one might think he did not constitute what has come to be called a 'single, unitary subject', and, of course, he would not be a possible participant in Socratic dialectic. Which head would Socrates question first? What would he do if he got a hundred separate answers all at the same time to a question like 'What is piety?' Or if he got fifty answers, forty hisses, squeals, roars, and discourses in a language comprehensible only to the gods? Second, Socrates is also afraid that he himself might be as uncontrolled and potentially incandescently violent as the monster. The assumption that these two things go together is not obviously true. Why couldn't a soul be unitary *and also* violent, or nonunitary in a way that prevented one from being violent, or at any rate effectively violent, at all?

Socrates says that his quest for self-knowledge was his way of trying to comply with the Delphic injunction to 'know thyself'. Socratic self-knowledge, though, seems a rather Procrustean thing. It is not a highly individuated understanding of my own unique features, properties, idiosyncrasies, fears, predilections, taste, the microhistory of my emotions and cognitions. It is not anything like what Freud would later call 'the story of my family expressed in the form of a novel' (*Familienroman des Neurotikers*).[24] In a lifetime of discussion with Socrates, I would most likely also get to know some of these things, but that would not be the point of the discussion, and everything would be filtered through and regimented by an abiding and overarching concern for defensible, general reasons. In practice Socrates turns the command of the god of Delphi into his own characteristic request that his interlocutor 'give an account' (διδόναι λόγον) of his opinions on whatever topic is at issue. Another way of parsing the Socratic project, then, is as the mode of life which tries to satisfy two commands:

1. Know thyself (γνῶθι σεαυτόν).
2. Give an account [of yourself, how you act and what you believe] (δίδου λόγον σεαυτοῦ).

These two—the question of who or what I am, and the question of what I can give an adequate account of—seem very different from each other, and each seems to be very different from questions of what is valuable or of practical necessity. Is it true that if I know myself, that is, can give an account of my opinions in abstract terms, I will also know what is the best form of life?

Modern philosophers often stand under the spell of some form of romanticism and do what they can to emphasise the novel, original, or even revolutionary nature of what they are trying to do, of their methods or views. To be sure, the most original modern philosopher, Hegel, was, oddly enough, almost completely immune to this and followed rather ancient practice. In the ancient world one was likely to understate the originality of one's position: philosophers tried to connect what they were doing with purportedly ancient forms of wisdom by inventing for their own views a longer and more distinguished pedigree than they really had, and Socrates has an especially amusing variant on this motif: he is just doing what the god of Delphi has been telling people to do from time immemorial. We are told that three inscriptions stood over the entrance to the oracle of Delphi:[25]

1. Know yourself (γνῶθι σεαυτόν).
2. Don't overdo it (μηδὲν ἄγαν).
3. Surety is next to catastrophe (i.e., stand surety for someone and you'll be sorry; 'take an IOU and you'll pay for it') (ἐγγύα πάρα δ ἄτη).

Socrates gives his own highly idiosyncratic reading of (1), which seems originally to have meant 'The god is busy and irritable. Don't pester him with too many questions; know what single question you want to ask before you enter the sanctuary'. Socrates does follow this injunction, thus interpreted, but only by virtue of displacing his importuning on to his fellow citizens. It is hard to see him as in any way conforming to the second demand; most other Athenians certainly thought he was definitely an extremist in that he asked distinctly too many questions. The history of philosophy would perhaps have been different if Socrates had interpreted the first two Delphic injunctions as meaning 'Know yourself, but don't overdo the pursuit of self-knowledge'. As far as the question of 'surety' is concerned, Socrates has no need of this advice for himself—he is so notably poor, no one would ask him to stand surety—but he accepts the offer of Plato and some others to stand surety (ἐγγυᾶσθαι [38b]) for the fine he proposes as his punishment. If the god at Delphi is to be trusted, this is not a very friendly way to treat Plato, whom the 'catastrophe' would be most likely to befall. Perhaps that catastrophe is precisely Western philosophy, although the full force of that calamity did not hit Plato so much as the whole population of Europe during the subsequent 2,000 years or so. In any case the purportedly Delphic genealogy of Socrates' project is another one of his ironic little jokes. His quest, then, has a shorter (but probably much more variegated) prehistory than he pretends; what, then, happened to it after his death?

# Chapter Two

# PLATO

The main character in Plato's *Apology of Socrates* seems clearly to think that I, and each one of us, could come to lead a better life by seeking wisdom and that that wisdom is constituted by ability adequately to answer questions and give reasoned explanations about what constitutes the nature of human excellence. The real historical person Socrates, as far as we can tell, will also most likely have subscribed to some version or approximation of this. We encounter in the *Republic* a figure called 'Socrates' who seems to have a different project. The Socrates of the *Republic* thinks that we, you and I, can lead a better life if we live in a society without laws and which is sharply divided into two classes. One class would contain a very tiny number of individuals; the members of this elite class would have an exceedingly rigorous training in mathematics and dialectics which would give them insight into 'the good', and they would rule over the rest. The great majority would be completely subject to the instruction of and control by members of this group of people who were presumed to know the truth about the world. People in the elite group, once they had that insight into the 'good', would also realise that it was incumbent on them, a sad necessity, to become (for a while) absolute governors of our societies, administering the details of the lives of each citizen in such a way that the general good and the ultimate common interest of all were realised (whether or not the members of the majority knew that).

Socrates, at least as represented by Plato in the *Apology*, tried hard to stand outside the usual sphere of everyday politics (31ff.). He knew his fellow citizens only too well and knew that he would never have survived as long as he did had he been at all involved in politics (31d–e). So he tried to improve the citizens of the city by discussion, one at a time, while at the same time avoiding all public office—as much as that was possible in democratic Athens, where every citizen was liable to be chosen by lot to fill a political post.

It would be completely out of character for the man who spoke the *Apology* to argue that philosophers should be kings and that they should tell the rest of the population what to do without any framework of public rules or laws. This, however, is exactly the way the Socrates in Plato's *Republic* describes how the purportedly 'best' city is to be run. The Socrates of the *Apology* is a man of a deeply sceptical disposition; he doesn't even completely believe the god of Delphi when he receives an oracle that seems implausible. And he is ironic, playful, (sometimes) tolerant; he doesn't even seem to be able to summon up any wrath against those who accused and those who condemned him. It is hard to imagine anything less like the usual conceptions of what is 'kingly'. Imagine Agamemnon, Lear, or Henry VIII in a comparable situation. Nietzsche, to be sure, thought this was a very clever mask which Socrates had invented in order to cover up the fact that he had the most tyrannical soul (we would say 'character' or 'personality') of any of his contemporaries, and that the mask did not simply cover it up but was an active instrument for furthering his aim of always being the one to come out on top.[1] Socrates invents a new agonistic game with new rules: get the opponent to make some substantive general claim, usually about the 'good human life', its preconditions and constituents; engage him in discussion; and tie him up in knots by making him contradict himself. You 'win' if you succeed; he wins if you don't. In fact, he always loses. From one point of view that does not seem very surprising. Socrates invented this new game (Nietzsche thinks it is one particularly suited to his own psychic deformity—a cancerous growth of the part of the soul devoted to ratiocination) and practices it continuously. So why shouldn't Socrates be especially good at it? The rules are so peculiar that even if he switched places with his opponents and let them do the asking of questions (as Plato envisages at one point in his dialogue *Gorgias*, 462ff.), they are rubbish at this. As Nietzsche also points out, the real trick is not to win the arguments but to get anyone (and eventually everyone) to find it perfectly natural to play the game all the time. Socrates does not do that by arguing; he is too intelligent actually to be taken in by his own propaganda about the effectiveness of argumentation. Rather he uses his charisma, his erotic power to tease and withhold. Plato, too, has Socrates say in *Symposium* (177d) that erotics is the one area in which he does have knowledge—and he was also fortunate to have as a follower the literary genius of Plato. Philosophy wins over the West to playing its peculiar game of argumentation, not by arguing but because Plato presents an irresistibly attractive literary image of Socrates as a model to be emulated (and eventually because philosophy comes to be seen to serve important social functions).[2]

However that might be, still the Socrates who emerges from the pages of *Apology* does not merely seem different from real or mythical kings such as Priam, Philip of Macedon, or Louis XIV, but he seems

48

to be very different in significant ways from the ideal 'philosopher-kings' envisaged in the *Republic*. For one thing, the philosopher-kings in the *Republic* are definitely presented as 'knowing' something, not as instances of Socratic ignorance. Furthermore, they are not merely said to know various things, such as astronomy, mathematics, geography, and music, but they are supposed to know that which is most important in human life, namely what is 'good'. They know what is good in general, in individual cases, and they know *why* doing, say, X in any situation Y is 'good'.

It would be disingenuous to think that Socrates' pretence of 'merely asking questions' was ever any more than that: a pretence. He almost always asks what are called in the context of legal cross-examination 'leading' questions, and even in *Apology* he says that he 'encourages' people to think about how they can lead 'the good' life, which is a way of going beyond merely asking questions. Nevertheless, he does not give anyone a direct order to do anything or to refrain from doing anything else. He does not either dispense the kind of 'good advice' one friend gives to another in our normal human affairs, nor does he give authoritative advice of the kind a physician would. He never commands as a king might, and he is as far from instantiating the Islamic ideal of 'commanding the right and forbidding the wrong' as anyone could be.[3]

There are two questions that arise about the kingly knowledge of the philosophers in the *Republic*. The first is whether such knowledge—knowledge not about the internal angles of triangles or the road to Ephesos, but about what is 'good'—can exist at all, or, more to the point (if it is not roughly the same thing), whether it can exist in a form that is accessible to humans. The second is whether possession of such knowledge could give an individual or group any kind of warrant to tell others what to do (and, if so, what the nature of that warrant might be). After all, a physician clearly has much more knowledge than I do about my current state and future prospects as a biological organism and also much more knowledge about what I might do to increase (or decrease) the chances that I will continue to live and flourish biologically without its being in any way the case that he or she can do anything more than give me 'advice' which I am free to follow, and sometimes do, or simply to ignore, as I occasionally do. Why should 'knowledge of the good' give those who possess it any more power or authority than that?

The *Republic* is basically an exaggerated further development of one particular strand of 'Socratic thought'. As we saw in the previous chapter, Socrates thought a good man did not need to fear death. The Socrates in this dialogue takes up this point almost immediately in book I, when he discusses the fear of death with Kephalos, the elderly millionaire. Kephalos is (oddly) confident: if one has never done wrong, never defrauded anyone, performed the sacrifices one owes the gods, and paid one's debts, one can have a 'sweet hope' (like Socrates' in *Apology*) as opposed to a 'bad hope' (i.e., expectation of suffering something bad). In that case one has no reason to fear what happens after death (330–331).

The macrostructure of the central part of the argument of the *Republic* is rather clear and proceeds in three steps. First, 'Socrates' tries to find something which is common to the various instances of things Kephalos has done and avoided doing, which, he says, give him confidence in the face of death. Roughly speaking, Socrates finds that common factor in the 'justice' of the actions Kephalos performed and the injustice of the ones he avoided. The second step consists in shifting the focus in the discussion of this 'justice' from what a person actually does—the concrete individual acts she performs—to the deep-seated psychological disposition which lies behind that. A just man must have such a unitary, deep-seated psychological disposition, and may not be simply a creature like the Typhon we encountered at the end of chapter 1. 'Justice' should be taken to refer in the first instance, not to a set of ways of acting but rather to a basic condition of the soul from which actions of a certain kind (usually? always?) spring. A just man is not so much one who pays his debts as one who has his soul internally so exactly and reliably in order and under control that he is not even tempted to commit murder, to renege on bets, to lie or defraud others, to leave the line of battle without permission, to neglect the cult of the gods, or not to pay his debts. However, although one can observe the actions an individual performs, how can one know anything about what takes place in the depths of the human soul? The *Republic* is an attempt to deal with this by drawing on a purported parallelism between the human individual and society as a whole. I am supposed to be a 'just' person if my soul instantiates 'justice', but no one can see into my soul, and what goes on in there is small, hidden, and difficult to observe. So in order to be able to see the internal workings of the soul more clearly, we are to look at a blown-up image of it: a functioning city. The question is transformed. Instead of 'What is it for a soul to instantiate the psychic unity, harmony, and coherence which is "justice"?' Socrates asks, 'What is it for a city (i.e., a functioning human society) to instantiate "justice"?' 'Justice' in the soul of the individual will mirror that on a smaller scale. This part of the argument, which is driven by the dodgy analogy between the soul and a city, contains an extensive discussion of what it is to get your soul in order. It turns out that, according to Socrates, the best and most reliable way to do that is to be very talented at philosophical discussion and reflection and to have trained and developed that capacity to a high degree. Anyone who does that will have a very clear view of the idea of the 'good' which turns out to be an ordering principle for the soul and for the city. If you are not

WHAT TYPE OF
GOOD IS THE ORDERS
PRINCIPLE FOR MY SOUL
IN MY COUNTRY

naturally gifted at philosophical discussion, there is still a second-best kind of life available to you: it is to live in a city ruled by such philosophers and to be completely subject to their commands.

Having established to his satisfaction that 'justice' in the individual is a kind of correct, harmonious ordering of the parts of the human soul, just as justice in the city is a correct ordering of the different social groups and functional parts, Plato ends the *Republic* with a myth that tries to give a final answer to Kephalos' question. If you have your soul in order, you need not fear death and what potentially comes after death because harmony of the soul is not only the source of all just action but also the basic principle of human happiness. If that is the case, the person with an ordered soul will always make the right choices in life and will always be happy. To be sure, according to Socrates, that 'order in the soul' can actually mean two slightly different things. Either, as one of the elite philosopher-kings, one can have had a view of the idea of 'the good' which stabilises all one's beliefs by connecting them in a reliable way with each other, or, as a nonelite inhabitant of a good city ruled by a group of philosopher-kings, one can have habitually lived a life of excellence because one followed the directives of the philosopher-kings. The fate of members of these two groups after death is different. However, to understand this part of Plato's view it is necessary to embark on a rather long digression about 'the good' and the idea of 'the good.'

Plato tends to use visual metaphors to describe what happens when we 'see' the idea of 'the good', but the most interesting way to think about it is not by trying to pursue those metaphors in any concerted way, as if what was actually at issue was some kind of mystic vision, but rather to start from the notion of dialectical discussion (516a–c, 532–535). Plato thinks that if we start discussing how we wish to act and live, making proposals about this, questioning our friends about their proposals and why they make them, and submitting ourselves to the questioning of others, the discussion, if pursued with vigour, will quickly move from individual points to more general topics and will soon become extremely wide-ranging. When people in such a discussion try to defend their proposals, they will give reasons for them, and these reasons will eventually appeal to some notion of the 'good'. Thus, I may propose that we in Britain should become vegetarians, renationalise our natural monopolies (railways, water, etc.), break up and severely regulate our banks, remain in the EU (but leave NATO), increase our level of tax support for state schools and for the NHS, reform the House of Lords and the archaic first-past-the-post electoral system, and so on. Needless to say, this proposal of a collective way of life will not and should not simply be permitted to pass without scrutiny and careful examination, and so should be made an object of discussion; dozens of objections can easily be raised to each of these proposals. If we are engaged in a proper dialectical argument, I shall be expected to 'give an account' (at least) of each component and of my reasons for supporting it. Thus, I may say that we should eat more vegetables and much less meat than we now do because this is *good for* our health. I might add that the rearing of animals for slaughter is not *good for* our environment: by some calculations the methane gas produced by cattle is a greater source of environmental pollution than any other (including industry and the internal combustion engine), and the demand for animal feed is a major cause of deforestation. I might add that the actual conditions under which meat production takes place are not *good for* the animals concerned (and perhaps also not morally *good for* those involved in the direct production process because of the attitudes toward living things which it engenders in them). If I hold that Britain should stay in the EU, it is because I think it is *good* to try to find collective solutions to collective problems, such as immigration, and because I think it is *good for us* to be able to resist the depredations of large multinational corporations and that this is possible only as a full member of a large and unified economic block. None of these reasons will itself necessarily be the end of the story because objections can be raised to each and every one of them as the discussion progresses and the arguments ramify. Plato's claim now is that the more thoroughly and persistently we discuss how to live and how to act, the more abstract the discussion is likely to get, and the denser the interlocking network of reasoning that appeals to some 'good' will become. The first impression may be that the discussion is getting more and more dispersed, leading further and further in a number of very different directions. Is there really any common concept of 'good' involved in discussions of a good diet (for humans), what is 'good' for animals who are raised for food for humans, what is 'good' for our environment, a 'good' form of political association, 'good' economic policies, a set of 'morally good' attitudes? Plato is committed to the view, though, that this is merely an initial impression of diversity which will disappear if the questioning is pursued with sufficient vigour, skill, and persistence. Eventually one will come to see that, as the discussion of proposals and reasons for them proceeds, there is very strong convergence in the reasons people give and accept and the ideas of what is 'good' to which they appeal. Thinking seriously about reasons in discussion with others leads us (eventually) to come to agree more and more. In particular, we come to realise that 'good', as it occurs in all these apparently different contexts, actually has a single central meaning and one which we can all come to agree on. The 'good' is really, despite its apparent multiplicity, one; every good is unified with everything else that is good and forms in principle parts of a single compatible whole; all the strands of reasoning that survive

54

dialectical investigation fit together to form a single whole, centred around the one concept of 'good'.

Furthermore, suppose that I simply have some opinion on a given topic but have never subjected it to dialectical discussion and found reasons for holding it that can be defended and integrated into a larger context of reasons. Plato now holds that opinions of this kind will have no stability for me. Because they are not connected tightly to reasons, and through those reasons to other reasons and other beliefs in a spiralling network, they can easily get lost; I can, and will, give them up or change them for adventitious, trivial, or even frivolous reasons. On the other hand, beliefs that are firmly embedded in the unitary system of 'the good' are very difficult to dislodge, because all the parts are held together by ties of ratiocination, and once the system is established, it will remain stably in place. The philosopher-kings, after ten or fifteen years of running through the reasons for their major beliefs again and again, reinforcing their connection with each others' beliefs and with the overarching idea of 'the good', will effectively have produced an immovable network.

Plato claims now that in the afterlife just action will be rewarded and unjust action punished, so three groups of people have nothing to fear: the philosopher-kings of the ideal city, run-of-the-mill virtuous citizens who have 'the good' fortune to live in an ideal polity ordered by the philosopher-kings, and finally certain heroic figures who were able to live well-ordered lives *outside* the context of the ideal polity (such as Socrates himself, presumably). The great challenge of the afterlife, though, is not to survive the torments imposed on major evildoers but to make the right choice of one's next life (614a–621d). Even if you in fact lived a good life, but the reason for this was only that you had 'the good' fortune to live in a well-ordered polity, there is no guarantee that, after drinking the waters of forgetfulness in the afterlife, you will choose a good life for your next stint on earth. On the other hand, if you have studied and practised philosophy, whether successfully on your own, like Socrates, or as part of a cohort of philosopher-kings in training in an ideal polity, you will naturally and unavoidably choose a good next life.

Kephalos was lucky in this life; however, we don't know how well he will choose his next life. Socrates was not lucky; rather he was a heroic, self-produced philosopher, like Odysseus; he not only led a good life of great excellence, but he will also know, as Odysseus does in the myth (620c–d), how to choose his next life.

If Socrates in the *Apology* puts the focus of ethics on types of human life considered as coherent wholes and takes them to be the primary objects of reflection and potential choice rather than individual acts that are to be performed or not, one can see the emphasis shift here even further away from the individual act. The superiority of the philosopher consists not in doing the right thing in some particular situation, nor even in choosing a particular life of excellence, but in getting his soul in such order that he will be able to continue reliably to choose excellent lives after death forever, through the infinite cycles of rebirth.

The myth about Er at the end of the *Republic* is an exceedingly impressive piece of imaginative writing, as befits one of the greatest literary artists Europe has produced. Yet there is something unsatisfactory about it. In general the *Republic,* apart from book I, has visibly less of the antagonistic cut and thrust of some of the other dialogues, but even its exposition is of a highly reasoned, discursive kind. Plato, like Socrates, always makes much of the need to guide human life by ratiocination and argumentation, so it comes as a bit of a shock at the end of this long course of dialectical discussion to be told *a story* about life after death. Wasn't the point to get away from 'what everyone says', common opinions, received doctrines, and mere stories?

It is not that Plato has not ever given well-argued reasons to think that the 'soul' survives the biological death of the individual. He actually has plenty of these in such other dialogues as *Meno*, *Phaedo*, and *Phaidros*. One might not find these arguments finally convincing, but they are clearly *arguments* and not just forms of story-telling. So perhaps the dialogue *Meno* does give us some reason to think, for instance, that our knowledge of geometry does not depend on the observations we make of the world around us, and thus is not empirical. Perhaps this should count as an argument that the 'soul' must have existed before birth, when it saw the archetypes of the shapes of things in our world. Furthermore, perhaps this means that the soul must be capable of existing independently of the body. One can discuss the plausibility of this in comparison with that of other ways of thinking about our knowledge of geometry. However, there still is a step, not to say a gulf, from this claim about some kind of antenatal existence for the human soul to the detailed story about the conditions under which the souls after death choose the form of their next life. In this story the details are not mere embellishments but have great bearing and import on the conclusion that can be drawn. It is important that drinking the waters of Lethe produce a highly differentiated form of forgetfulness. It makes people completely forget the accidental actual opinions they formed during their lives, so that the memory and mental slate of nonphilosophers, even those who were virtuous in their lives on earth because they lived in a just city, are wiped clean. However, imbibing these waters does not cause philosophers after death to lose their grip on the system of well-grounded beliefs and reasons which they managed to construct through dialectical argumentation and which is held together finally by the single idea of the 'good'. This detail is essential to Plato's argument that the genuine philosopher has some advantage over the person of merely accidental and habitual virtue who has led a good life only because he or she has happened to grow up a member of a just city. What warrant do these details have?

At the beginning of book II (357a–368b) Socrates undertakes to show that 'the good', virtuous man, the man of excellence, is not just more praiseworthy but is actually happier than the unjust man. What would it mean to show this? What about the 'happiness' of those who live in the ideal city?

If asked to list human goods, both ancients and moderns would tend to include 'happiness' in the range of things that are human goods. However, this masks an important difference. In modern usage 'happiness' is generally taken to refer in the first instance to the subjective state of an individual, as that individual herself judges of it. She is 'happy' if she is in a psychic state of being pleased, satisfied, or content and is willing to say so. The ancients, and this includes, it seems, even nonphilosophers in the ancient world, tended to construe 'happiness' in a way that made it much more strongly refer to some objective state of affairs, as a state of doing things well, functioning well, being fortunate in one's undertakings, and having success in one's enterprises. A good sprinter sprints well— that is what sprinters do—and is successful; a good human being does what human beings do well and is successful. We say such a human being is 'happy'. The very word that was used most commonly, *eudaimonia*, signifies the property of living *as if* one had a good spirit watching over one's life and one's endeavours to ensure that one functioned well and one's affairs prospered. A happy life was one in which the agent flourished. To be sure, the ancients also thought that if one was overwhelmingly successful, one would be subjectively pleased with one's life—why on earth would one not be?—but that is rather a natural consequence of being happy rather than the thing itself. This is different from saying that being happy is just being content or pleased with one's life.

What one can see happening in Plato is a development of the ancient line of thought very much further and very much more consistently than many of his contemporaries accomplished, with the result that it began to crack and split at the seams. If being a happy human was doing what a human did well, then the orderly inhabitant of an ideal city of the kind described in *Republic* would surely be 'happy' because the city was constructed precisely to allow people to do well what humans did. This would seem incontrovertible. However, Socrates' interlocutors take one look at the ideal city and are horrified. They agree—well, at any rate, they have been cajoled and chivvied along by Socrates into 'agreeing'—that the city is a framework that will allow humans to do well and prosper, but they can't help noticing that no one would *like* to live in a city like this. Life there would not be satisfying or pleasing to the inhabitants, and they would not be content. It is as if they become aware of the potential split that was always there in their conception of 'happiness': on the one hand there is functioning well, prospering, having success; on the other hand, enjoying, being satisfied by or pleased with the life one is leading. Under normal circumstances one did not have to become aware of this split, but being confronted with Plato's ideal city brings it very vividly to the fore and makes it almost impossible to ignore.

My use of the contrast between 'objective' and 'subjective' in this discussion might give rise to a further confusion which it is also important to avoid. One might argue that Plato's Socrates does not at all work with an 'objective' conception of 'happiness'. After all, the whole point of the discussion is that 'happiness' does *not* consist in objective—that is, external—success: in being a powerful politician, an always victorious runner, a farmer whose fields yield huge crops. Rather it consists in an inner state of the soul, a state of proper order and harmony. Isn't that 'subjective'? The answer is no. The term 'subjective' is ambiguous, as between 'being a property of the human subject/soul' and 'being whatever a human subject judges it to be'. Examples of the second are things like being tasty. For a dish to be tasty is *just* for someone to judge that it tastes, or would taste, good. There is nothing beyond that; judging makes it so. The properties of the human soul are not 'subjective' in that sense for Plato. To say that my soul is in order is definitely not merely to say that I judge that my soul is in order and to say that I am pleased with my life as it is, because I could be wrong. To be sure, if my soul is in order, Plato thinks, I will find my life pleasing and will correctly judge that my soul is in harmony, but the converse does not hold. The order/disorder of my soul is, paradoxically, not a subjective but, if one uses this terminology at all, an objective phenomenon.

To return to the crucial question raised at the start of book II in light of the rest of the dialogue, it would seem that the happiness which Socrates vindicates as the property of the just and virtuous man has almost no relation to our immediate human situation and our judgments about it. It does not consist of the satisfaction of desires, healthy living, psychic harmony, or really any discernible property of this life, nor even as a property of my own immediate afterlife. Rather it is an abstract property of my soul that expresses itself in an infinite series of decisions I will reliably make after death about which lives I wish to lead in my next stints on earth. If the mythic story was to be the final outcome anyway, why bother with the dialectic at all? Why not just say from the beginning that the life of virtue/excellence was 'inherently' better than any other?

In the long central part of the *Republic* Plato discusses how to construct a virtuous city 'merely in words' (369a). The Platonic Socrates and his friends start from a number of assumptions about human beings and the societies we can form, and they agree from the beginning on some clear, basic principles that will guide them in their construction. He writes, 'Let us then make our city in speech from the beginning, and, it seems, it is our need [χρεία] that makes it' (369c) and 'The first and biggest of our needs is for provision of nourishment so we can live and be' (369d). The basis from which they begin includes assumptions about the basic goal of human societies and an analysis of the structure of human needs. Societies, they assume, exist for the purpose of satisfying human needs, and we can know with some degree of security which needs are real, genuine, and urgent and which are false, illusory, superfluous or perverted. Real needs are, among other things, easily recognised, historically and sociologically invariant, and uncontroversial: need for nourishment, clothing, protection against inclement weather. What goes beyond this—complicated dishes, ornaments, perfume, etc.—is no longer a necessity of life but a luxury (at best), a waste of precious resources, or a vice.

This starting point, that the satisfaction of human needs should be the primary goal of society, might be questioned from several slightly different angles. First of all, one might deny that 'needs' is at all a sufficiently well-defined category to play an important role in social philosophy. Desires, preferences, wants constitute a clear enough category, but to say 'I need' is really just to say 'I want very much'. It is to say it, though, in a way that is mystifying, giving to what is really just the strong desire of an individual the appearance of something more (such as an objective imperative).[4] A second objection does not directly attack the notion of 'need' or its distinction from (mere) desire or preference but points out that what we

61

'need' will have to be set at either too low or too idiosyncratically 'high' a level. By setting the level of recognised 'needs' at too low a level I mean connecting 'needs' too strictly to biological necessities. Setting the level too low would mean ensuring that people got the absolute minimum of calories necessary for them to continue to function and had protection against the cold just sufficient to prevent them from freezing to death, but this would be all. Recall, however, the point that the description of this society was supposed to have: it was to be the framework within which one could see most clearly how human excellences operated. Do forms of human excellence show themselves most clearly in rudimentary societies just barely above the subsistence level? It is not impossible to think this, but is there any argument for it? To set the standard of 'need' too high would mean identifying needs as conditions that must be satisfied not just if bare-minimum biological subsistence is to be preserved but if a certain minimal form of social and perhaps even cultural life is to be maintained. The difficulty here is not so much that the level of need satisfaction set would seem to be rather arbitrary but that, once cultural needs of any kind are at all admitted, it is hard to see how one can avoid prejudicing the whole construction by building into the set of 'needs' culturally specific value-notions. How is one to adjudicate conflicts between, for instance, excellence in (some kind of cultural) expressivity and excellence in production of cereals? Is restraint or exuberance a need? Or both? Do cultures that cultivate Nōh plays and cultures that cultivate *opera seria* compete with or complement each other? A final concern about Plato's approach to 'needs' would emphasise that actually needs themselves, contrary to what Plato seems to assume, are not fixed and invariant but develop historically. It makes perfect sense in modern Western societies to speak of a 'social need' for wide availability of access to medical procedures like surgery to deal with conditions that can easily be treated by such procedures, like appendicitis, and to distinguish this from the mere desire on the part of the population for the local team to win lots of races at some international sporting event. This is true despite the fact that such a 'need' did not and could not have existed in the fifth century BCE, when appropriate surgical techniques, antiseptic regimes, and so on did not exist. To give a proper account of human needs which recognises appropriately that they have a historical dimension and yet does not simply conflate them with mere desires, wishes, or wants requires a much more complex theory than any that Plato envisages.

Plato proceeds, however, to assume that 'needs' are fixed and relatively unchanging, and then asks this question: How can one ensure that all the genuine needs of the members of the city are satisfied (even if this requires one to neglect certain artificial or illusory needs)? His answer is that the best way to ensure that this takes place is to see that there is a fixed occupation which is specifically directed at satisfying each of the real needs, and that the society contains enough appropriately gifted and adequately trained people to exercise these occupations. Peasants, that is, produce agricultural goods to nourish us; shoemakers make shoes for us; physicians heal us when we are ill. These different occupations are assumed to be highly individuated and distinct from one another, and it is further assumed that they will be more efficiently exercised if they are performed by exclusive specialists:

Πλείω τε ἕκαστα γίγνεται καὶ κάλλιον καὶ ῥᾷον, ὅταν εἷς ἓν κατὰ φύσιν καὶ ἐν καιρῷ, σχολὴν τῶν ἄλλων ἄγων, πράττῃ. (370c)

There is more of everything and everything is finer and easier to acquire and use, when each person does only *one* thing, that for which his nature especially fits him, and leaves every other activity alone.

So a farmer is a better farmer if she is nothing but a farmer, and the best physician will be someone who is exclusively and nothing but a physician. This principle of exclusive division of labour turns out to be absolutely crucial for Plato's construction, and it is difficult to see how it can be compatible with later humanist and neo-humanist views about the need for the development of all sides of the human personality.[5] This neohumanist view holds both that you won't be an especially good physician if you try *only* to be a physician (and do not also to some extent have some of the skills of a family therapist, social worker, old-style pastor, etc.) and that you certainly won't be an especially good human being.[6]

Plato, however, is keen on the exclusive division of labour and proceeds to use it as a basis for the social structure of his ideal city, adding to it the further, and in fact highly implausible, assumption that each person is born with an exclusive natural talent for some one occupation. So the theory will to some extent be a hostage to the specific way in which the occupations are defined and specified as distinct from one another. Are people simply born with a natural predisposition and aptitude for food production (as opposed to war) or as cereal farmers, hunter-gatherers, pastoralists, or rice growers? The ideal city, therefore, is one in which each person does exclusively that for which she is 'by nature' and birth suited. The similarity of this structure to certain especially rigid forms of traditional society is striking. If part of the historical significance of Socrates was the hope he held out that one could get some distance from the social role assigned to one through ratiocination, argument, and the appeal to reason, and if this is what really frightened the Athenians, then Plato has rehabilitated him very effectively, although at what we might think is a very high price. Society, on this account, need not fear reason: Plato can show how reason can solder individuals even more closely together and bind them even more firmly to their assigned roles than the historically contingent confusion of existing Athenian social institutions ever could.

If one now wonders why Plato's city, which is trumpeted as being so especially rational, beautiful, and generally good, does not already exist, Plato has three responses. First of all, there is no guarantee in nature that in each generation enough people with the right kinds of natural talents will be born so as to fill all the necessary occupations in the city. If that does in fact happen, it is a fortunate accident, but no one can count on it. Sometimes there are simply not enough naturally gifted physicians available to train, and if this phenomenon is repeated on a large scale, it will be impossible for an ideal city either to be established or to maintain itself in existence. Second, although the Platonic principle of exclusive division of labour is, perhaps, admirably rational, it is not self-evident. It would have to be discovered, recognised, and implemented. So people can simply and nonculpably be in ignorance of this fundamental truth. Without knowledge, no ideal city is possible. Plato's third reason for the nonexistence of the ideal city is that up to now no one has had both enough power and enough insight into the necessity of implementing the appropriate division of labour actually to set up a whole city based on this principle. Our human situation is hopeless, Plato thinks, as long as we fail to give absolute monarchical power to a group of correctly trained philosophers or until a powerful king has himself trained in the proper way as a Platonic philosopher and practises what he has learned (473). This final demand is really a tautological requirement for Plato, given that he thinks you have only really 'learned' something about the proper way to act if you actually reliably act in that way. The shift in Plato's usage during the course of the *Republic* between speaking of a group of individuals being trained in dialectic (and then potentially forming a *collegium*) and speaking in the singular about 'a philosopher-king' is not perhaps insignificant. In any case it is the nonconjunction of power and knowledge which is the third reason for the nonexistence of the ideal city.

The question about what is a 'better' or the 'best' human life has a number of different dimensions. Some of the interlocutors in the dialogue themselves bring up the question: Even if we assume that the inhabitants of the ideal city will be 'good' or leading 'good lives', will they also be happy?[7] To this question Plato gives the mind-numbing nonanswer that they may not perhaps seem to be very happy, but they are 'as happy as it is possible for them to be'. This is an especially unhelpful response in a slaveholding society which saw in slavery an absolute social necessity but was under few illusions about the fate of slaves. Some later philosophers were to develop ideological constructions that cast an inappropriately comforting light on the grim realities of being a slave—true freedom and happiness lay within, so slaves could be as happy as free people—but philosophers in the fourth century did not in general engage in that kind of cosmetic exercise. Plato knew that slavery was necessary and that no slave could lead a happy, or even fully human, life;[8] he was a tool or instrument used for various purposes and of no real value beyond that use. It was an unmitigated disaster to be a slave. For slaves to be 'as happy as it was possible for them to be' was not to be *happy* at all. If this was clearly the case for slaves, then equally the ordinary citizens in the ideal city might not be at all relieved to hear that they were to be permitted to be 'as happy as it was possible for them to be'.

This brings us back once again to the question of 'goodness' and its relation to happiness. Earlier I suggested that there might be some reason to wonder whether 'good' really was a term with as unified a meaning as many ancient philosophers assume. Some philosophers have claimed that 'good' is a simple perceivable property,

like 'blue', 'warm', or sharp',[9] but that both seems inherently unlikely and also would be of little help in trying to decide what kind
of human life is 'good'. If we really could look at a human life and
just intuit whether or not it was 'good', as we simply touch a pot to
tell whether or not it is warm, it is hard to see how there could be
so much fundamental disagreement about which lives are good. So
it seems to make more sense to start out from the assumption that
'good' refers to a relative or contextual property of something. This
might be thought to account for the wide variety of senses and us-
ages of the term, because the context in which the judgment about
the 'good' is made is highly variable. So what is basic is not 'This is
good' but 'This is good *as* . . .' 'This is good *for* . . .', 'This is good
*to* . . .' Examples are easy to find or invent: 'She was *good as* a
university lecturer, but has been terrible as an administrator' (or
vice versa); 'That performance was *good for* a beginner, but for an
advanced student it would not be good enough'; 'This brick is no
good to build with (because of its nonstandard shape), but it is
very good to break windows with (because it fits nicely in the hand
and is aerodynamically streamlined)'; 'This dress is good to look at
but not to wear' (the *Guardami, non toccare* principle that applies
to much Italian design). What is important is that, prima facie, this
covers a wide variety of different forms of contextuality. Each is the
context given by an envisaged form of activity: lecturing, building,
breaking a window, stroking for pleasure.

The 'good human life' would mean 'good *as* a human life to live'
or 'good *for human living*', just as a 'good knife' would be one
'good *for* cutting' or 'good *as* a cutting tool'. This discovery (or assumption) would be more gripping if we knew more clearly what
'human living' was. We know what 'cutting' is , but what is 'human
living'? It clearly is not supposed to be simply 'continuing to conduct a certain biological process', because the one thing almost

universally rejected by early philosophers is the view that you are leading a good human life if you do whatever is necessary to save your skin in any given situation. 'Cutting' is a relatively clearly defined activity; biological life is also a rather clearly defined activity; but surely, specifically *human* living is a mess of different activities: drinking vodka, writing letters to the editor, sleeping, sacrificing some of your children to a god, currycombing a horse, tattooing a neighbour. The varieties seem infinite. You might not approve of human sacrifice, but it is hard to say it is not part of a specifically human way of living. Or do animals sacrifice their offspring to their gods? So one cannot even say that specifically human living is doing those things that are distinctive of humans and distinguish them from animals (such as human sacrifice, laughter [?], card games, religious persecution). If 'human living' is not just a matter of biology, then we seem to be returned to the question that has arisen already in a slightly different context: How do you avoid simply building a conception of the 'good' into your concept of 'truly human' living? Why is that not circular?

There is, however, another dimension to this ambiguity. At first blush, 'good' seems not to be what is sometimes called an 'objective property' but to be doubly dependent on a relation to a human subject. If a circle has a diameter of 2 centimetres or if a block of cheese weighs 200 grammes or if this knife can cut a certain type of wood (of a certain size), these seem to be properties these entities have that do not necessarily require reference to any human plans or projects. To be sure, the choice of 'centimetre' or 'gramme' as a unit of measure is a human choice and thus subject to all the usual conditions of such, but that is a different matter. It is difficult to specify in what this 'objectivity' is supposed to consist, but that I can't give an account of X certainly does not mean that X in no sense exists and cannot be used in suitable contexts in a way that is perfectly unobjectionable. On the other hand, if I say 'This action is good', it seems natural to ask 'Good *for whom*?'[10] One of our aboriginal experiences as grown-ups is that what is good for me may not be good for you. It seems plausible that there is some close connection between 'what is good for me' and my happiness, even if it is difficult to say exactly what this connection is. Surely, one might also suggest, there might be some connection between what is 'good for "*you* (in general)"' and 'morality' (in some appropriately broad sense). Surely, that is, one could construe 'you' in the phrase 'good for you' in a way that was sufficiently all-encompassing yet not completely empty of human content.

Plato holds that the operation of dialectical discussion, if correctly and very thoroughly prosecuted by people with natural gifts for it and appropriate training, will smooth out the differences between what is good for me and what is good for you, leaving a single conception of something that is both at the same time. Can happiness and morality (in some broad sense of each) fit together so harmoniously?

One of the ambiguities of 'good' is: Good for me, or good for you (indeterminate who)? There is, however, a second ambiguity which is not identical with this first one but is also important. We often distinguish between what I think is good (for me, for you, for whomever or whatever) and what someone else thinks is good (for me, for you, etc.). Lots of things are good for me *although I don't know it* and despite the fact that other people (e.g., doctors) know it. Doctors might know that evil-smelling, unappetizing, and unpalatable potions or painful surgical procedures would give me the health I desperately would like to have but which I reject out of ignorance of or false belief about their properties. So the doctor's judgement of what is better *for me,* her version of what is 'good', may be different from my own judgement (and better). So now whose version of 'happiness' is to be compatible with whose version of 'morality'?

Plato's central claim is that there is such a thing as an objective good, something that is not identical with what is either (merely) good for me or (merely) good in my judgement; through dialectical discussion, knowledge of this good is supposed to be accessible to us, at least to those of us with the right natural gifts and training and who use that training in optimal contexts. Those who are capable and attain real knowledge at the end of the dialectic see the idea of 'the good'; this, for the philosopher-king, will be his warrant to rule others. So 'the idea of the good' cancels the merely apparent contextuality of 'good' in all the dimensions mentioned earlier. Plato's 'good' is, as it were, good for anything (plays a positive and valued role, even an essential role) in any activity, good for anyone, and finally good in anyone's judgement (provided that judgment is fully rational).

Why, however, should dialectical discussion, at least of a seriously Socratic type, ever come to an end? Or rather why should it come to a 'natural' end, in the sense of a definitive, agreed-on conclusion? Clearly it can be interrupted, repressed, or abandoned because of fatigue (or for other reasons). Do we, however, actually have *any* example of such a discussion reaching not just interim consensus but a proper Platonic conclusion? If we look at the model of Socrates, the early Platonic dialogues do not exactly give us any special reason to be sanguine because they all end in a failure to find any kind of agreement or consensus. In some of the cases where a minimal 'consensus' seems to be attained, as with Thrasymachus in book I of *Republic,* this is so patently a result of the bullying and fancy footwork by Socrates (and the literary artistry of Plato) that it is hard to take it seriously.

There would, of course, be a way out of this, if we could return once again to the idea of a 'human life' (where that is not construed as a life of mere biological survival) and give it some kind of deter-minate, singular teleological content. If there was some kind of cre-ator of humanity, and that creator set humans up precisely so that a particular kind of activity was what they were 'there for' and what they were intended to do, then performing that activity well would be being 'good at human living'. Just as we make knives 'in order to cut' and a good knife is one that cuts well, a good human would be one who was good at doing what God's plan envisaged for her. Maybe human life is, then, to be understood relative to some divine plan for humanity.

*Chapter Three*

# LUCRETIUS

What if the god(s) has/have no Plan? What if the very idea of a plan for the world as a whole made no sense and the very idea of a god having sufficient interest in humans and their affairs to try even to notice and comprehend them, much less to map out a possible future for them, made no sense either?

In the early fifteenth century the Renaissance humanist Poggio Bracciolini discovered the manuscript of a poem in Latin in the library of a monastery in Germany, where it seems to have lain unread and almost unnoticed since it was copied, probably in the ninth century (when it will, in turn, have been copied from some ancient manuscript).[1] The poem, which comprises just over 7,000 lines, was eventually identified as one which was known to have been written by the ancient Roman author (Titus) Lucretius (Carus), who lived in the late Republican period and died about 55 BCE. Ancient sources reported that he had left his philosophical poem unfinished at the time of his death and that the editor who arranged for posthumous publication was none other than Cicero.[2] There is some uncertainty about the title of the poem, but the phrase 'on the nature of things' (*de rerum natura*) occurs several times in the text of the poem itself (e.g., I.25), and it is as good a way as any to refer to the work, so I shall call it *On the Nature of Things*.

The first thing that will likely strike a contemporary reader who approaches Lucretius for the first time is that he writes in verse rather than in prose. The verse form he uses is dactylic hexameter, which every educated person in the ancient world would have recognised as the metre in which the Homeric epics were composed, but from early on this metre was also widely used for a variety of other purposes, including didactic poetry. Lucretius was by no means the only author in the ancient world to write a philosophical text in verse; we have significant fragments by the 'pre-Socratic' philosophers Parmenides and Empedokles (written in the same metre as that employed by Lucretius) and also by Xenophanes (in a slightly different metre), and we know by report and ancient testimony of much other work of this kind.[3] Lucretius stands, then, at the end of a long tradition of Greek philosophical theorising in verse, but he is probably the last major philosopher whose works have survived and whose most important work is a poem. One might even wonder if he felt slightly self-conscious about writing in verse because he feels the need to give a special explanation for it; his message, he says, is harsh and bitter but in the long run salutary: we are no more than conjunctions of atoms in a void, and death is the end of everything for us. So, like a physician who must give a bitter draught to young children, Lucretius anoints the rim of the cup with the honey of his verse (IV.10–25). This particular interpretation of Lucretius' intentions seems to me misguided and based on hindsight. He did not know that he stood at the end of a long tradition. The impression one gets from his poem is exactly the reverse. He belonged to that generation in the late Roman Republic who were proud to be inaugurating something; the very idea that one could discuss technical questions of philosophy in Latin rather than Greek was a new one, and Lucretius was well aware of contributing significantly to this by his inventive use of the Latin language (I.135–145)

Ancient philosophers, as has already been mentioned, did not strive for doctrinal originality, and Lucretius specifically eschews any such claim. The basic truth about the world had already, he thought, been discovered by the Greek philosopher Epicurus,[4] and Lucretius' goal is simply to express that truth in a way that will make it comprehensible and optimally palatable (especially to speakers of Latin). As Socrates traced his quest back to the god at Delphi, Lucretius traced his back to the 'god Epicurus' (V.1ff.). Lucretius is clearly less interested in novelty than he is in truth and in ridding humanity of what he takes to be one of its greatest evils, fear of death. And who can blame him?

Initially Lucretius seems to have an unfair advantage over other philosophers in that so much of what he thinks is self-evidently true. One of Plato's students said about the pre-Socratic philosopher Anaxagoras that he was like a sober man among a crowd of drunkards who are spouting nonsense.[5] One might say something similar about Lucretius. This 'advantage' is, of course, a bit of a double-edged sword in that much of the interest in reading philosophers is watching them squirm, gambol, and engage in the most unheard of (but for that reason alone often highly entertaining) antics in their desperate attempts to find some way to support their more hopelessly implausible views, for instance about the conjunction of happiness and morality, the essential goodness of our world, the motivational force of 'reason', natural teleology, the unique place of Man in the universe, and so on. Lucretius doesn't have to go through any of the contortions needed to try to defend any of these outlandish positions; for him the world is atoms moving at random in a void, and the final truth about humans is that we pursue pleasure and avoid pain, and should do that with greater clarity than we have yet managed. If there are any gods—and there probably are—that is not important because there is no reason whatever to expect them to have any interest in us or our affairs.

*On the Nature of Things* treats what we would call the area of conjunction between religion, physics (or perhaps cosmology), and ethics (or morality). 'Natural philosophy' was an afterthought, or even less than an afterthought, for Socrates and Plato. Plato's Socrates says at one point that he was interested in the structure of the universe when he was a boy, but that as he grew older he outgrew this childishness and turned his attention to the issues of how it is best to live. Mathematics had a kind of special epistemic status for Plato as an instance of a form of knowledge that offered certainty, and therefore it also had a special place in the education of the philosopher-kings, but whatever 'cosmology' we find in *Republic* appears in the final myth. In 1913 a fragmentary manuscript came to light, written in Hegel's hand (1797) but possibly not composed by him or, at any rate, not composed exclusively by him, which scholars have come to call the *Ältestes Systemprogramm* of German idealism. The anonymous author(s) of this text state that metaphysics is to be construed as a subdivision of ethics (*Moral*) and that the basic philosophical question is 'How must the world be constituted for a moral agent?'[6] This sequence is important to note: first morality, then how the world must be for there to be moral agents and for this morality to have its grip on us. It sometimes looks as if Plato's philosophy also instantiates a structure like this. There is, of course, an explicit and powerful ethical motivation in Lucretius—to free men from the fear of death and of the gods—but the structure of the argument is different. The physics/cosmology is by no means an afterthought, and the possibility of ethics is not taken to determine the limits of how the world must be. That the world is composed of atoms moving at random in a void can't in any way be deduced from the requirements of ethics; it stands, Lucretius thinks, as a truth in its own right and the best explanation of the appearances of our world. Any patterns we might think we are able to perceive in the ordering of our world are merely apparent and merely local configurations that mask the true nature of reality. They are like the patterns one might find in the production of an infinite number of monkeys tapping on the keyboard of an infinite number of typewriters. Even if they did eventually one day produce texts that were identical to the complete works of Homer or Shakespeare or one of Gödel's papers, this would be an accident, and it would be folly to expect that their next production would make any sense at all. Given that it is true that randomness is the basic final feature of our world, certain things follow for human living. The physics purportedly lets us know what we can hope for, what we should and what we need not fear, and this is the basis of an ethics.[7]

Book I of the poem begins with an invocation of the goddess Venus, who presides over the fertility of the natural world. Lucretius then immediately initiates a savage indictment of the crimes and outrages committed in the name of *religio*. So is this a work containing the type of ancient polytheistic views with which we are familiar, or is it something novel—for instance, a handbook *in nuce* for atheists?

'Moralising criticism of religion' by philosophers in the Greek world has a long history, although one must be careful about the exact conceptualisation of early instances because of unclarity both in the notion of 'moralising' and in that of 'religion'. In the case of some early philosophers there is even unclarity about whether their remarks are intended as 'criticism'. Thus we have a fragment from the sixth-century BCE philosopher Herakleitos about certain rites of the god Dionysus, involving apparently public celebration of the phallus.[8] This would be 'most shameless', Herakleitos says, if it were not done in the name of Dionysus. Later philosophers took this as a criticism of popular religion, but it is at least as likely, given what else we know about Herakleitos, who was keen on the coexistence of apparently contradictory things, that this was just another remark like 'asses prefer straw to gold' (Fr. 9). That is, it is an expression of his view about context dependency: in one context (that of human life) gold is more valued; in another (asinine life) straw is more valued. Equally, in some contexts (such as religious rites) singing the praises of a publicly displayed phallus is 'pious' (although the fragment doesn't tell us what exact word Herakleitos would have used for the opposite of 'shameless'); in all other contexts it is shameless. One should further note that even if this passage is not just another value-neutral remark about the coexistence of opposites but a *criticism* of popular cults, it would not be clear that it is a 'moral' or 'moralising' criticism. Are decency, decorum, and propriety necessarily matters of morality rather than of etiquette, good manners or good taste, tact, or judgement? This depends partly on whether one has a clear idea of a distinct realm of the moral which is sharply distinguished from the aesthetically pleasing, the socially conventional, the personally offensive. If it isn't at all clear that that set of distinctions or any like it exists, and it seems to be the case that it does not exist for the very earliest period, then the idea of a specifically 'moral' criticism doesn't make sense either.

With figures like Xenophanes and then Plato, we are on slightly firmer ground in ascribing a critical intent and one that has something like a 'moral' basis and content, but it is not clear that it is directed at 'religion', for two reasons. First, the Greeks had no single simple substantive to designate what we call 'religion' that is at all parallel to our concept. The closest expression they had was τὰ τῶν θεῶν, 'the things/matters/affairs of the gods', which is not the same thing at all. In some dimensions 'matters concerning the gods' is much more indeterminate and open-ended than 'religion', including all sorts of things which a post–Judeo-Christian society would not really consider to be part of 'religion' in the strict sense, such as questions about the ownership and upkeep of temples, common stories people told about the gods, and details about the clothing of statues. In another dimension, to be sure, τὰ τῶν θεῶν is more limited than most contemporary Western conceptions of religion, if only because no Greek god, nor indeed the totality of them, ever made claim to the relentless universal surveillance of and control over *every*, even the smallest, aspect of human life, which makes monotheists in general such a potentially nasty group of people.

Second, the older criticism is mostly directed specifically at one group of humans, the poets, and their stories—Homer and Hesiod usually being singled out for the scandalous tales they told about theft and adultery among the Olympians. This mode of criticism can be thought of as resting on three assumptions. First, that our basic moral conceptions—for instance that adultery, theft, and lying are bad—are relatively clear and can be taken to be unproblematic. Second, that they apply (in principle) to gods as well as to humans. Third, that the gods must be only good and in no way evil. On those assumptions, some of which people like Herakleitos would have rejected, Homeric tales about the gods must be false. Why, however, should we assume that the gods are always and absolutely good? Why is this not simply a Platonic prejudice? The poets were, to be sure, generally thought to define or give shape to the gods, so they were more exposed than they would be in certain other cultures. Still, it is the poets who are banned from the *Republic,* not the priests, and criticism of the poets is clearly thought to be perfectly compatible with traditional religious practices.

The contrast with Lucretius on both of these accounts is striking. He does not just have a simple substantive *religio,* but this makes him able to personify *religio* as he does from the very beginning of book I. *Religio* can 'show her head from heaven, treading down on humans from above' (I.64–65). That is, *religio* can and does act and do things. In Greek you could say that some god had done something (e.g., showed his head), or that some human had done something (e.g., told a lie about the gods), but you could not even linguistically say in Greek that Religion did something because that would mean that 'the matters of the gods did something', which doesn't make much sense. This shift in form of conceptualisation is anything but cognitively insignificant and philosophically neutral. As a potentially personified, distinctive realm of human action, *religio* could itself be criticised for what it did.

Lucretius' motivation and goal—to free man from fear and psychological upset—are ethical, but his cited reasons for rejecting *religio* are not that it causes men to do terrible or immoral things. It is true: that the gods can be and often are terrible and can cause men to do terrible things, was a commonplace in the ancient world. Much ancient tragedy is based on plots that illustrate this. Lucretius' favourite example is Agamemnon, who sacrifices his daughter to regain the favour of one of the gods, but there are plenty of other cases. The god Dionysus drives Pentheus' mother and a group of other matrons insane and causes them to tear Pentheus limb from limb because he was disrespectful toward the god (in Euripides' *Bachhae*); in another play Hera takes out her pique against Herakles by driving him mad and causing him to kill his children (*Hercules Furens*). In this latter play some of the humans on stage actually comment on how badly the gods are behaving—they are much worse than humans—without there being any suggestion that this means that they do not exist, or even that it is not necessary to act reverently toward them and discharge all cultic obligation. Being able to appreciate tragedy at all requires, one might even claim, being able to envisage and embrace this possibility, namely that the gods can harm us. In any case, Lucretius does not assume that these stories must be false because they attribute immorality to the gods; he thinks the stories about the gods should be rejected because they are based on complete cosmological misconceptions. They take the bad luck arising from an unfortunate random conjunction of atoms to be a sign of the teleological malevolence of an agent who, we can know, could not possibly have any plans or purposes, good or ill, toward us. The reason for this is that all gods are by definition perfect, and thus they must be completely self-sufficient. This, however, implies that they must be wholly unconcerned with human affairs, because if they were concerned, this would be a form of dependency and thus a lack of self-sufficiency.

From the fact that Lucretius' word *religio* developed historically over the centuries into our word 'religion', it does not, of course, follow that they mean the same thing. One could argue that *religio* does not mean 'religion' at all but is much closer to what is expressed by the modern words 'superstition', 'fanaticism', or 'fundamentalism'. It does seem to be the case that *religio* comes from a root (*lig*) which means 'bind, tie, fetter'. *Religio,* then, would refer to a force that binds us, that is, to the specifically coercive aspect of certain theological beliefs and cultic practices. *Religio* is what *compels* Agamemnon to sacrifice his daughter, Iphianassa. She suffers because her father believes that he must sacrifice her to a goddess so that the winds will blow to take him and his fleet to Troy. As Lucretius puts it, she suffers 'from religion' (*tantum religio potuit*

*suadere malorum* [I.80–101]). But of course Agamemnon, her
father, also suffers 'from religion' because he has the false beliefs in
question in the first place and acts on them, and they, in the long
run, do him no good at all: because he sacrificed Iphianassa, he is
eventually murdered by his wife, Clytaimnestra. Such dark compul-
sion resulting from false beliefs might be thought to have nothing
to do with, for example, a contemplative admiration of the power
of Venus to bring forth flowers and make the birds fly through the
air. Lucretius' rejection of *religio* thus clearly does not make him
an atheist in the sense Meletus accuses Socrates of being an atheist,
that is, thinking that no gods exist at all (*Apology* 26b–d). However,
this still leaves open the question of his relation to 'religion' in our
sense of that term. To understand this, it makes sense to begin by
recognising that in the West, at least three rather different strands of
thought have come together in our contemporary conception of 'religion'. For purposes of exposition and as a first approximation, let
me distinguish 'cult', 'received morality', and 'theology'.

First, there is the idea that a religion is a collection of specific
cultic practices, rituals, ceremonies, and community observances
that are understood to have a special status and be distinct from
everyday activities. I mean by this, to take some examples from re-
cent societies in the West, such things as keeping the Sabbath and
Passover, abstaining from certain foods that are not deemed to be
kosher, putting a mezuzah on the doorjamb (for Jews); wearing
scapulars, using rosaries, and crossing themselves (left to right for
Catholics; right to left for Orthodox Christians); snake handling,
speaking in tongues, full-immersion baptism, or Bible study (for different Protestant sects). Some of these practices might be thought to
be mandatory, others merely meritorious. In some religions the
number and significance of the distinctive practices may be maxi-
mised, often to such an extent, in some sects or some of what Max

Weber calls 'virtuoso groups', that virtually every action in life can have a specific cultic form or significance;[9] in others, such as some versions of Protestant Christianity, these rituals tend, for various reasons, to be de-emphasised. No matter how extensive the range of ceremonies and rituals becomes, it seems unlikely that one could ever really make every action a ritual action, thus obliterating any distinction between cult and everyday action. This is compatible with being able to give any individual action, including a nonritual action, some kind of religious 'interpretation'. Some hyperreligious believers might think this 'interpretation' is not just part of the action but its essence and the only reason they perform the action. They do not keep the peace *because* that is in itself a good thing to do, or even because it is a good thing to do *and also* part of what their god requires of them; rather they assert that the *only* reason they keep the peace is because it is a religious duty imposed on them by their gods.

Retrojecting this conception of religion as a set of cultic, ritual, and ceremonial practices back to the ancient world, one can equally identify different types of cultic and related practices: foodstuffs were sacrificed to different gods in differing ways; the Romans distinguished between sacrifices in the Roman style (with head covered) and sacrifices in the Greek style (without a head covering but wearing a wreath). Such practices, rituals, and ceremonies are inherently social in their nature, even if the rituals are performed by individuals. It is the communal context which is important: in the nineteenth and twentieth centuries rosaries were used by Catholics in Europe for prayer by individuals, but what makes using one a case of a religious practice, and not just a case of someone playing with some worry beads, is its reference to collective practices and beliefs.

A person who does not belong to any of the communities of observance and does not practise the rituals recognised by any group

in a given society can be said not to have (a) religion (in one sense
of this term, obviously). I'll use a calque of the German expression
*konfessionslos,* 'without a confession', to refer to people like this.
Obviously, nowadays we all think that people without a confession
need not necessarily behave in morally objectionable ways in their
everyday life,[10] and, for that matter, they need not deny the existence of (some kind of) god, nor even the belief that god imposes
some moral demands on humans. This brings us to the second
strand, that of a 'received religious morality' (θέμις).

Generally, when we speak of 'religion' we don't have in mind
merely the set of ritual practices; we also think that there are, originally associated with these practices but perhaps to some extent
independent of them, certain forms of feeling and acting which belong to everyday life that are held to have a distinctive positive
value. There are perhaps also some that are held in particular dises-
teem. The ancient Greeks thought it bizarre, and not a little absurd, that Persian followers of Zoroaster put such great emphasis
on truth-telling in everyday life and expressed such detestation of
lying.[11] Similarly, it is not implausible to claim that certain variants of
Judaism developed a specific, recognisable concept of 'righteousness'
to refer to an everyday social ethic, while Christians claimed for themselves a certain style of practising charity. Roman *fides* in all their
dealings with non-Romans was highly trumpeted by apologists for
Rome, but it was in fact a bit of a joke, and anyone who depended
on it was a fool (or, more likely, a slave or a corpse); nevertheless it
was an important ideological construction. To make this idea of a
received religious morality work, one probably has to have some
notion of 'common morality' as a foil against which some specific
forms of action can be contrasted and designated as specifically religious in their orientation, origin, or structure. As Achilles says to
Agamemnon, every normal man loves his wife; there is nothing

special about that (*Iliad*, 9.341–343). That is 'common morality'. To be distinctive, Christian love would have to be different from, and presumably in addition to, that kind of love. So the construction will depend on what contrast class is chosen. Naturally, though, the distinction might still make sense and be analytically useful even if it exists only in the realm of the imaginary. In fact, not every man loves his wife, and perhaps there is nothing distinctive about Christian love, but it might still be an important fact about a society or group of people that they think there is a difference. Arguably for a long time in our society, lots of things were considered to be specifically 'Christian virtues' that were only common sense or common morality, but that they were taken to be specifically Christian was itself a very important thing to understand, if one wanted to grasp the thought and explain the action of that society.[12]

If one accepts this distinction between rituals and a received religiously informed morality, it seems obvious that in some cases the two can diverge. One can fiddle with one's rosary all day long, go to Mass every morning, and participate correctly in every ritual while failing to lead a life suffused by 'Christian charity'; equally, particularly in our post-Christian societies, there may be some perhaps only residual but nonetheless not nonexistent commitment to what are recognizably 'Christian' forms of charity that are not attended by any ritual or ceremonial action at all.

Finally, the third strand is 'theology' strictly so called, that is, a set of beliefs about the gods. It does not seem unreasonable to think that having a theology, that is, some beliefs about gods, is a part of what we call a 'religion'. In one sense, then, 'atheism' is clearly a theology, namely a belief about the gods: that none of them exist. Even religions that lack gods, then, like Buddhism, have a theology. Buddhists think it is an important truth that there are no gods; what appear to be gods or are taken to be gods are just part of the fabric of illusion from which it would be good for us to escape. Believing that no gods exist is different from the, I think, more characteristic modern attitude, which is not to deny that any gods exist or even to express reasoned agnosticism but simply to be uninterested in the whole question and wish people would stop concerning themselves with it. Modern indifferentism is not even agnosticism, much less atheism.

One can distinguish at least three potentially overlapping origins for belief in god(s). The first is fear, especially fear of the unknown. Thunder and lightning terrify, and our response may be to attribute them to the actions of a postulated god whom we would do well to soothe and placate. This can be seen as a way of trying to get control of the situation, and, depending on how we understand the situation, placatory rituals may or may not be successful.[13] They won't, we think, ever get rid of the thunder and lightning, but they may well calm the fear to some extent.

A second origin of belief in the gods is from speculative curiosity, which itself can take at least two slightly different forms. First, people simply enjoy imagining things, making things up, especially exaggerating, inventing, and listening to a well-told tall tale. It isn't as if people are naturally afraid of an eight-legged or a winged horse which was faster than any known horse, or a whole mountain made purely of gold, or a man who could easily throw a rock such as two normal men couldn't even pick up (*Iliad*, 5.302–304), but they simply enjoy imagining and speaking about these things. The more speculatively inclined populations eventually begin to think about the exact nature of these god(s), who, at least initially, are presumed unproblematically to exist. Gradually there develops a kind of cognitive pressure in the direction of construing them not merely as 'bigger and more powerful' than humans but as *maximally* big and powerful, and then as 'perfect' (*teleios*), that is, not capable of any improvement. Xenophanes in the sixth century uses this as part of an argument for one of the very first full-blown forms of monotheism, claiming that there could only ever possibly be *one* such perfect being, because the idea that he is maximal excludes competition.[14]

Furthermore, people wish not just to exercise their imaginations but also to make sense of the world and to have an explanation for things, and this wish seems to have an inner dynamic which causes us to try to encompass more and more of the world into a unity and have explanations for how things are in the present that go further and further back. So there is a speculation that expresses itself in imagining bigger and better things than those around us, and one that tries to make more and more sense of the world, especially by getting better explanations. These are not exactly the same thing and need not necessarily be connected, but in the West a conjunction tends to be made. God is both the biggest thing there is and the final explanation of all that is. One can wonder whether our speculative impulses are not very deeply connected with some existential anxieties, but on particular occasions they can certainly be activated without active fear. One difficulty that arises for Mosaic and post-Mosaic theism in construing its God as such a 'god of speculation' is that it tends to become increasingly difficult to see that there is any point in having an attitude of appropriate reverence, or indeed any affective attitude at all, toward him. Why bend the knee to what is merely a principle of final explanation? Why circumcise your boys in its name? In the case of gods that arise from the second variant of the speculative impulse, real explanations that will actually satisfy curiosity take an increasingly abstract form, but why pray to something that eventually turns out to look like a mathematical formula rather than a man with a beard?

The first kind of speculation gives rise to gods that are of special interest to Lucretius. Although he shows little interest in following

Xenophanes down the road to strict monotheism, for simplicity of exposition let us now assume that there is only one god. Imagine a god who is not merely good, not merely very good, not merely the best ever, but who is completely perfect. However, part of what we mean by 'perfect' is complete in itself, self-sufficient, wanting and lacking nothing. To have a plan or design or project, however, is to *lack* something and be trying to, or about to be trying to, attain it. To the extent to which I don't already have what I am trying to attain, I may even say that I am distressed or 'pained' by that—perhaps only very mildly pained, but a perfect being would never be even mildly in distress. So a perfect being could not have plans or designs, certainly not in anything like the sense in which we could imagine them. In a memorable passage Lucretius draws the conclusion:

> *omnis enim per se divom natura necessest*
> *inmortali aevo summa cum pace fruatur*
> *semota ab nostris rebus seiunctaque longe;*
> *nam privata dolore omni, privata perclis,*
> *ipsa suis pollens opibus, nil indiga nostri,*
> *nec bene promeritis capitur neque tangitur ira.* (I.44–49)

> The gods by their very nature must enjoy immortal life with the highest peace, remote from our affairs and far removed from them; the gods by their nature are without any pain; nothing could count as a 'danger' for them; by nature they need only rely on their own resources to be powerful, and have no need of ours, so they cannot be swayed by our meritorious actions nor touched by anger.

A third origin of conceptions of gods is human inadequacy, weakness, failure, and neediness, originally an unsatisfied need for real practical help, eventually sublimated in various ways.[15] So in the *Iliad* various heroes ask for help from the gods (in general or from one or another of their special 'patrons' among the gods) in killing their enemies or defending themselves. Eventually this can mutate into Ajax's prayer to Zeus when the Greeks are pinned against their ships and are fighting in a mist. This prayer comes to be taken as the very epitome of the sublime, because the 'help' he asks for is so impressively elevated—not to live, but only to die in the light: 'Take away the mist and kill us in the light, if that's what you want' (*Iliad,* 17.645–647).[16] I take the need for consolation, comfort, and psychological solace which becomes increasingly important in modern forms of religiosity to be an instance of this neediness.

One can immediately see the problem that arises from any conjunction of gods of speculation and gods of consolation. The more in my life of misery I need consolation from a god who is big, powerful, and, eventually, perfect, the less will it be clear why any god so conceived could possibly have an interest in providing the requisite comfort (or indeed anything else). Or to put it slightly differently, Lucretius punctures the infantile fantasies of a Big Brother or Omnipotent Father who will succour and take care of us, on the grounds that they are incoherent illusions. He leaves us, on the other hand, with a kind of consolation in that equally no Terrible Persecutor or Great Judge could exist, or, if he did exist, could have any interest in the *nugatoria* of human life, so any fear on this account is unfounded. When Vergil asks 'How could any heavenly being have such great wrath as that which Juno directs at Aeneas?' (*Aeneid,* I.11), Lucretius' answer would be that the question is so ill formulated as not to permit any answer, because a truly heavenly being would not be at all amenable to anger.

If 'religions', then, are historically extended conjunctions of rituals, forms of received morality, and theological speculation, what does Lucretius think of them? He had no objection in principle to rituals, ceremonies, and established religious practices. Although believers in the major contemporary monotheistic religions will most likely find it odd or even perverse, there is nothing irrational about participating in and cultivating various existing religious rituals even if one is agnostic about the existence of the god in question or even if one believes that no such thing as a god exists. These rituals may have special standing in giving a group a sense of identity; they may foster community spirit; they may increase solidarity; and they may be thought to confer innumerable other benefits, such as calming people down or providing a protected, nonutilitarian space for general reflection in overly busy human lives. Think of Kafka's story about Josephine:[17] mice come from all around just to hear the famous mouse-singer Josephine sing, but actually she can't sing, any more than any other mouse can; she just squeaks a bit (as any other mouse could). But the mice keep coming, because sitting in the audience and listening to Josephine gives them a chance to get together and think quietly and uninterruptedly while she is uselessly squeaking about up on stage.

The reverse phenomenon also occurs. The theologically atheist rabbi or priest who is nevertheless devoted to the religious rituals and the moral and spiritual welfare of his community is a common figure in literature and in life. Catholic doctrine even has a special provision (the distinction between *ex opera operantis* and *ex opere operato*) to ensure that the validity of its sacraments does not depend too closely on the actual psychic state of the priest who administers them.[18] An atheist priest can administer valid baptism, provided he minimally intends to do that, just as Niels Bohr insisted on placing a horseshoe over his door even though he didn't believe in the superstition that doing so would keep his house safe. He did it because he had been told it worked even without supporting belief from the occupant of the house. In principle it is even possible for the whole congregation to be theologically atheist, provided no one knows that the others are. Feuerbach in the nineteenth century proposed that Christian rituals be retained, but explicitly given a new naturalistic meaning, with the Eucharist indicating the importance of common nourishment in a community and a corresponding reinterpretation of the other basic rituals. To be sure, it might well be that in the long run these ceremonies and practices have the appropriate effect of contributing to social solidarity and well-being only if a sufficient number of members of the community continue to think that they are not mere mechanisms for fostering good community relations and spiritual growth but have some foundation in a transcendental reality.[19] That, however, is a different, and a sociological, question.

Lucretius' invocation of Venus at the beginning of *On the Nature of Things* may be seen in this light as participation in a kind of literary-religious ritual. Although the ritual may seem to appeal to Venus to come to Lucretius' aid, that is, to intervene, his own theology excludes this. It need not exclude, though, the possibility that the ritual of appeal is *actually,* as it were, directed at Lucretius himself and his audience, intended to put them in the right frame of mind and inspire them, just as the contemporary atheist may in a court swear on a Bible to tell the truth, not as an expression of a belief in any particular god but to express seriousness of purpose and contribute to creating and maintaining an atmosphere of judicious care by participating in widely cherished rituals.

On the issue of received morality, Lucretius must reject all forms of what he calls *religio*, that is, forms of action based on a purportedly binding requirement to do something because some deity demands it. This is compatible with a belief in the importance of noncoercive forms of morality, that is, of a morality based not on 'you must' (because the god wills it) but on 'this is a better way of acting or living'. This noncoercive morality might even have a certain theological component in that the gods (correctly construed), although they do nothing at all, could be considered paradigms. Even if they are not concerned with and never interfere in human affairs, they can perhaps have a role in ethics because they instantiate in an exemplary way the tranquillity to which humans should aspire and a form of peace which is a model for human emulation. They do not do anything at all, but *we* can change ourselves by contemplating and perhaps even worshipping them in the right way (which includes not imagining that they can 'bind' us in any way).

One half of Lucretius' project in *On the Nature of Things* is to take away fear of the gods, which he does by developing the arguments described earlier. The second is to free men of the fear of what happens after death. Plato places a myth at the end of the *Republic,* one component of which is the idea that there is reward for good actions and punishment for evil, or at least monstrously evil, actions after death, and also that it is important to develop harmony of the soul in this life based on knowledge of 'the good', so that we will chose our next lives wisely. Lucretius pulls the rug from under this because 'we' are an accidental conjunction of atoms which is dissolved at death. There is, thus, no 'we' who could be punished after death, or rewarded, or suffer, or enjoy, or make wise choices or poor choices. Death can't be an evil for me, because death is a state in which there is no more 'me'.

Before leaving Lucretius it is right to correct slightly the picture which I have given as a first approximation of his view. I have emphasised that for him it is important that the ethics does not by itself simply require us to develop a physics of a type which will function to calm our troubled minds, but that peace of mind can be attained because there really is no afterlife that could be relevant to us, and it really is the case that the gods can have no interest in us and our affairs. This means that it is important that what we would call a 'materialist' explanation of all natural phenomena, one that uses as its final principle the idea that the world is a random conjunction of atoms moving in a void, is possible, and that one such explanation is the correct one. So far, so good. However, there is another side to this that is different from anything we might be inclined to accept. Although it is important that there is a true materialist explanation of everything and that we hold fast to the insight that this is the case, it is not terribly important *which one* (of perhaps several possible materialist explanations) it is, or that we know exactly which one it is. We can and should relax about the choice among particular materialist explanations. After all, Lucretius has no desire to replace fear of the gods with another form of mental and psychic distress resulting from an obsessive pursuit of detailed accuracy in understanding nature. Atoms move, on his view, at random, and thus with a certain indeterminacy or at least unpredictability. They 'swerve' or 'deviate', so there are in any case limitations on the possibility of human calculation, explanation, and prediction. We should accept this indeterminacy with equanimity. People in the modern world are liable to see this laissez-faire view about the explanation and prediction of natural phenomena as perhaps suitable for ancient forms of society in which the study of nature was a contemplative activity, but not appropriate to a society which depends as much on technology as ours does.

*Chapter Four*

# AUGUSTINE

Augustine is the only one of the authors of a work explicitly treated in this volume to have professional training in shaping words into what was, for educated members of his society, a pleasing form: he was a successful practitioner and professor of rhetoric, a highly regarded discipline in the Roman Empire. Nevertheless his works are particularly rebarbative for the modern reader, for a number of reasons. Partly this is a consequence of his (to modern taste) thoroughly repulsive personality, which emerges very clearly from his texts—he is completely humourless, extremely self-obsessed, vindictive, and deeply misogynist, while also being fixated on his mother. A seeker-out of heretics and principled partisan of intolerance in his later years, he was one of the first Christians to call for state coercion of religious deviants and has some claim to be considered the patron saint of the Inquisition.

Augustine's style of thinking and writing is also very alien to us. One of the things that makes his literary performances seem perverse is that many of them look like transcriptions of *oral,* virtually stream-of-consciousness interpretations of a set of *written* texts that he takes to have special ('canonical') standing. These are what Augustine calls 'Scripture'—essentially what in Europe is now usually called 'The Bible'. Passages from these texts are subject to intense and sometimes excruciating scrutiny, as if literally every jot and tittle and even every mark of punctuation had deep significance, and they are tortured in the most fantastic way so as to 'reveal' what Augustine takes their 'meaning' to be.[1] This is even more peculiar given that Augustine was working not with original texts but with translations, in some cases translations of translations (via the Septuagint from Hebrew or Aramaic to Greek to Latin). This fact, conjoined with the vagaries of the text (resulting from the difficulties of faithful reproduction under ancient conditions), means that to the modern eye, he seems to be treating almost random bits of text as if they contained the solution to the riddle of the universe. His exegesis is closer in spirit to the kind of thing Panurge indulges in (in book III of Rabelais' sequence of books on Pantagruel and Gargantua) when he consults the text of Vergil, and an especially corrupt edition of Vergil at that, about whether or not he should marry, than to anything we can recognise as 'interpretation'.[2]

Furthermore, our literary tastes are no longer those of late antiquity, in which a particular kind of oral fluency was especially highly prized and in which *copia*—the ability to deploy a wide variety of different expressions for the same thing and to go on speaking without stumbling, interruption, or ever being at a loss for words—was a highly regarded virtue. Instead of finding this style lush, evocative, and deeply fulfilling, many moderns are more likely to be reminded of an unskilled veterinarian charged with the mercy killing of hopelessly wounded soldiers who makes repeated thrusts with his needle at the base of the skull without being able to locate the spinal chord. Augustine's texts are at the same time crabbed, digressive, and repetitious, and the works as a whole often seem to lack any discernible overall shape, much less any aesthetic properties; rather they seem deeply decadent in the sense that the individual details get out of control so that the larger structures are difficult to discern. Highly patterned individual sentences pullulate and are strung out in merely associative strings, with the whole held together by, at best, a kind of perpetual looping back toward some purported central topic. This is particularly the case for *The City of God,* which may seem at first glance to ramble on unconscionably for several hundred thousand words. There is no doubt some underlying coherency rooted in Augustine's singular religious sensibility which is expressed in this logorrhetic stream, but it requires considerable energy and focus to discern it. Perhaps the idea is that God is the only adequate reader of Augustine's texts; he can make them make sense; for the rest of us, reading them remains a penitential exercise. Nevertheless Augustine is interesting partly because he compels one to admire him by his sheer intellectual power despite what he shows us of his repellent self and despite the unattractive flabbiness of his written style.

Of Augustine's many works only one, the *Confessions,* has remained a continual major intellectual presence up to today as something most people will have read. Part of the reason for that is, no doubt, that this work can be made to fit in relatively comfortably with specifically modern concerns about subjectivity, individual psychology, and personal development. Thinking of Augustine as a precursor of Rousseau and Freud is not false, but it gives an extremely one-sided and distorted image of what one can learn from his writings, and it in fact distracts attention from some of the more important and distinctive things that can be learned from his work. Augustine's massive *City of God,* despite its shortcomings as a work of literature, develops a way of thinking about human life and the world which is completely and interestingly different from the models other philosophers have been trying to inculcate in us. This is the reason why it is *The City of God* that will be the focus of what follows.

Let us start from an observation that might seem trivial and superficial. *The City of God* is explicitly described by its author as a response to a specific, dated historical event, the sack of the city of Rome in 410 by the Visigoths under their king Alaric. In contrast to the works of Plato and Lucretius, the backbone of Augustine's text is the telling of a sequence of stories, the narration of a history of particular events: Adam's Fall, the founding of Rome, the Flood. Furthermore, whatever one may think of the status of stories like this, that is, whether one takes them to be fables or to be true, there are others that are undeniably real events: the Punic Wars, the Exile of the Jews, the destruction of Nineveh. The intention of Augustine in *The City of God* is to try to discover not the immediate causal antecedents but the meaning of these events. So there is no long account of the complicated (failed) negotiations between the Visigothic king and various factions in Rome that led to the occupation of the city; Augustine tries to determine the 'meaning' of this event. As with many of the best philosophical books, he starts with one question, 'How are we to understand the sack of Rome?', but in the course of trying to answer that question, he gradually begins to investigate its presuppositions, and they turn out to be complex. He then ends up also asking the metaquestion 'What should count as having an "understanding" of some real historical event?' To understand the event is to grasp its 'meaning', but this is no help if we don't know what specific kind of 'meaning' it is that we should be aspiring to grasp. The most philosophically interesting part of the account is trying to say what the 'meaning' of an event could be such that grasping it would allow us to have a full understanding of the event, and that is one of the things Augustine tries to do in the work.

In addition to the discussion of events, *The City of God* is full of references to the lives of named people—Regulus, Alexander of Macedon, Ambrose of Milan, Paulus and Palladia, Sulla, Jacob and Esau, Hannibal, Cyprian, Romulus and Remus, Adam and Eve—and to particular relevant moments in their lives. We might first say that this is not a list of 'real' people because some of those on it, for example Romulus and Remus, plainly belong in the realm of 'myth'. Augustine clearly distinguished the categories of 'myth' and 'fable'—the chimera does not exist; the *Ara pacis* does—and he is perfectly content to acknowledge that some of these figures are, let us say, 'legendary', in that many of the stories told about them may or may not be true. That real charismatic persons, such as Alexander of Macedon, Frederick the Great, Lenin, or my former teacher Sidney Morgenbesser, attract and accumulate around themselves a stock of tales and purported bons mots, and that they never actually said or did many of the things ascribed to them, doesn't mean they did not exist. Whatever we might think of the historical reality of Regulus, Jacob, Hannibal, Romulus, or Eve, it is clear that Augustine did not think of them as mythic in the same way that the chimera or Pegasus are, and, although he might in fact be wrong about this, it was of the utmost importance to him that figures like Jacob and Eve actually existed and were not just literary fictions or inventions of the imagination.

This particular intention, the orientation toward concrete, historical reality, makes *The City of God* different from most of the other books of philosophy one might encounter. It has often been pointed out that in Lucretius' poem *On the Nature of Things* Epicurus is specifically named only once (III.1042; the rest of the time he is simply 'a Greek man'). No biographical fact about his life, apart from his birth in Greece, is even mentioned; none is considered to be of any relevance to the argument. Similarly, the Punic Wars are referred to only offhandedly (III.830ff.), by way of illustration, and the only thing about them that is mentioned is that in the past they shook up the whole world; because, however, they took place before Lucretius' time, he and his contemporaries (not yet being born) didn't notice them, and *hence they are irrelevant.* The point is precisely their irrelevance, despite the fact that they were, objectively speaking, major events. No actual historical events play any particular role whatever in the *Republic,* and the people named in it are either simply lay figures, repeating in succession 'Yes, Socrates', 'Indeed, O most marvellous companion', or 'How true, preternatural master', or they are used as examples or illustrations of general points. Socrates' *Apology* might look to be an exception to this, because its historical location and the details of the events described are anything but irrelevant, and in fact the situation in many of the dialogues is too complex for one actually to claim that reference to specific events is completely irrelevant. However, it does seem to be true that if one ignores Plato's own actual practice and focuses on the version of his views that comes to be established as canonical, this encourages one to suspend consideration of biographical and historical details. Socrates himself keeps repeating in other Platonic dialogues that he himself is really superfluous to the process of reflection that is taking place. Whether or not he is the one conducting the conversation makes no difference; in fact his real historical presence is irrelevant, because the discussion (*logos*) is proceeding, pushing ahead, following its own laws. In a famous passage (*Theaetetus,*148–150) he describes himself as a mere 'midwife' to the thoughts of others. The midwife doesn't herself bear, but simply helps others to bring forth what they have conceived and can produce. Generally, they would eventually bring forth anyway, although perhaps not so quickly, safely, and comfortably. So the detailed circumstances of the midwife's own life and of her demise should not be important. In principle Socrates is as superfluous as the midwife is. It seems, however, highly implausible that the real existence of certain people and the reality of what they do, say, and suffer can always be treated in so cavalier a way.

Compare for a moment the story of the last days of Socrates and that of the last days of Jesus, the latter a narrative of infinite significance for Augustine. Imagine variants on the standard Christian story. For instance, variant 1: suppose there was a mix-up and the Romans crucified not the Galilean rabbi who was upsetting the Sanhedrin so much but, say, Simon of Cyrene. Since Simon was forced to help Jesus carry the cross, this is not an inconceivable confusion (see Monty Python's *Life of Brian*). Or suppose, variant 2, the confusion took place in the Garden of Gethsemane and Peter killed Judas, allowing Jesus to escape to Edom and live out his life there. Or what if the Roman soldiers had killed both Judas and Jesus side by side in the scuffle (variant 3). Or consider the Russian variants. If the Son of God was *really* to take on all of human nature in the fullest sense in order to redeem humanity, this would have to include the deficiencies, errors, depravities, and weaknesses which are an inherent and constituent part of human nature. So the Son of God, in order to be able to be the Lamb-who-takes-away-the-sins-of-the-world, would have to know such depravity from the inside, that is, not merely by observing it in others but through direct experience by actualising it himself. However, there is nothing morally degraded or degrading about being the innocent victim of a judicial murder. Only the traitor Judas, who had plumbed the depths of human evil, would be able to redeem human nature. So Judas would have to be the Messiah. Which one, then, was crucified: the innocent (but then anodyne) rabbi Jesus (variant 4) or Judas (variant

5), the potential Redeemer? Which fate is worse for Judas (and thus better for a potential Saviour)? Surely in Augustine's view, if *any* of these variants were to have been the case, this would have a profound effect on the nature of the truth he was trying to propound.

Now compare this with a similar sequence of variants on the story of Socrates. Would it have mattered if the jury had acquitted Socrates? What if Socrates had made a libation and there was not enough hemlock left to kill him? What if Krito had drunk the hemlock by mistake or had sacrificed himself in Socrates' place, while Socrates himself went off to the fleshpots of Thessaly? The literary effect would be massively different, but on the 'official' Platonic story none of this would make any difference or in any way be relevant, provided Socrates himself did not do anything morally outrageous at the end. The Socratic project of self-knowledge and the search for wisdom remains valid, regardless, just as the propositions in Euclid's *Elements* would not be affected if it should turn out that Euclid did not exist, or that the book had been composed not by a Greek scholar in Alexandria in the third century BCE, but by a Scythian herdsman 200 years earlier (or later).

Here the early Nietzsche would interrupt to point out that the official Platonists were being, at the very least, disingenuous, and that thinking about the way in which they were not being honest would bring out an important limitation in their official programme. Plato must be committed to some thesis about the motivational force of ratiocination alone, but would Socrates really have had the effect he did if he had led much the same life for most of it but scampered off to Thessaly at the end? Nietzsche's view is that Plato needed to replace the model of the tragic hero with another, equally powerful, aesthetically irresistible image: that of the hero of reason. This will work only if the 'hero' acts in a way that is 'heroic'. Nietzsche takes this to suggest very strongly that the whole project of reason itself is limited, and actually self-undermining. It gets going and maintains itself only because of the powerful aesthetic images with which it is associated, but the appeal to which it must explicitly repudiate. To the extent to which it gets clarity about itself, it sees its own incoherence.[3]

Augustine would not need to have read Nietzsche to take a version of this point, although he would have conceived and phrased it differently. Plato's main obsession is that humans are fundamentally speaking, conceptualising, and reasoning beings—that this is the most important thing about them and the faculty that must, before others, be cultivated, developed, and refined. But both Augustine and Nietzsche would agree that this is an exceedingly shallow and superficial way to think about people. For Nietzsche, human impulse, drive, and desire and the human preconceptual image-making capacity are much more fundamental and important than concepts or reasons, and for Augustine, man is a creature not of ratiocination but of love. Augustine's way of putting Nietzsche's point would be that Plato tries to get people to give priority to a certain form of 'reasoning' by getting them to love (the image of) Socrates.

The 'image-making capacity' which Nietzsche (in some of his many moods) takes to be fundamental is an ability (and in fact a *need*) to generate individuated pictures not general concepts.[4] I recall, or see, or imagine my cat Tabitha, not 'a cat in general' (whatever that might be) or 'the concept of cat'. Concepts arise only by a secondary process from these images. 'Love', for Augustine, is equally individuated and concrete in its object and in its development, and it is a necessary precondition to cognition. I don't know and then love; rather, unless I love, which means in the first instance 'have an affective relation to an individual', I cannot know.

At one point in his life, before his conversion to Christianity, Augustine came very strongly under the influence of Platonism (or perhaps Neoplatonism, but for our purposes the distinction is not important), but it is of sufficient importance in understanding his mature position correctly to see how he differs from Plato on two major points, even at the cost of a certain amount of repetition. The first point of difference is Augustine's assertion of the priority of love over reason, the second his views about the constitutive role of history in human life.

Augustine accepts, of course, all the banalities to which we have become accustomed to hear for at least the 2,500 years since Plato: man is an animal who has language, is capable of forming concepts, argues, uses reason; therefore he should use his reason ... (and every undergraduate nowadays would be able to continue this sentence along the well-beaten track for several paragraphs at least). This is not completely false, but for Augustine it does not get at the real heart of the matter. From the fact that we can reason, and that reasoning plays a significant role in our lives, it does not follow that reason is an autonomous power, nor that it constitutes 'the human essence', nor that 'reasoning being' is what I finally truly am, nor that my highest goal must, or could, be to cultivate reason. Rather Augustine believes that a human being is essentially not an instance of reason, a rational agent, but an affective configuration, that is, specifically, an individuated configuration of what he calls 'love' (*amor*). 'Love' here is to be taken in a very general sense of any kind of engaged attention, and it encompasses the whole desiderative, voluntative, and aspirational dimension of human life; it also encompasses both negative and positive forms. Thus it includes impulses, preferences, predilections, attractions, forms of admiration, empathy, and commitment, but also (negatively) disinclination, dislike, revulsion, contempt, and animosity. Augustine is deeply committed to the view that some kind of attention and affective engagement, some kind of 'love' (including, of course, possibly hatred) is a necessary condition for any form of cognition, and that the form this love takes has an effect on the kind and extent of cognition which is possible. To be sure, once I love and this permits me to know, the knowledge can increase my love in various ways, and in some happy case a virtuous expanding cycle of increased loving and increased knowing can be established—something like this is a central idea in the *Confessions* when Augustine speaks of love of/knowledge of God[5]—but the love is more basic and must come first, although both the nature of that primacy and the exact relation between love and cognition must remain something of a mystery. One might say that love is not so much a precondition of knowledge as itself a form of knowing.

Nevertheless, I am a finite and fallible agent, and so my self-knowledge will always be fragmentary, limited, distorted, and acquired only by dint of great exertion, despite the fact that I might be thought to be 'extremely close' to myself: 'quid autem propinquius meipso mihi? . . . Ego certe laboro hic et laboro in meipso; factus sum mihi terra difficultatis et sudoris nimii.' [What is closer to myself than I am myself? . . . I am at work here and labour in myself; I have become for myself a plot of land to be worked with difficulty and much sweat (*Confessions*, X.16).][6] The idea that I am myself a plot of land that needs to be worked with much sweat is the opposite of the early modern idea that I am immediately transparent to myself: 'Nec ego ipse capio totum quod sum.' [I do not grasp completely what I am (X.8).] Furthermore, for Augustine, humans are sinful creatures whose wills are distorted by self-love. One will not get anywhere by simple introspection because any such introspective process will be irremediably distorted by perverted forms of self-love, and those forms of self-love will not be dissolved and cannot be corrected for merely by further introspection.

If, following Socrates, my project is that of knowing myself properly, then, following Augustine, one might say that it is that of loving myself properly (a condition of which, he thinks, is to learn to love God properly). Again, knowing plays a role in this process, but it is neither the beginning and foundation of it nor the basic motor nor the final goal, but just a constituent part of a larger process of developing love. In this process particular people and events play a crucial role because love can get no grip at all initially on abstractions and can never develop in such a way as to leave behind some attachment to particulars. There is a diabolical complication here in that you can only love God properly to the extent to which you know him, but you can know him only if you already love him. So how can this process come to be initiated at all? Augustine's answer, which forms the basis of the main line of Christian doctrine for the next 2,000 years, is that basically there is nothing I can do on my own; the initiative must lie with God to jump-start the process by flooding me with his grace, which causes me to begin to love him. I can perhaps cooperate with this process—the details of this are highly obscure and very controversial—but I cannot initiate it. Whether or not God will give his grace is something completely up to him and, from our perspective, utterly arbitrary. This sense of being essentially a creature of passions, desires, and loves, not of reason, and of being, finally, completely out of control of my own love and thus of my own life is characteristic of Augustine's approach.

Once God has filled me with his grace (to the limited extent to which I am capable of receiving it), the first thing I can come to know is that it is possible to 'love' God. Or rather, stripping off the misleading temporal structuration, to be filled with God's grace is in itself to know that it is possible to love God. This might seem an odd thing to claim, because as participants in a post-monotheistic culture it may seem obvious to us that *if* God existed, it would be possible to love him. But this just means that we stand on the hither side of a kind of conceptual revolution. Pre-Christian Greeks may have honoured, feared, celebrated, lusted after, married, or even and in some extraordinary cases (Odysseus and Athena in the *Odyssey* and Hippolytus and Artemis in Euripides' *Hippolytus*) had a long and close companionable relationship with a god or goddess, but they did not have a kind of relationship that Augustine would have called 'love' of God, which is supposed to be neither a form of erotic desire, friendship, approbation, or benevolence nor a companionship based on long association and shared interests. When Augustine claims that only through knowing about the historical fact of the Incarnation—that is, the Christian view that in the person of Jesus God actually became man—and interpreting it correctly can one realize that it is possible to love God, this is as much an assertion about Augustine's rather deviant conception of 'the love of God' as it is a formulation of his conception of the deity, or rather it is *both*.

(Possible) knowledge of myself, knowledge of God, and awareness that it is possible to love God are, however, also bound up with having a correct understanding of certain historical events, two in particular: the Fall and the Incarnation. Adam was given a free choice between following the deepest dictates of his own nature and obeying God's command or wilfully choosing to pervert his own nature by trying to love himself more than God and following his own inclination rather than the divine command. He made the wrong choice. This is called Original Sin, and Augustine thinks it is inherited from Adam by all subsequent humans. Because of Adam's sin, our nature is perverted (*Confessions*, XIV.1). This gives rise to a kind of paradox in that we usually think of 'natural' and 'perverted' (if we use those terms in a substantive way at all) as being opposites, but according to Augustine, for humans after Adam, that is, all the humans anyone could ever have known since the Fall, it is natural to have a perverted form of love. The second great event, the Incarnation, is also a historical reality for Augustine: at a certain point in time God became a concrete particular man who lived on the eastern fringes of the Roman Empire, died, and was raised— or 'raised himself'—from the dead. By Augustine's time the view that Jesus had raised himself from the dead, rather than, for instance, being raised by some other agency, had effectively become part of Christian doctrine. The Incarnation changed everything; in particular it gave humans the power to reverse Adam's perversion of human nature itself. As one of the early Christian texts puts it, it gives men 'the power to become sons of God'.[7] To have this power is to have a transformed nature. This is not a theoretical truth, or not only a theoretical truth, but also a historical one. As already mentioned, for Plato particular people and events are relatively unimportant. Whether it was Er or someone else who had the vision of the underworld does not matter; in fact, whether or not he 'really' saw the Underworld does not matter; the point is in the deeper meaning of the myth. His story stands on its own as expressive of a series of fully general truths about the importance of getting one's soul in order and making that order fixed through the study of philosophy. Er himself and his 'real' existence (or not) is of no importance. He exists only as a literary fiction to transmit a message. On the other hand, for Augustine, Adam's sin is supposed to be a real event and to have real consequences for all humans. Equally, if God did not *really* become man at a certain point, or if I have misidentified this man (thinking he is Pontius Pilate, Judas, Tiberius Caesar, or Manes, for instance), the construction is thought to make no sense at all. History and the particular actions of particular people in it make a real difference, and to know myself is to know my place in that concrete historical succession of events. Knowing the history of what are taken to be real people with real proper names is essential.

The history we must know is real history, but we must also understand this past reality correctly, which means that it is absolutely important to use appropriate concepts which highlight what actually happened rather than focusing attention on superficial aspects of events. We must see what happened not as the story of the Greeks versus the Persians (Herodotus) nor of the Romans versus the Carthaginians (Ennius) but as the story of the City of God versus the City of Man. Neither the City of God not the City of Man, however, is a city in the same sense in which Rome, Pergamum, or Alexandria were cities. Neither one has a concrete location in space and time. Both are in the first instance theoretical constructs which provide lenses through which to view the real events of history rather than individual parts of the story told.

Since humans, as we have seen, are for Augustine essentially configurations of love, it is not surprising that the two cities, too, are defined in terms of forms of love (*The City of God*, XIV.28, XV). The City of God is constituted of all those whose love is essentially directed at the one true God, whereas the City of Man is composed of all of those whose love is not so directed. Since the humans who love God are scattered around the *oikoumene,* the known inhabited world surrounding the Mediterranean basin among the nations in different communities—in a handful of cities in Syria, scattered throughout Cappadocia, in small groups in Italy, on Greek islands, and of course in the towns of North Africa—it requires a powerful theory even to see them and distinguish them as a single distinct community. What is more, the City of God contains not just visible, living members but also all those who have loved God and are now dead (but enjoying eternal life with him).

he City of God becomes visible only to the eye trained by
theology, so the City of Man forms a unit only if one
to ignore all the variegated surface differences between
humans who do not love God (sixth-century Greeks, fourth-century
Persians, pagan tribes in northern Europe) and to focus on the one
essential feature which made it imperative to group them together:
they were all (in one way or another) devoted to (more or less
sophisticated forms of) self-glorification. Augustine projects, as it
were, his own monotheism on all others, and this forces him to see
in others a parallel kind of mono-idolatry. Just as he has only one
God, they must also, despite appearances, have only one. Instead of
lots of different gods, different objects of human love and aspiration, there is really a unity in 'paganism'. All pagans really worship
themselves, albeit sometimes in different disguises. Their many
gods are, however, only one: man. Therefore, it may look as if there
were an almost infinite spectrum of possible objects of love—God,
Baal, Apollo, Jupiter, family, self, fame, Rome, the European Union,
Humanity as a whole, Reason, and so on—but the spectrum is not
infinite because all the possibilities after the first one collapse, when
correctly understood, into one; namely they are all ways in which
man tries to worship himself (in one form of another). So the choice
is simple: love God (and belong to the City of God) or love man (and
belong to the City of Man).

Augustine's conception of 'love of God' is monolithic, all-
consuming, and strongly teleological, being focused on attaining the
greatest unity of object; it is usually at least faintly, and sometimes
properly, totalitarian. It is only *real* love if you love only one thing,
a thing having all the properties which make it optimally worth
loving, and if you love this 'thing' in the right way. Thus there must
be only 'one' object of love, God, and while it/he must in some

sense encompass all possible such objects, it/he must also be in some sense construed as excluding all others, except as possible subordinate parts. Something can be acceptable as a possible part only on terms set by the one real object of love: God. Augustine's God is not the pantheistic softie of Goethe, but a being of terrible wrath, his unlimited anger being considered the natural pendant to his infinite love. The answer to the question asked by St. Jerome, 'Can I love God and also Cicero?', is no.[8] Jerome may, of course, read Cicero, but not because he takes inherent delight in this, only to the extent to which he can see this reading as playing a subordinate role in some project mandated by the love of God—such as learning to write in a good Latin style in order to translate sacred books into proper, comprehensible, and attractive Latin.

To love God in the right way is to love him according to the doctrines of 'true religion', but to have 'true religion' is to have the right theology, to know and accept the correct historical story about the way God intervened in history in singular, unpredictable ways, and to participate in the correct cultic practices of God's community on earth, the Church. That an action is performed from a motivation which is given by 'true religion' is the only final standard for judging whether or not it is morally good

Augustine's view that true religion is the only final standard of good action has some highly counterintuitive consequences, which he, however, is intelligent enough to see and honest and consistent enough explicitly to draw. It means not only that there is no salvation outside the Catholic Church, but also no virtue. If being virtuous means doing what one ought to do, and doing what one ought to do means being motivated to one's action by a correct understanding and love of God, that is, by 'true religion', then no action not motivated by 'true religion' can be virtuous.

*Quod non possint ibi verae esse virtutes, ubi non est vera religio . . .*
*Proinde virtutes, quas habere sibi videtur. . . . Rettulerit nisi ad Deum,*
*etiam ipsae vitia sunt potius quam virtutes. Nam licet a quibusdam*
*tunc verae atque honestae putentur esse virtutes, cum referuntur ad*
*se ipsas ne propter aliud expetuntur ; etiam tunc inflatae et superbae*
*sunt, ideo non virtutes, sed vitia iudicanda sunt. (The City of God,*
XIX.25)

That there can be no true virtues where there is no true religion.
Unless [the virtuous person] refers the virtues he appears to have on
his own back to God, they are vices rather than virtues. By some
people it is thought that virtues can be true and honest when they
refer only to themselves and are not sought for the sake of anything
else. But then these purported virtues are puffed up and haughty, and
so are to be judged to be not virtues but vices.

So no Roman who sacrificed herself for her children performed a
virtuous act because its motivation was wrong; it was, we might say,
a higher form of selfishness ('acting to benefit *her* children'). No
Roman who sacrificed himself for 'humanity as a whole' acted vir-
tuously because to act for the sake of humanity (rather than God)
is to act on a false religion which does not see that love of God must
be all-consuming. No Roman who sacrificed herself because it was
the ultimately rational thing to do (as a member of the ancient philosophical sect called Stoicism might have put it) was performing a
virtuous action because even this is choosing to act for the wrong
reason and with the wrong motives, namely choosing to do what
Reason demands, not what the love of God demands. Even following Reason for its own sake is a way of perversely worshipping
ourselves.

This analysis of human and divine love is also used by Augustine
to try to show that only through and in the love of God can humans

ever attain happiness. If happiness means attaining what I desire, then one of the things I clearly desire is, he thinks, to live forever. Human love and desire, that is, is in its own way as monomaniacal and imperious as God's love is. This means that the only object of love that can satisfy us is one that can be loved eternally, but that in turn means an object who can *give* us eternal life, because otherwise we eventually die. Poets may speak of 'eternal fame', but nothing on earth is eternal, and Augustine spends several hundred pages at the beginning of *The City of God* showing that the pagan gods are not real gods, not worthy of love, and certainly not in a position to give man eternal life. So this leaves him to conclude that only the love of God can be the vehicle of human happiness.

Augustine does discuss one objection to this, which would be made by philosophers of a number of different persuasions, among them Lucretius (*The City of God,* XIV.25). This objection starts from the observation that one should not simply acknowledge the desires one happens to have at any given time, and then see to what extent they can be satisfied. Rather one should take a critical attitude toward one's own desires, distinguishing between those among them that are reasonable and those that are incoherent or otherwise impossible of satisfaction. Then happiness should be construed as consisting not in the ideal satisfaction of *all* desires but in the satisfaction of those desires that are reasonable, coherent, possible. Since the desire for eternal life is not one that it is possible to satisfy— pagans must assume—given that we all die, it is deeply irrational and we should try to control it rather than pandering to it. In any case, the fact that this desire cannot be satisfied should be counted as no denigration to our attaining the happiness that is possible to humans. Against this, Augustine makes what is a very telling objection. He says that what this amounts to is telling us to try to be content to be miserable. To try to devalue and vilify some of our desires by calling them 'irrational' or 'unreasonable' is just muddying the water. One might think this is a bit rich coming from someone with Augustine's own polemic practice, but let's ignore that for the moment. We have, then, Augustine continues, the desires we have; no amount of high-flown vituperation of them is really going to get rid of them or change them. If you are going to discuss happiness at all, you have to deal with these desires as they are. One of them is the desire for eternal life, and it is so central to us that failure to satisfy it implies misery, and no amount of empty ratiocination is going to change that. Only finding a kind of love that will satisfy the desire will do.

However, this still does not really answer the question, because one can still ask whether two of the assumptions of the argument are correct. First, is it really the case that all people always wish to live forever? In my experience this is not at all the case. Lots of people I know express the view, once they have reached a certain age, that they are ready to die and would actually prefer that their life not continue indefinitely. Both my parents, for instance, said this repeatedly and in ways that gave me no reason to think they were not serious. There is perhaps a kind of illusion we can fall victim to here. It might be the case that at (virtually) any moment, I would prefer to continue to live (a bit) more rather than die immediately at that moment. Although logically this might seem to imply that I desire to live forever, that may not be the case. I may genuinely not wish to die immediately at any given point and yet deny that this means I have a desire to live forever. Augustine himself famously reports that for years he prayed to God to make him chaste, 'but not yet' (*Confessions*, VIII.7). This is not exactly a parallel case because Augustine did eventually drop the 'not yet' clause in his prayer, but he does not deny that for all those years he did have a genuine desire for chastity, although one couched and formulated

112

in such a way that it would not be realized. Even if he had got to the end of his life without explicitly repudiating the 'not yet' clause, is there reason to deny completely that he actually also had (in some form) the desire to be chaste? The second assumption of the argument is that my life *as a whole* is miserable if I don't get all my desires fulfilled. This seems an extreme and implausible, not to say neurasthenic attitude to have.

Essential history, then, is the story of the relation between God and man, or between the City of God and the City of Man. The City of God is the invisible assembly of those who stand in the right relation to the proper object of love; it is the Church considered not as an actual sociological reality but as an idealised communion of living and dead saints. However, one can fully understand that the temptation is virtually overwhelming to identify this ideal construct with the actual Catholic Church as an empirical institution. All the more so since for Augustine my 'loves' are not disembodied, internal, psychological states; they exist only as embodied in external forms of institutionally structured action, and these external forms must be those of the Catholic Church.

This externalist and corporativist conception—any individual's love of God is not an individual activation of an inner psychological disposition but is mediated through the external social structures of the Church—finds expression in the slogan *Extra ecclesiam nullus est salus* [There is no salvation outside the Church]. It also means that no human is truly capable of love (of self and of God and thus of salvation) except in and through the Church. To be sure, the slogan is ambiguous, with a space between the two meanings which is easy to overlook; this is characteristic of ideological constructs. 'There is no salvation outside the Church' is a tautology if by 'the Church' is meant the City of God (because the City of God is by definition those who love God). 'There is no salvation outside the

Church' if by 'the Church' is meant any given real social institution is by no means a tautology. Much of the history of Christianity will be played out in the space between these two.

In Plato and Lucretius nothing is ever going to change. For as long as the world and humans exist, the souls will drink from the waters of Lethe and return to life on earth. The atoms that form one man will disperse, but some of them may form another human: *Eadem sunt omnia semper*. [Everything is always the same (*Lucretius* I.945).] However, in the world of Augustine things are very definitely *not* always the same. There are real essential differences between different kinds of people that are not all simply covered over and flattened out by appeals to 'our common human nature'. Adam before the Fall had a different human nature from that which he had after the Fall: before the Fall he was not subject to death; after the Fall he was mortal. A Christian is radically and essentially different from a pagan because a Christian has the power to become a son of God, and a mortal Christian sinner is radically different from a human saint who has already died and now enjoys life eternal. Adam is not at all like Nimrud, who is not like Jacob, who in turn is not at all like Tiberius or St. Paul. Real change is possible. Look at Adam; look at Paul.

# Chapter Five

# MONTAIGNE

Lots of philosophers have been terrible busybodies, never happier than when sticking their noses into other people's business, reproving them, putting them to rights, correcting them, giving them unsolicited advice. Socrates was clearly able to be agreeable and even very amusing when it suited him, but he was also an exceedingly irritating little twerp, who, if Plato's account of him is to be believed, had more than an occasional whiff of the (highly sophisticated) intellectual bully about him.[1] His preferred stance, of mildly curious bystander who just happened not to understand what was going on and had a few innocent questions to ask, was a mere pretence, all the more infuriating because it provided no clear focus for negation or resistance. When the prophet shouts 'Smite the Ababelites! Kill their unborn children in the womb!', one can respond 'No, I don't feel like smiting any Ababelites today' or 'Hey, my sister-in-law once had an Ababelite cook and nanny, and she was okay'. This form of resistance won't work when one is confronted with a

115

seemingly polite, even self-deprecating, request for enlightenment: 'Euthyphro, you're a priest, and a great expert in matters of religion; tell me what piety is, won't you? I've never understood that. I need your help.' Socrates found an absolutely ingenious way to make even asking a simple question an impertinent intervention in others' lives, thus potentially destabilising and disorienting them completely. Alcibiades in *Symposium* (215–223) says that Socrates' questioning 'almost' had the effect of making even him, notoriously both unbelievably successful and utterly shameless in his behaviour, ashamed of himself. Socratic irony and the Socratic mode of questioning were monumentally inventive ways of being irritating.

You couldn't ignore Socrates' questions, reject them, or deal with them; they stuck and festered. Plato has Socrates say it himself: he is a gadfly. Not a cicada, chirping agreeably in the foliage, or a honey bee about a useful occupation, or even a wasp, a creature with an elegant shape in addition to its sting, or a harmless ant, but the insect equivalent of vermin, a fat, ugly, *pointless* pain in the neck. Of course the city, compared by Socrates to a horse (noble steed), wanted to swat the little *emerdeur,* and the gadfly's pathetic claim that he is useful, nay necessary to the horse is ridiculous. Horses don't need gadflies to remain active; they gallop around perfectly well even in regions where no gadflies exist. And what's wrong anyway with a horse that is indolent? If he doesn't feel like galloping, why should he gallop? To say that Zeus *must* be the one who sent the gadfly to make the horse gallop is just special pleading. Just imagine what Socrates himself would have done to an opponent who brought forth this kind of mythic nonsense to justify himself in an argument.

If Socrates' persistent, unsettling interrogation was at the origin of what came to be called 'philosophy', and some form of this questioning continued, in whatever etiolated way, to be its internal motor, it was Plato, the man who, in contrast to Socrates, seemed to claim to know everything (of importance), who created the paradigm that established itself in the West of what it was to be a philosopher. The philosopher is someone who, usually after a long and highly disciplined intellectual quest involving complicated processes of reasoning, has come into possession of certain invariable ('eternal') truths which bear on the structure of human life and action. The philosopher must try to shape her life according to these truths: if she succeeds, they will give her character maximal stability, constancy, fixity of purpose and substance, where these are assumed to be good properties. Success here gives the philosopher authority: by knowing the appropriate 'truths' and embodying them in her own life, the philosopher acquires the right (and perhaps also the obligation) to give advice to others, to correct their opinions, and to regulate their behaviour. For Plato the philosopher is a king with a responsibility to instruct and a right to command.

In this way, as we have already seen, the as yet not institutionalised bully / busybody can mutate into the schoolmaster-cum-commissar who is Plato's philosopher-king, or into a particularly annoying form in the Christian philosopher-turned-preacher such as Augustine, who has a (more or less) 'reasoned' interpretation of his revealed Scripture, is never shy when it comes to telling people in the most straightforward way what to believe and what to do, and is only too keen to call in the 'secular arm' to enforce his conception of correct belief or proper morality.

Montaigne is almost completely free of all of these pathologies. One cannot imagine him wagging his finger, asking an impertinent or intentionally embarrassing question, thumping a Bible, or butting in where he is not wanted. As he says of himself and his work, 'Autres forment l'homme; je le récite et en représente un particulier, bien mal formé, et lequel, si j'avoy a façonner de nouveau je feroy bien autre qu'il n'est'. [Others form men; I tell of him, and portray a

117

particular one, very ill-formed, whom I should really make very different from what he is, if I had to fashion him over again'.][2] The word *former* means 'give shape to' and designates the pedagogical and advisory functions of philosophers: they give shape to lives, to their own and to those of others, by writing, teaching, advising, preaching, haranguing, intervening. It is not Montaigne's intention to do any of these. Rather he wishes simply to recount (*réciter*) the flow of his thoughts and reactions. Since he is under no illusions about the mediocrity of his character and of the life he has led, he does not think that in describing his life he is painting the portrait of some ideal, which could serve even indirectly as a model for others (III.2, III.13).

Montaigne knew of some philosophers who were exceptions to the general penchant for instructing and forming others' lives. The 'sceptic' Pyrrho was one. He had no doctrine to preach; he simply acted in a certain way: considering matters carefully and suspending judgement in cases that were unclear.[3] These turned out to include all outstanding theoretical issues, but Pyrrho did not *assert* that this was or would always be the case; he simply failed to commit himself one way or the other in each given case that came up. He gave no instruction and did not claim that his way of acting was any better than others'. Montaigne clearly appreciated Pyrrho as an admirable deviant from the existing paradigm. Prolonged reflection on the role of 'philosophy' in life had convinced Montaigne that being 'a philosopher' in the traditional mould was undesirable. He had several reasons for thinking this. First of all, philosophers claim to be able to 'form' lives because they have some kind of knowledge about the world and about human life, but Montaigne is deeply doubtful about the very possibility of 'knowledge' of the world, if one means by that a body of systematically interconnected, theoretically articulated propositions which are certainly true. The world is not a system but a confused mass of chaotic events which only sporadically and accidentally exhibits any kind of order at all, and humans have no contact with any form of 'being', that is, any substantial continuing objects or structures (II.12). The senses, to be sure, seem to put us directly into contact with this world, and that contact, one can say, has the property of certitude: 'Fire burns, there is no denying it', but the *impression* of certainty is a sure sign of uncertainty, and what the senses can give us or tell us is too indeterminate in itself to count as 'knowledge' (II.2]. Thus, there is a certainty of (or 'in') immediate sensation—if one wishes to call it that—but this is not correctly described as a form of 'knowledge'.

The mere fact that my eyes are capable of vision and are assaulted by light of the right kind may cause or motivate me to do any number of things, but we can begin to speak of 'knowledge' only when what seems to be the content of our sensations is put into words and into a propositional form. In so doing it always loses the 'certainty' it had. 'Knowledge' must be embodied in the linguistic form of a knowledge-claim. Only when I undertake to say 'This is red light' or 'This is bright' or 'The sun is shining on me' do I make a potential knowledge-claim, and in the passage from immediate sensation to verbal formulation, any possible certainty is irretrievably lost. Equally, Montaigne argues, 'reason' alone does not have the power and consistency which philosophers attribute to it; it can give us no clear rules for life and thus has no special authority. In addition, if living like a philosopher includes giving advice, it is bad form, a violation of basic principles of etiquette and of civilised social intercourse. This attitude on Montaigne's part is partly just a question of his own sense of propriety, good taste, and discretion, but it is not *merely* that. Paradoxically enough, then, 'doing' ethics in the usual way is either completely pointless or an obstacle to leading a good life, or even mildly reprehensible (because so often a prelude to preaching or pushing people around).

Any reader, then, who opens Montaigne's *Essais* for the first time and approaches the text with expectations formed by the reading of other works of philosophy is liable quickly to be disappointed, bewildered, and disoriented. The book does not contain anything like a set of universal, rational principles, categorical moral rules, laws of nature, or even general guidelines, approximate rules of thumb, or clever maxims to live by. There are no such general rules (III.13). Rather one is immediately confronted with detailed discussions of a welter of concrete historical cases—and some mythological and literary ones.

The beginning reader of book I will notice that Montaigne seems almost obsessed, at least at this early point in the *Essais,* by a certain small range of situations. Many of the examples he describes concern the populations of besieged towns or beleaguered garrisons. Should the people in a besieged garrison resist at all, put up a token resistance, resist to the very end, resist until even after the end, when the town is clearly defeated, or should they beg for mercy? Under what conditions is it a good idea to parley with an enemy? How can envoys, ambassadors, or negotiators expect to be treated? Montaigne's point in narrating these tales seems clearly to be to illustrate the variability of the ways in which humans act in different situations, and in particular the very great variety of ways in which they react to each other and to each other's behaviour. The human world is just as chaotic and unpredictable as the nonhuman world. Sometimes, to take Montaigne's example of a beleaguered city, an enemy will respond positively to immediate abject submission and spare those who yield; sometimes they will take this as a sign of cowardice and it will unleash their fury. Sometimes prolonged, persistent defence of a hopeless position will gain their admiration; sometimes it just enrages them and stimulates them to greater severity than they would otherwise have exhibited. One simply can't tell beforehand how people will react. How, then, could any general rule for moral behaviour be of any use?

Perhaps there are no universal rules, like 'Never under any circumstances lie' or 'Never under any circumstances take without permission what belongs to others', but there might be some context-dependent general guidelines or crude rules of thumb. For instance, if the besieger is himself a man of great courage, he will be more likely to appreciate the courage of a defender, so defend yourself strongly to the bitter end, and he will show mercy; otherwise, it is better to submit without resisting. However, Montaigne immediately cites counterexamples even to this kind of contextualised rule. Perhaps, then, the rules have to be even more detailed and suited to the particular context. But the greater the number of specific conditions introduced into the apodosis (the 'if' clause) of such a rule, the narrower the range of cases is likely to be to which it could apply and the less like a useful rule it looks to be. Whether or not this is the case, at a certain point the resulting 'rules' will become so complicated and unwieldy as not to be of any practical use to human beings.

Well and good, one might think; this is not a work which constructs and defends either an abstract and universal moral system or a set of contextual rules for action. Maybe the author is an extreme 'particularist' and thinks there is nothing more to ethics than the investigation of concrete cases and the resolution of the problems they throw up by appeal to some kind of individualised insight. Maybe individual judgement does not work according to principles, laws, or rules (contextual or not) at all but rather by some kind of perception or direct insight into the essential qualities of particular situations; some philosophers call this 'intuition' (III.13). Perhaps it is a question of learning to *notice* what is important, essential, or salient about certain situations, something which is a quasi-observational not a ratiocinative power, or is based on a nonrationalisable reaction to given situations. Perhaps you could cultivate and refine this power by investigating concrete examples, even though you could not give rules to follow. The *Essais* might then be a book of practical or exemplary casuistry, a discussion of a variety of individual cases discussed in terms that will sharpen our powers of individual discrimination and judgement, even though it proposes no rules (and in fact asserts that none exist).

In a sense, of course, it cannot but be true that the *Essais* are a work about individual judgement. Still, the usual way of thinking about casuistry is that there are some individual problematic cases that cannot, for one reason or another, easily be resolved by applying some simple principle, but that by studying each case in detail one can work one's way around to a 'solution' to the problem it presents. However, the *Essais* do not present 'solutions' in any obvious sense, only questions which Montaigne discusses but leaves unanswered. 'Should I negotiate or resist?' The *Essais* leave the clear impression not merely that Montaigne does not present an answer to this question but that he thinks there is no 'answer' or 'solution'. This does not necessarily mean that thinking about the factors involved in a variety of different situations is pointless, but it does mean that whatever is happening there does not have the structure of finding a single preferable solution to a distinctly formulated 'problem' or 'question'. Careful reflection on a concrete case may sometime, but not always, permit me to come to a sensible decision, but even when that is possible what happens is not at all like the subsumption of an individual case under a general rule.

Second, recall that Montaigne does not merely think that the world exhibits infinite variety and is constantly changing, but he also thinks that human judgement, including his own judgement, is variable in the same way, and he thinks that this is true for most people. One year's crop of apples is sweet, the next year's is sour. However some years I may prefer sweet apples, but other years more sour ones; some years I may be off apples altogether. The world changes and I change, and there is no necessary coordination between the two. Maybe exceptional people like Socrates (III.12) and Cato (II.1; II.28) are different, but we should definitely not assume we are like them. He even says that when his opinions on things, and presumably his judgements, too, *do* exhibit consistency, that is a happy accident (II.12/F428). So once we have investigated carefully, we cannot expect to come even to a stable (much less a highly well-grounded) judgement on any individual case.

If Montaigne is not a scholar, a savant, or a scientist and does not claim to be one, and is also not a philosopher, an adviser, preacher, or a pedagogue, what is he doing? Two of his intentions seem clear. First, human judgement is at best weak, changeable, and unreliable, but this does not imply that it cannot be in any way improved by repeated exercise and observation. The effect here, though, is likely to be extremely limited. Second, the study of the opinions I hold, the judgements I make, and how they change can contribute to making me more aware of the kind of person I am: I don't necessarily judge any 'better' (whatever that might mean), but I can come to know how I tend to react to a wide variety of situations, and that might be called a kind of 'self-knowledge'. So does Montaigne subscribe to the received philosophers' opinion that some kind of self-knowledge is a goal, or even 'the goal' of human life?

To speak of 'the goal' of human life usually means that there is *one* such goal (for all people) and that everything else should be subordinated to this one goal. Montaigne, although he tries to come to know himself as well as he can, does not seem to suggest that.

After all, one of the most engaging and attractive features of his writing is the catholicity of his ability to admire the most varied kinds of human lives. He admires ancient philosophers, political, military, and literary figures like Cato, Socrates, Pyrrho, Epaminondas, Alexander, Lucretius, and Vergil; Julian the Apostate; Henri IV; a thieving peasant in Armagnac (III.2), who stole 'in moderation' and made arrangements for partial restitution of the stolen goods after his death; the Inca king Atahualpa; but also the Swiss female camp followers of armies (I.14), peasants of Aquitaine who make no great fuss about dying, and the lives led by members of various tribes in Brazil. It is true that there are certain properties that many of the people he admires seem to share. These include endurance and the ability to bear adversity without complaint, consistency of thought and action, and lack of pretension, but none of these people has *all* these properties, and most of them do not share a high level of self-knowledge. The peasants certainly have nothing at all like self-knowledge, and at one point Montaigne even says (III.13) that we need a school of stupidity.

Admiring the people who live a certain kind of life or who aspire to or realise some 'ideal' to a high degree is not the same thing as positing that form of life or that ideal as 'the' (or even 'a') goal or end of human life. There may well be a variety of different ways of living and character traits that I find admirable without its being the case that they have anything significant in common (apart, perhaps, from the fact that I admire them). When Plato's Socrates asks Meno what 'excellence' is, Meno replies by saying that 'excellence' is different things in different contexts:[4] excellence in a cook is not the same as excellence in a carpenter, for instance. Socrates stops him right there and says there must be some one thing in common to all excellences, by virtue of which we call them all excellences; excellence must have the same form everywhere. Why must there be? Montaigne would disagree with Socrates: *distinguo*, he says, is the basic principle of his logic (II.1). Tranquillity of soul, self-knowledge, consistency of thought and of action, self-expression, 'stoical' endurance of pain and misfortune, living according to nature, and absence of remorse for the life one has led, to mention just some of the traits that Montaigne seems to admire in others, are not at all obviously the same thing or an instance of some one discernible property. I can, of course, admire in others traits which I do not wish myself to have or ways of living which I do not wish to follow myself. This pluralism extends not just to what I admire in others but also to the things I find valuable for myself. Montaigne was very keen not just on coming to know himself better but also on certain kinds of personal freedom, especially his own freedom of movement. He does not, however, take freedom and self-knowledge to be at all the same thing, nor does he assume that these things are orshould be as important to others as they are to him.

One might think that this approach to Montaigne was incorrect because he really did come increasingly to accept one overarching goal for life, 'living according to nature', which is, in addition, a traditional formula used by various ancient philosophers to designate the goal of life. Even when Montaigne seems closest to adopting this principle as a guide to life, he registers two qualifications (III.12). First of all, this is not a universal principle but just a crude rule of thumb used for first approximations, which, like every other such rule, admits of exceptions. Second, part of what it is to live according to nature is precisely not to force oneself into conformity with any set of *ordonnances* but to let oneself go ('Je me laisse aller, comme je suis venu, je ne combats rien' [III.12]). Even putting aside for the moment these two massive reservations, if one looks at his discussion carefully one will recognise that he very clearly thinks that no such thing as a 'natural law' or a 'law of nature' exists in any sense that would give comfort to philosophers who hold that such a law is ethically fundamental.

Discussions of 'nature' go back to antiquity: the sophists are usually credited with introducing the distinction between 'nature' (φύσις) and 'custom/law/convention' (νόμος; θέσις), that is, what is 'natural' and what 'artificial', and they used it to some effect as a critical tool for analysing social institutions.[5] By 'law/convention/custom' some men were citizens of Athens, but some were not; however, this customary distinction had no standing in nature, because in both cases men are men. For this critical function to make sense, the distinction between custom and nature has to be sharp, and 'nature' has to be construed as a positive source of some kind of moral orientation; that is, it must be in some sense presupposed that it is 'good' to act according to what is natural, as opposed to what is merely customary.

From the very beginning there are, to be sure, difficulties with this distinction, the main one being that if you take it seriously and construe 'nature' in anything like the usual sense of the term, such as 'what other animals who live outside human control do', you end up with a life like that of the Cynic Diogenes: performing all 'natural' functions in public, and perhaps engaging in incest, sodomy, and cannibalism.[6] All of these are widely found in the animal kingdom. They seem, then, to be wrong only 'by convention', but they were precisely the kind of thing which doctrines of natural law were supposed to exclude as 'unnatural'. Diogenes was never refuted, just ignored, because the appeal to some normatively loaded concept of 'nature' seemed just too useful to give up. So, as usual in cases like this, refuge is sought in metaphysical constructions: 'nature' doesn't mean what animals (including humans) usually do, if not forced, but something completely different, which has to do, for instance, with a hidden but inherent teleology. With the dominance of Christianity these metaphysically loaded views about 'nature' and its laws become increasingly tortuous as they are forced to pass through the sieve of a highly idiosyncratic religious sensibility.[7]

Of course, there is an anodyne sense in which one can appeal to 'nature' and say we must follow it. It is a 'natural law', one might say, that humans cannot live if they are totally deprived of water for two weeks, so if my planned action takes no account of this 'natural' law, it will be unlikely to be successful. Montaigne does not deny such natural necessities, but he also warns us repeatedly about judging what is possible and impossible by our own conceptions; the accidental customs of our own society strongly affect what we imagine is possible or impossible in a way which we cannot control or correct for. So even if there were 'natural laws', we wouldn't be able to recognise them and distinguish them clearly from laws we take to be 'natural' but only because of our customary ways of thinking. In addition, natural facts like the need for water would function only as conditions, as something to be taken account of, not as something which *prescribes* to us positively what we should do. Hunger strikers can sometimes have good reasons—morally good reasons—to refuse to drink.

If there were such things as 'laws of nature' (II.12), not as common sense conceives them—'Don't try things you have reason to believe are impossible'—but in the sense which some philosophers came to claim, that is, substantive, normatively prescriptive, positive rules for how we ought to behave that were recognisable by the study of nature, there would be only two possible ways of discovering them. The first way would be through some form of ratiocination—but Montaigne devotes a whole long essay ('The Apology of Raymond Sebonde') to showing that reason is too weak and its results too variable and contradictory ever to demonstrate anything like what would be needed. The other way would be universal consensus on them, but in fact there is no such consensus. Societies vary enormously in what they permit and consider to be 'natural', what they prohibit, and in the laws they give themselves, so 'laws of nature' that could positively guide us do not exist.

For Montaigne, 'living according to nature' is not really to be contrasted with following custom, because each society has its own customs, and in whatever society we live, we will hold to be 'natural' just what we have been accustomed to. In the essay 'Of Cannibals', he is also most insistent in claiming that no particular thing, no practice or institution, is considered to be 'natural' everywhere and always. The whole notion of what is 'natural' is a social construct based on habitual forms of behaviour. Thus Montaigne says that speaking Latin seems 'more natural' to him than French ('Le langage latin m'est comme naturel, je l'entends mieux que le François' [III.2]), but this does not mean that he was born 'naturally' speaking Latin. (As he tells us himself, he became a 'natural' speaker of Latin by virtue of the strenuous and peculiar education his father provided for him [I.26].)

Since for Montaigne nature has no laws, or at any rate no laws that are in any way discernible by us—at best it has something like occasionally recognisable habits to which there are always exceptions—so, too, the best life for a human would be a life not based on any purported 'certitudes', a life without principles (II.12). A life conducted according to rules (*ordonnance et discipline*) is 'the most stupid' (III.13) imaginable.[8] I note that this does not mean that there can be no rules or that discipline is useless; in the making of shoes or the navigating of a ship they may be both possible (within limits) and useful, but it is foolish to think one could live one's life as a whole in its important dimensions according to rules.

'Living according to nature' is, then, for Montaigne, not an alternative to living according to the changing, accidental customs or habits of the place where we live; these habits partly constitute what we mean by 'natural'. Rather, in human affairs 'living according to nature' is supposed to be the opposite of living according to *ordonnance et discipline*. If, however, *that* is the case, the real contrast is between Christian monks and certain dogmatic philosophers who live according to 'rules', and everyone else. 'Everyone else', to be sure, doesn't actually mark out any real group with discernible properties, so the concept has no real positive value as a guide to life. 'Living according to nature' means *not* to impose on one's life (through *ordonnance et discipline*) a model of living which one has come to know through some kind of cognitive insight and which is utterly at odds with the local customs.

This view and attitude may seem unacceptable in any number of ways. In particular we might suspect that it is quietistic and conformist, but it is certainly not a 'natural law' view in anything like the usual sense. So when Montaigne says that the cannibals of Brazil are 'closer to nature' than we are, this means that he thinks their life as a whole has been less structured by purportedly cognitive *ordonnances* and disciplines than was his own life in sixteenth-century Aquitaine. That is compatible with thinking that there is no way in which we could, as it were, peel away from *their* life artificial accretions to get back to a true, pure, basic Nature, much less that we could do the same for our own lives.

Montaigne does not pretend to start from nothing and nowhere. He is a man of his time and place, and he knows it, so he starts from the opinions he has, which he knows are local and provincial, those customary in his circles, and he reflects on them. ('L'homme ne peut ester que ce qu'il est' [II.12].) Part of this accepted, customary intellectual apparatus, which he shares with other members of his social class and his epoch, is a set of views about 'nature' and what is 'natural'. On reflection, however, Montaigne comes to see that the usual views people have about what is 'natural' do not at all have the standing which people attribute to them. In fact, rather than there being a strict dichotomy between what is 'natural' and what is merely 'customary', people *call* 'natural' simply what is customary in their own society. The *Essais* document Montaigne's growing realisation that this is the case and his attempts to come to terms with this realisation. However, even when he has seen through the normative concept of 'the natural', this does not at a stroke abolish the hold which this concept has over him, and why should one assume that it will? Important and centrally located social concepts are notoriously 'sticky', and one does not in general get rid of them merely by seeing that they do not really make much sense. After all, seeing through the concept of 'nature' (as his contemporaries tend to use it) does not automatically give Montaigne another, better way of thinking about the world, another set of concepts; in addition, he needs to live *with* the other members of his society for whom this concept is structurally important. So in the *Essais* we see him using appeals to 'nature', coming to see that they don't make sense, trying out various alternative ways of thinking, falling back into modes of speaking that still presuppose some (very indeterminate) notion of 'nature', and distancing himself from these, in a continual cycle. The *Essais* are intended not as pieces of canonical legislation but as a record of a process of thinking; this is one of the reasons they seem to be in such constant motion, and also one of the ways in which Montaigne seems to me to be particularly close to the situation in which we find ourselves in the twenty-first century. Just as he knew that there was something deeply wrong about the sharp distinction between nature and custom, but continued to speak of 'nature' and what is 'natural' (as if anyone knew what that could be), so most of us know in our more reflective moments that much of what our contemporaries think and (especially) say about democracy, human rights, and the free market is irremediable tosh: an incoherent combination of completely false statements, distorted half-truths, and utterly unwarranted fantasies presenting themselves as irrefutable facts. Just as Europeans *really* got rid of talk about 'natural laws' not by analysing the internal incoherencies of the conceptions associated with it but through the gradual development over centuries of a civilisation dependent on and devoted to a form of scientific enquiry which had no place for 'natural teleology', so we, too, won't get rid of the free market or the idea of human rights by analysing the incoherencies in what people say and think about them, but rather by a long historical process of economic catastrophes, recoveries, further catastrophes, and radical transformations in our society of a kind we cannot describe in detail, which will render markets and rights obsolete; it will then be easy, retrospectively, to see how ludicrous these views are, and people will wonder how it was that we could have failed for so long to draw the proper conclusions from their palpable incoherence. The answer is that some do see this, but seeing is not enough.

We remain to some extent dependent on the institutions we have, the language we share with our contemporaries, and the common opinions that arise from living together in the way that we do. Montaigne is particularly sensitive to the role of language here; Pyrrho would have needed a new language to express his philosophy correctly, because our language is composed of 'affirmative propositions' (II.12). Montaigne makes no attempt to introduce a new technical vocabulary, but one can see him shifting the weight attributed to different concepts that were thought to be important. In reading the works of a thinker, even one who, like Montaigne, very definitely did not present himself as a systematic philosopher, it is almost always useful to try to distinguish between what one might call the 'weight-bearing' concepts—the ones that are in constant and central use and play an important role in allowing the flow of thought to proceed—and other concepts that are merely decorative, rhetorical, or gestural, part of the established decor, historical reminiscence, colloquial *façons de parler* that are not to be taken too seriously, accepted pieties that have to be repeated for one (usually political or religious) reason or other, or window dressing. One of the most interesting aspects of Montaigne's thought is his replacement of the usual categories with a rather different set of concepts. 'Replacement' here does not mean that he breaks with and eschews the old concepts completely and intentionally invents, introduces, and adopts a striking new way of speaking; it means that a certain old vocabulary, and the concepts associated with it, just seem gradually to wane in importance, and he tends to prefer to use another set of terms, words that had been around before but had not been used with such insistence, but gradually come to be employed with greater frequency and more weight.

There is, then, an older approach—I'll call it the 'standard' approach simply to have a convenient way to refer to it—which focuses on a complex *instrumentarium* consisting of the interrelated concepts 'opinion/belief', 'argument', 'observation', 'confirmation', 'justify', 'rational', 'science/knowledge', 'authority', and 'truth'. These are not just one more set of more or less optional concepts; they are concepts which older philosophers thought a serious person *must* stay focused on and must use in discussion. The reason for this is that the main human task is to try to transform (mere) opinion into proper knowledge of the truth, to attain well-grounded self-knowledge, and to know how to act and live, and these are the terms which one must use to discharge any of these tasks. These terms and concepts are tightly bound to each other, even virtually

defined in terms of each other: 'Knowledge is justified true belief'
runs one commonly accepted formula. However, the 'self-knowledge'
which we find in the *Essais* is not actually tightly connected with
the other items in this complex (truth, argument, etc.). Rather it is
located in a network of reflections centring around a completely different set of concepts: experience, judgment, practice, and a highly
important one which I will refer to as 'getting on well with' or
'being on good terms with'.[9] The French word is *s'entendre*. It isn't
that Montaigne claims that there is no such thing as 'argument',
'rationality', or 'truth', or that the concepts we have of these phenomena are completely incorrect. Rather he thinks they are both
not as clear, authoritative, or powerful as they are often taken to
be and not nearly as central and significant; he demotes them to
the status of side issues, matters of secondary or tertiary importance. We do not need to analyse human life through the lens which
this complex of concepts provides; there is another one which is
equally good or better. Or rather, there is not necessarily one single,
well-defined alternative to the standard *instrumentarium*, but in
principle a wide variety of other conceptions that, in varying com-
binations, could give structure to life. So we do not have to worry
too much about these standard concepts. Of course, it might be
important to discuss 'justification', 'confirmation', and some of the
others because they have infiltrated common speech, and, as such,
it might be important to clear up some errors about them, but that
is different from making them the centrepieces of a system or way
of life.

The basic sense of *s'entendre* is 'pay attention to each other; listen
to each other'. Then it comes to mean 'understand', and finally, 'be
on good terms with; get on with'. 'J'aymerois mieux m'entendre
bien en moy qu'en Ciceron.' [ I should prefer to be on good terms
with myself and understand myself than to do so with Cicero

(III.284).] To say that I get on with one of my friends or that I am 'on good terms with' them means neither that I can formulate true propositions about how they will act nor that we agree on everything—how boring if that were true. For Montaigne, friendship is a central model for a wide variety of human phenomena. My friends may surprise me, and often when I am able to predict how they will judge a situation or what they will do, I can't specify any reasons for this prediction that would stand up to scrutiny. To 'get on with' them implies also that I will be able to continue to live my life and manage my relations with them even when they change (as people do). It is also the case that one can get on with lots of people whose specific beliefs, both about the world and about how we should act in it, are radically different from one's own. Human collective life would be impossible if that were not so. This is why one should be careful in putting too much emphasis on the role of the dangerously ambiguous word 'consensus' in thinking about human society.

If I can 'get on' or fail to get on with others, I can also do so with myself, and in fact the social dimension of the process of coming to know myself is very important for Montaigne. It is easier to see myself if I look in the mirror provided by others and by the process of writing about myself. The real friendship with his friend La Boétie, the literary engagement with writers of the past, and the process of writing, publishing, and noting reactions to the *Essais* were part of Montaigne's way of getting on with, becoming familiar and comfortable with himself. Just as I do not try to force my friends into patterns of living that are contrary to their impulses and the way they live, so also in my own case, understanding myself means, among other things, not trying to force myself into a pregiven pattern that is not compatible with my impulses and the way I am. 'The way I am' and 'the way he/she/they is/are' is partly a question of natural talents and propensities, partly of social customs, and partly of habits, where these three are so inextricably intertwined that one can never in any individual case sort out with irrevocable sharpness and clarity what is 'nature' and what is 'custom'. If, in some desperate case, I do need to discriminate, my judgement will not be arbitrary, but it will never be infallible. Doubt will be ended by judgement, but when Montaigne refers to the scales as his motto (II.12), this example can mislead the unwary reader. '"Que sçais-je?", comme je la porte à la devise d'une balance.' The scales in the marketplace have two pans and represent measuring of two objects that are commensurate at least in that both have a weight. They are level when the weight of one is equal to the weight of the other. If I tried to place two incommensurables in the pans, say, 'hope' in one and the prime number 7 in the other, I would get no result. Indeed I would not even know how to begin to try to make the comparison. However, Montaigne's model of 'judgement' is not the measuring of the weight of commodities but juridical judgement—he was, after all, until his retirement an officer of the law—and the *Essais* are full of examples of cases in which judgement requires one to take account of noncommensurable aspects of a situation. How do I take account of such factors as the intention of the criminal, the actual severity of the crime, the need for social order, the existence of extenuating circumstances, and the Christian obligation to mercy in coming to a judicial judgement? These considerations belong to completely different domains. There can be no algorithm for comparing these things: they are incommensurate. It isn't that there is an ideal scale (in heaven) but that *we* merely have weak access to the judgement which that would give. Rather, human judgement is inherently a matter of trying to put together things that cannot really be measured on the same scale at all. What I know is a matter of judgement in this sense. In many cases I need to discriminate and decide; my judgement need not be arbitrary, but it will never be infallible.

There will be a tendency in the minds of those in thrall to traditional distinctions to think that Montaigne's 'judgement' and 'being on (good) terms with' are just ways of replacing the more exact epistemological terminology of 'belief', 'agreement', and 'consent', and a language of 'skills' and 'knowing how', with something much vaguer and more approximate. Thus 'I am on terms with her' really just means 'I agree on a sufficient number of beliefs and have the skill to negotiate some kind of compromise with her on matters of belief and action'. One wonders what argument could be propounded for this view. First, it is not obvious that the preferred vocabulary of the common run of philosopher has any greater clarity than Montaigne's. It is more familiar—in particular it is more familiar if one has been subjected to a curriculum which trains you to do this kind of analysis—but that is a separate issue.

To return to a question that Montaigne poses in his introduction, is it a waste of time for the reader to engage with the *Essais*, given that they do not propound some kind of universal ethic? Only the reader can answer that question, each one for himself or herself. If you read and find you wish to get on good terms with Montaigne, even in the ethereal way which literature makes possible, this will be one answer to the question. If not, that is a different answer. Some may feel a sense of discomfort at this. 'If we look at the world in the way Montaigne did, how are we going to find an ironclad moral justification for forcing others to do what we think they ought to do?' To which Montaigne's response would, I take it, be 'Precisely.' We might be inclined to add to this that those who feel the force of this question very keenly might consider thinking about what that fact says about them. What it says may not be complimentary. The rest of us might reflect on what this tells us about some of the people with whom we need to remain on good terms. Most important, perhaps, we might ask whether we don't find in ourselves, if we look closely enough, at least strong traces of what we see in them, even when that is not something we approve of.

*Chapter Six*

# HOBBES

For purposes of discussion and action, we can group humans together in a variety of different ways. I can choose a number of people at random from the world population and study them, or I can pick people not completely arbitrarily but according to some criterion of selection, such as all those who are left-handed or who have a certain form of colour blindness, or I can group together the speakers of Portuguese or Bahasa Indonesia or Wu, or assemble theoretically all the people who live in Normandy or the European Union. I might antecedently have better or worse reasons for making one kind of choice for grouping people rather than another, and, perhaps only in retrospect, my choice may turn out to have been fortunate and useful, or the reverse. What it means to say that my choice has been 'fortunate' or the reverse depends in part on what I am trying to find out: certain groupings may make it easier or less easy for me to discover what I want to know. If I am trying to eradicate kuru, a disease that is transmitted by eating the brains of people who carry a particular protein-based pathogen, I will not make much progress if I study all those people who are ambidextrous or who speak Portuguese. On the other hand, if I concentrate on the populations inhabiting a certain region in New Guinea, I may eventually notice that the people who get the disease are those who participate in religious rites of funerary cannibalism in which carriers' brains are consumed. Primarily, it seems—before the Australian colonial officials banned the practice—it was the tribal women and children who considered the brains of the deceased to be a special delicacy; the men avoided this dish because they thought it made them weak and soft, hence the much higher rate of incidence of kuru among women and children than among adult men. What sort of grouping should I make if I do not have a highly specific subject of research such as kuru but wish to understand 'in general' how people interact with each other?

Hobbes has a clear answer to this question. You will observe that some people 'submit' to (the will of) others; others do not. Farmers in East Anglia systematically do what the British Ministry of Agriculture tells them to do but also systematically ignore rulings by the Peruvian Ministry of Mines. By tracing the relations of submission, you can come to mark out a series of groups, and by structuring your study around the groups so picked out, you will come to an understanding of very important features of what is going on in human societies. To 'submit' to another's will does not mean simply that I do what you want—I may do that for reasons of my own or for other reasons completely independent of your wishes. Nor does it mean that in some particular case you overpower me and force me to do what you want. If you literally throw me bodily out of the aircraft, I have not submitted to your will, but I have been propelled by an external force that I have been unable to resist. Physical coercion takes place, of course, and probably more of it than we realise, given that in societies like ours much of it is hidden from public view. Yet direct coercion alone is obviously an extremely poor *general* model for what goes on in any human society. For one thing, direct physical coercion is exceedingly inefficient. If, from one point of view, societies can be seen as structures oriented toward trying to increase and accumulate human powers, then direct, continual use of force is not a good way of going about achieving this goal. If you need a police officer in every car to force the driver physically to obey the traffic code, you will need a lot of police officers. That you submit does not mean that someone needs to coerce you directly in each individual instance, although the eventual possibility of some direct coercion as a last resort remains, and in some individual contexts (e.g., US police forces and black men) the direct use of force may be so close to the surface that 'last resort' is a misnomer. In fact, one might argue that in some cases the absence of overt coercion is a sign of how extreme the submission is; no one even thinks of resisting.[1]

I 'submit to your will' when there is a continuing relationship of asymmetrical power that plays the right kind of role in giving me an effective motivation for acting so as to do what you wish; I have in some sense 'internalised' the possible coercion. This does not preclude the possibility that you might order me to do things that I can myself see are reasonable in themselves or in my own best interest. In these cases coercion might not actually be necessary, although I do not, when left to my own devices, always do what I can see is reasonable or in my own best interest, and so the possibility of being coerced would still be useful in focusing my mind and jolting me into action. The point is that the internalised relation of dependency does not depend on either of these factors—that I recognise the rationality of what I am commanded to do or that I see that it is in my own interest—for its motivational force. The basic question then is how the 'internalisation' of my state of inferiority of power takes place, so that I fill out my Inland Revenue forms each year correctly without the government needing to put an actual inspector in my study, even if one could be accommodated among the detritus.

Civil war is a situation in which established relations of submission and domination have broken down or are in the process of breaking down. Hobbes, who himself lived through the English Civil War, thought that civil war was the worst catastrophe that could befall a society, and his *Leviathan* is essentially a treatise intended to show people how they could avoid this ultimate horror. The politics of peace for Hobbes was not a matter of simply following nature, slightly modifying and refining our natural inclinations, or improving our spontaneous and 'natural' modes of living together, but required the establishment and maintenance of a highly artificial construct, called 'the state'. *Leviathan* purports to show why it is rational to resort to this artificial construct, points to the dangers of allowing it to crumble or relax its grip on us, and, in so doing, purports to show us a possible way out of the purgatorial state of permanent war which will otherwise be our fate.

In *Leviathan* Hobbes discusses three forms of organisation that crystallise submission of the will. He calls these dominion acquired by generation, by force, or by institution. The first is the family. Here the children are subject 'by nature' from the very beginning to the truly overwhelming power of the parents (i.e., the father and occasionally, but more rarely, the mother) and grow up with their will in submission. That the infant and the small child are utterly dependent on the will of others seems reasonable, and that in most cases this state will be internalised into something one can call 'submission of the will' might also be accepted, but at this point Hobbes makes a claim that seems preposterous. The parent has dominion, he asserts, not because he begat the child, because the dominion consists not in the mere occasional overpowering of the child (even if only in case of necessity, such as when it is about to put its hand

141

into the fire) but in submission. This submission, however, is an internal state, which Hobbes uses the magic word 'consent' to describe. The parent has dominion (I.22) 'from the Childs consent, either expresse, or by other sufficient arguments declared'. This in fact just shows that 'consent' is a virtually useless, empty word, used to spread an attractive odour of acceptability over what, from another point of view, can be seen to be an exceedingly ugly or, at any rate, unavoidable but grim reality.[2] If one takes a position outside the Hobbesian framework, it certainly looks as if the child has no 'real' choice; but that is irrelevant. No amount of complex argumentation is likely to be able to convince most people that there is freedom without real choice. As Hobbes says, when describing the second form of dominion, that acquired by force, even if I, while facing 'the present stroke of death', and to avoid that execution, speak the words that the man who is wielding the sword requires of me, I have 'consented' to his dominion and covenanted with him. Archetypically and characteristically, this second form of domination can be seen as a kind of slavery. In return for my life, I become the slave of the man with the sword. This is in some sense, Hobbes thinks, a 'natural' phenomenon, just as submission to the father is a natural phenomenon because in both cases I submit to a 'natural person' who has greater power than I do, the father or a human being threatening me directly. I might prefer not to have been in the situation of expecting the present stroke of death, but, given that I am in that position, I 'freely' submit my will to the man holding the sword. One might see this as a reductio ad absurdum of this notion of 'freedom' or of the whole view, which takes concepts like 'freedom' and 'consent' to be of extreme and central importance but operates by emptying them of content. Perhaps this objection itself, though, is a way of taking the concept of 'freedom' much too seriously.

Hobbes' real primary interest in *Leviathan,* however, is not in these 'natural' phenomena: family groups living together or dominion acquired over humans by direct use of force or war. Rather he wishes to focus instead on a specifically 'artificial' construct, what he calls 'the Common-wealth or State'. This takes place not when some individual or group submits to the will of a natural, preexisting person, a father or a conqueror, but when a new artificial person is created, the 'Sovereign' of a 'State'. Such a new and artificial person is created, where none existed before, through the very act of joint submission by all those who, by this very submission, will become the subjects of the Sovereign and the members of the state thus constituted.

So the claim is that if I want to understand the human world, it is good to start by picking out groups held together by shared, collective forms of submission. This submission is based on 'consent' (in Hobbes' exceedingly etiolated sense of 'consent'), and that, in turn, is based on fear. I submit to slavery for fear of the Master, and I agree to construct a state and live in peace under a Sovereign within that state because I fear my fellow subjects. What could and would they do to me, if we were not all under this Sovereign? One might find something refreshingly realistic in this acknowledgement of the role of power, force, and the fear of the use of force even in relations within the family, and it can also be saluted as more honest than the approach of the many theorists who proceed as if families were always radiant nests of warmth, intimacy, appreciation, and love and fortresses against the external cold of the wider social and political world.

Hobbes was rather clear that his political philosophy presupposed a kind of philosophical anthropology, which he describes explicitly and at length in chapters 1–9. Thus he assumes that we are all individuals who are naturally separate, one from the other.

In addition, we are all by nature physically equal to each other; at least to the extent, as he says, that the weakest can in principle kill even the strongest. We fear death more than anything else, and we are endowed with a highly developed sense of self-preservation. Associated with this there is even a natural right to self-preservation. Yet we do not merely seek to avoid death, but each of us is also driven by a strong positive desire to pursue what seems good, though what seems good to each individual will be different. Contrary to Plato, Hobbes does not think there can be a science of 'the good'; such a discipline has no place in the tableau of sciences which he presents. The reason is that there is no determinate content to 'the good'; the term is used relatively by each speaker simply to designate what that speaker desires. Since people's desires are shifting and fleeting and no two people agree about what is desirable, there is no steady object designated by the term 'good'. And since power is always a means to get some good, the only generalisation possible about positive motivation is that there will be a general inclination among men to pursue power after power (chapter 11). Since, however, to repeat, 'the good' is just whatever I desire, variable, bizarre, and unexpected as that may be, no one can know what the object of my desire might be (chapter 6).

Finally, we are all epistemically opaque to one another. If I encounter someone, I don't know what she desires and thus what she takes to be good, what she intends, and how she will use such power as she has. Consequently, I will also not know what course she will pursue, nor what she judges to be the salient aspects of the circumstances in which we find ourselves. This variability in the judgements which the Other makes about any given situation, even the present situation, is a further factor of uncertainty, in addition to the nontransparency of her desires and intentions. Does the Other see this to be a commercial exchange, an opportunity to gain glory in combat, a time when it is appropriate to show especially great courtesy, or a case where her gods require a particular kind of ritual behaviour or sacrifice? Does she see my gesture as courteous or offensive or incomprehensible or potentially threatening? How am I antecedently to know? This variety, independence, and mutual opacity of judgements of 'the good', judgements about situations, and intentions is a fundamental problem for which the proposed answer is the invention/creation of a single overwhelming Sovereign to whom we are all subjected. The Sovereign will wield overwhelming power and will be the final definitive judge in any situation.

This construction does not require that *everyone* be evil and aggressive or that they set out intentionally to harm me. I can know on general grounds that the Other whom I encounter pursues the power to obtain what he thinks is good, but it is perfectly possible that this good is, say, geometric knowledge, and thus of no immediate threat to me. The crucial fact is my ignorance of his conception of 'the good' and his intentions. I do not *know* about someone I encounter at random how he will wish to treat me and whether or not he is a threat. If there is any possibility that his intentions are hostile, it is in the local context rational for me to be fearful and untrusting. If he is a harmless geometer, no harm is done by proleptically getting out of his way, but if, as could well be—who knows?—he is a slaver, I spare myself infinite distress and degradation by hiding before he sees me.

The general situation, however, is even worse than this would suggest. If I don't antecedently know what the Other's intentions and her reading of our situation are, it makes sense not to trust her. However, suppose I have no way of simply avoiding her or hiding, but must deal with her. It then makes sense for me to be proactively threatening in order to discourage her from taking advantage of me. It is obvious on a moment's reflection that the same line of reasoning could and will easily occur to her, so that even if her intentions are peaceful, it makes sense in this situation, in which she is uncertain about my motives, for her to act in a way that is threatening. If this happens, each of us now has not just a general propensity to be careful but a potential 'reason' to become more aggressive: she is not now just an opaque black box but is acting visibly as if she were trying to threaten me. The structure of uncertainty in the situation makes escalation a perfectly understandable, indeed rational response on both sides. This is the situation, the 'state of nature', in which humans found themselves, according to Hobbes, before the institution of the state, and one in which they shall find themselves again should the state structure fail in any serious way. This analysis of the rationality of mutual mistrust and proleptic aggression is one of Hobbes's first and most powerful contributions to our understanding of the human world.

This view of human nature makes certain widely practised approaches simply impossible. There are no reliable bonds of natural affection or sympathy to which I can appeal in building up social relations; there is no common 'good' which could be invoked—the 'good' is just constituted by whatever unpredictably flickering desire the others happen to experience at any given moment; it is difficult even to know how to appeal to your advantage, since I antecedently can have no idea what you desire. I cannot even be sure that my individual coercive force can be relied on, because the assumption of an approximate equality of strength between humans means that even the weakest can in principle kill the strongest. In this situation the only way out, Hobbes thinks, is via an appeal to reason. Each of the parties to the escalation described in the paragraph before the previous one is in principle able to understand the logic of the symmetrical situation in which they find themselves, even though they do not know what particular desires, other beliefs about the situation, and intentions the Other has.

If we can agree to authorise someone, a 'Sovereign', to act for and govern us, lending to that Sovereign all our power, we create a new structure which did not exist before, an overwhelmingly strong Leviathan, and when that occurs the humans who compose the Leviathan are no longer in the aboriginal situation called the 'state of nature'. I now no longer encounter opaque Others who may or may not be a threat to me and who are potentially strong enough to do me a fatal injury. The Others may remain untransparent in their individual beliefs, motives, and intentions, but I now know that they will act toward me only within the bounds placed on them by a power much greater than they and who will protect me from anyone who tries to overstep those bounds. If all humans really are physically equal, capable of rational thought, and overwhelmingly motivated by a desire for self-preservation, and if all are distrustful of others because they have no sure idea which of the infinite variety of possible other motivations (apart from self-preservation), desires, and intentions others may have toward them, then we all can see that it is rational for us to agree to this authorisation.

The Sovereign must be absolute; no one can have the power to withstand him nor have any power over him. He can and must function as the final authority for what counts as 'good' in the society and as the final interpreter of actions by members of the state (chapters 6, 26). What is 'good' is, to be sure, just what is 'good for me', and that depends on my varying desires, but the Sovereign can impose on society a public definition of the 'good' and an interpretation of which forms of behaviour are to be construed as permitted, which are forbidden, and which are threatening. This imposition takes place through the public, potentially violent *action* of the

147

Sovereign. Crudely speaking, the Sovereign imposes his interpretation of the laws he might give by executing those who do not conform to *his* conceptions, or, if the state is already very firmly established, by threatening to do so or to impose other, equally public punishments on those who fail to accept his interpretation. In addition to 'the good' which is nothing more than what any individual at any time desires, there comes to be a publicly recognised 'good' which is defined by the Sovereign's laws.

There are, however, two issues that deserve further consideration. First, is it really correct to assume even theoretically that we can begin with the idea of a 'diffident' individual, that is, one who knows nothing about the motives of those around her and thus has reason to be wary of them (chapter 13 on 'diffidence')? Certainly this would seem to be contradicted by what we know about the real situation of human beings. We all grow up as members of 'families' of one form and structure or another. Outside *some* kind of family, no infant would survive.[3] Part of what that means is that, even if the family is not a model of benevolence and altruism, in families we learn to rely on others for nourishment, protection, and minimal support and to depend on other family members to have reliable and appropriate motivations sufficient to satisfy at least our most basic needs.[4] There is no reason to sentimentalise this. I may have what are now called 'primary caregivers' who treat me badly in various ways, force me to conform to various ill-judged or destructive protocols, and so on. Still, if I did not get a minimal amount of human attention, I would not have survived physically, and I would not have become an adult capable of reasoning, discussion, and potential consent unless I had had various forms of *predictable* (even if minimal and in some respects oppressive) emotional support. Infants who have not built up some form of confidence in their caregiver (predictably nasty as he or she might be), will not survive into adulthood. In addition to the physical dimension, this simply seems to be a psychic necessity of human development. Epistemic opacity also does not seem a natural way to characterise relations like these. My cat Tabitha knows that it is 6 p.m. and time for her supper— when we move from British Summer Time to Greenwich Mean Time, she expects it at 5 p.m. for a while until she gets used to the new regime—and I know that she knows it, although she only vocalises and does not verbalise this knowledge. Reliable knowledge and associated forms of confidence seem to be necessary conditions for human existence, and so complete 'diffidence' is an unlikely candidate for a basic human trait. It would seem to be a high-level achievement to become suspicious, sceptical, or mistrustful, rather than something basic. 'Diffidence' needs to be learned against the background of a fundamental sense of something that it would probably be too much to call 'trust' but which is certainly not active mistrust. No one in the grip of complete and radical mistrust/diffidence could survive. Pyrrho needed a student, on whom he depended completely, to shepherd him around; equally even minimal human family units need to cooperate with others in working, even if that working means no more than jointly collecting ripe fruit in the jungle. That a young animal growing up in such a functioning group is best understood as a diffident individual consenting to 'dominion paternal' in Hobbes' sense (chapter 20) seems at the very least a highly speculative construction for which one would like to see some evidence. Why could not the commonwealth or state arise from the union of such cooperating groups or bands, each one held together by a robust, if not invincible sense of dependence on, knowledge of, and confidence in each other, rather than from a mass of isolated individuals? This would mean that the dynamics of state formation had a completely different form from that envisaged by Hobbes. Groups coming together need not be as obviously 'equal' in strength as isolated individual humans are. Bands would have strength by virtue of the strength of their members, but also by virtue of their general internal coherence, their experience in working together and cooperating, and the relations of trust that exist between the members.

Trust, confidence, solidarity, reliable expectation—I have been treating these as though they mean the same thing or are functionally interchangeable, and shifting back and forth from one to another in an uncontrolled way. Of course, they are not exactly the same thing, and a complete analysis would need to deal with them more extensively and show how they perhaps coincided or failed to coincide in different cases. Nevertheless, for someone seeking an alternative to Hobbes, this need not be an objection. All that is needed is that there clearly be a set of informal ties that hold people together so that it is not rational for them to be completely diffident. Furthermore these ties must *not* be 'artificial', in Hobbes' sense; that is, they need not arise in the way Hobbes envisages as the result of the combined operation of fear and rationality on isolated, mutually opaque, and wary individuals. What is at issue is this mechanism which Hobbes claims is the only rational solution to what he presents as the universal state of the human being prior to the institution of the state.

Forming a state from existing groups (probably of very different kinds) would likely mean that what 'reason' requires would be completely different from what Hobbes presents in *Leviathan*, which is based on the conjunction of isolated individuals. Would groups of different strength agree to the same conditions as individuals who are all presumed equal? I note again that these remarks are in no way intended to denigrate or reduce the role in politics of sheer force and of calculations of the outcomes of different uses of force. At issue is not the amount of force but the different ways it impinges on humans who already have complex relations with others.

Of course, one might reply that the theory of the 'state of nature' was never intended to be a description of how things really (ever) were with humans, but a thought model or an exploration of a set of possibilities that permanently threaten us. It isn't that the human species was ever a set of diffident, isolated individuals, but this is a fate that can strike at any time and must therefore always be taken into account as an open possibility. Change of climate that wipes out our staple crops, leaving me the last survivor; an epidemic that deprives me of my fellows, after which I then encounter another survivor whom I have never seen—that is fair enough, but it does mean that, even in these extreme imagined cases, the 'isolated individuals' in question are socialised individuals who have been *reduced* to a state of isolation. It is not at all obvious that their diffidence, if they are diffident, is other than an artefact of their particular history rather than anything that can be seen as part of 'nature'. Finally, it is unclear what status should be given to any of this. What relevance to us should it have, if it were true that survivors in these extreme circumstances could be expected to enter into some specifiable set of relations with one another?

This raises the second question about Hobbes' anthropology: Is it really the case that I always pursue self-preservation and rank it ahead of other human goals? As an empirical generalisation about human behaviour this is highly implausible. Take the case of Cato of Utica, a staunch supporter of the Roman Republic during the Civil War which Caesar inaugurated by crossing the Rubicon. Caesar made much of his 'clemency'; he took great pride in not being vindictive to his enemies but forgiving them and treating them well. It was exactly this 'clemency' which especially infuriated republicans because clemency was a 'royal' virtue, something one might value in an absolute ruler with the power of life and death over subjects. Republicans were supposed to be 'equals' between whom condescending behaviour such as the offering of 'clemency' was inappropriate.[5] So when Cato saw that the republican cause was lost, he committed suicide, much to the irritation of Caesar, who would have liked to exhibit his superiority by granting him pardon. When Caesar heard of Cato's suicide he memorably said, as Plutarch puts it, 'Cato, I envy you your death, because you begrudged me the sparing of your life' (which is more pithy in Greek because Plutarch/Caesar uses the same word for what I have translated as 'envy' and 'begrudge').[6] So Cato preferred suicide in order to avoid a merely symbolic act of submission, which would almost surely have permitted him to preserve his own life. Hobbes wishes very much to convince people that it is a bad idea to follow your desires and conceptions of 'the good' if these lead you to put any perceived good ahead of self-preservation. Opinions and beliefs are light, fleeting things, uncertain and epiphenomenal; how could anyone visibly and directly risk their very life for anything so insubstantial and insecure? The difficulty is, of course, that in fact people do. What becomes of Hobbes' argument, however, if one takes a different view of human motivation, such as that of Montaigne? Montaigne claims that people will allow themselves to be tortured and killed in order to maintain even relatively trivial beliefs they have once adopted, and even beliefs they have taken over from others and do not themselves fully understand.[7] This seems to be a simple empirical claim that he makes based on observation of the world, and of course it does not mean that any and every difference of opinion will be the source of a struggle to the death—it means only that one cannot ever exclude the possibility that some difference of opinion will become disruptive in this way.

A defender of Hobbes' construction might reply here that for Cato to have acquired his highly sophisticated views about the correct form of government and the ethical consequences that should

be drawn from these, he must already have lived in a civilised commonwealth because he never would have been able to acquire those
beliefs in the goodness of republicanism in the brutal conditions of
the state of nature. Perfectly true, but since it begs the question
about how things are in the 'state of nature', it can't be considered
a definitive reply. A more plausible response is to grant that it is not a
strictly universal truth of anthropology that people always in fact
prefer self-preservation to any good, but just a rough first approximation. It is true for a sufficient number of people so that in most
circumstances it would be possible to form a commonwealth, or it
would at any rate be rational to try to form one. Of course there
can be no guarantee that people in the commonwealth will not
come to value some purported 'goods' (including the assertion of
some opinion) above self-preservation. Monotheistic religious beliefs are a particularly toxic danger, Hobbes thinks, because they
tend to be taken to have transcendental warrant and thus make a
claim that they should be held with special force, tenacity, and ferocity, regardless of any other considerations, and perhaps imposed
on others with equal ferocity. If it happens to one or a small number
of dissenters that they value some belief or custom more than self-
preservation, they will be dealt with, perhaps executed, by the Sovereign. If there are too many for the Sovereign, mobilising all her
resources, to deal with, then there is civil war. Hobbes need not be
taken, implausibly, to be trying to demonstrate something which is
clearly not true, such as that no commonwealth could ever break
down into civil war. The text then could be read as asserting that
most people tend to put self-preservation first, and thus to point to
a *possible* mode of civil peace, if you have the good luck to avoid or
the discipline to eschew theological or other forms of fanaticism.

Putting aside these two serious objections, one might still see
in Hobbes' analysis a convincing account of an important social

phenomenon. Human political society (and that means for Hobbes any civilised society) is not just an artificial construct but a kind of self-levitation or pulling oneself up by one's bootstraps. The point of the project is to make social order as much as possible independent of individual judgement, but of course this will work only under highly specific circumstances and will never be absolutely realised. The judgement of what counts as 'insult', 'assault', or 'injustice', that is, is to be relegated from each individual's judgement to that of the Sovereign, and the reason the Sovereign is effective and that it is rational for individuals to delegate this judgement to the Sovereign, is that she has overawing power. But of course, his overawing power is not a physical property he has—as Montaigne's cannibals observed (I.31), the king is no stronger physically than the man-at-arms—but is rather an ability to mobilise through commands the actions of others who have subjected themselves to him. As Hobbes says, 'Reputation for power is increase in power' (chapter 10). But 'reputation' is an inherently social phenomenon which can in principle make itself independent not only of the physical powers of the Sovereign but even of the first-order beliefs of the members of society.

To see this, consider an example given by Keynes.[8] He pointed out the differences between different kinds of competition. In the first ('simple') one, suppose I were asked to judge something like how many beans there were in a certain bottle or how much precipitation would fall on a certain city during a certain period of time. Although there can often be the usual problems of defining terms here (does 'the city' have clear boundaries?), there is some sense in which we think there can be an objective answer to this question. In contrast, the second case is one in which I am asked to judge among poems and decide which one is most beautiful. A third possible case is that I am asked to decide which poem is 'the nation's favourite'. 'Beauty', one might expect, is 'subjective', a question of individual taste, like 'the good' on Hobbes' analysis. To say that someone or something is beautiful is the expression of a preference rather than a claim about some objective state of affairs. We make this assumption because we have experience of the way in which human taste does vary. There may be some kind of general default preference for regularity and symmetry, but we also know of societies which value precisely the asymmetries and blemishes. Thus it is said that the best haiku are characterised by lack of absolute grammatical smoothness. Beauty spots on human beings were so highly valued in certain places in the late eighteenth century that people who did not have them would try artificially to produce the effect of having them by the use of cosmetics. We also know that in asking for an overall judgement of something like beauty, we are asking individuals to take account of different aspects, and the weighting individuals will give to these aspects may differ. So you and I may find different poems beautiful. I like Pound's *Cantos;* you prefer *A Shropshire Lad.* So on Hobbes' analysis the *Cantos* are good (for me); *A Shropshire Lad* is good (for you). In the absence of some definitive judgement by the Sovereign, we may try to resolve this disagreement by discussion between us, but if one of us fails to convince the other to change his or her judgement, there is nothing more to say. In the second case I am asked to judge what the result would be if each person was asked *individually* about his or her own particular preference, each one voting individually and the preferences then cumulated. Here, I might very well predict that, say, *A Shropshire Lad* is likely to be voted most beautiful, even though it would not be my preference. I judge this because I think most other people would actually prefer this poem. But if I am asked, as in the third case, to predict the outcome of a contest for 'the nation's favourite poem', the issue is not which poem *I* find most beautiful but which one would be judged *by most people* to be most beautiful. In that case, I am trying to predict not which poem each individual would actually prefer but which poem a majority think 'most people' would prefer. I can, then, end up not merely voting for a poem I do not prefer but voting for one which no one actually prefers (but enough—a majority—think most others will be likely to prefer). If political power is at all like this, that is, if it is a matter of judging whether most other people will think that most people will obey the Sovereign (if that is demanded of them), it has an exceedingly fragile constitution. It depends on the fact that 'enough' members of the society think that 'enough' others continue to authorise and will support the Sovereign. If that is the case, the Sovereign will be able to repress individual dissidents; otherwise perhaps not. The fragility of the configuration depends on my lack of direct information about others' preferences and opinions in a given case.

Hobbes' view about social order and civil society has philosophically the overwhelming advantage that it does not require acceptance of any number of highly problematic, if not outright dodgy conceptions: 'natural' principles of legitimacy, justice, rights, or even notions of the 'common good'. Still, the twenty-first century has not been kind to him, if only because many of the phenomena that seem to have been most significant in driving action belong to a register that he has particular difficulties in recognising and accounting for. He was no stranger to religious fanaticism, including religiously legitimated violence against others, but did not seem to have much understanding of martyrdom—the willingness of people to sacrifice their lives for some ideational construct—or of nationalism, including in its racist, ethnic, or religious versions. These are significant limitations.

*Chapter Seven*

# HEGEL

Philosophy, Hegel wrote, was its time grasped in a concept, but it was also inherently retrospective.[1] To know your present was to understand it as the outcome of its past. A certain philosophy appeared, then, not as the dawn of new era but when a historical period was drawing to a close, to sum up what it had been. That Plato could write his *Republic,* the ultimate philosophy of the Greek city-state, was a sign that its heyday was over and that the future belonged to large territorial empires like those of Alexander and his successors and, of course, to that of Rome. This thought was to have long historical legs. Marx believed that if he could get a full and correct understanding of the capitalist economic formation, this could be an important weapon in the class struggle, but he also thought that if he could bring *Kapital* to a successful conclusion, the very fact that he had been able to grasp fully what was going on would be a sign that this system of production had entered its terminal phase. Like the Greek polis in the fourth century, it might totter on for a bit, a walking corpse, but the 'good hoplites' which the city-states would still train their young men to be would prove no match for the Macedonian phalanx, just as even the phalanx would be unable to resist the Roman legions.

Myth would have it that Hegel had actually been in Jena in 1806 finishing his *Phenomenology of Spirit* when he heard the cannonade that announced the opening of the battle of Jena/Auerstedt in which Napoleon's forces all but annihilated the Prussian army just outside the city.[2] That battle, he thought, meant the definitive victory of the French Revolution over the ancien régime. Not even the restoration after the defeat of Napoleon and the Congress of Vienna could fully undo this, because in order to succeed the restoration had been forced itself to adopt (often without explicitly acknowledging it) some of the central principles of the revolutionary project. To be able to compete with the élan of the French citizen-armies, the Prussians needed to create something like citizen-armies of their own, so they abolished serfdom, began to appeal to 'patriotism', and in general embarked on a course of action that spelled the doom of any serious form of feudalism. That was the reality of Hegel's present. By the 1820s and 1830s that was the reality of Hegel's present.

The *Phenomenology of Spirit* is Hegel's first major publication, and it has a somewhat unusual status in the corpus of his work. He describes it as at the same time an 'introduction' to his 'system of philosophy' and the first part of that system.[3] The ambiguity involved in this dual focus and dual intention is difficult to grasp and express clearly, so it is necessary to take a step back and embark on what might look like a slight digression in order to understand it. We are familiar from Plato's *Republic* with the idea of philosophical development and progress. The 'prisoners' in the cave are in thrall to what they take to be common sense—opinions about the shadows on the walls. When they begin to engage in dialectical discussion, they are freed from the delusions they have about these shadows, and as the discussion continues, they get a better grasp on reality and on their world. Through a series of rationally motivated transitions, they eventually move up from the cave to a place in which they can see 'the idea of the good' directly and from which they can survey the whole landscape. Now imagine that there could be a similar process of cultural development, from shadowy confusion through a series of steps each of which is a certain way of organising social, intellectual, spiritual, and cultural life, and suppose that this sequence, too, could be seen as a progressive ascent toward clarity, self-transparency, and rationality, ending in the developed political and social world of the nineteenth century. Now imagine further that one could put these two sequences—that of the individual's ascent from common sense to full self-knowledge and philosophical clarity, and that of our culture's ascent to its present fully developed form—in parallel. This is what the *Phenomenology* tries to achieve.

I stated earlier that the *Phenomenology* had a dual focus, but it would be more correct to say that it has *three* distinct perspectives. First, it is as if the *Phenomenology* were the logbook or diary kept by one of those prisoners, describing how she saw the world at each point in the dialectical ascent—how she saw through each illusion, starting with the illusion that the shadows around her were real, and passed through a series of stages. At each stage the prisoner interpreted herself, the surrounding world, and the relation that existed between her and that world in a slightly different way. Second, this diary of discussions and changes of belief is *also* a history of the cultural forms Western civilisation has passed through in attaining its perfect culmination (in nineteenth-century Europe). Thus, we watch societies based on slavery generate Stoicism, Stoicism break down into scepticism, which in turn engenders various forms of religious life (Hegel's 'unhappy consciousness'), and so forth until we

159

reach the present. The *Phenomenology* maps this motion, too, exhibiting the underlying rational structures which the transitions instantiate. Third, at the end of the 'ascent' the individual path and the sociocultural path are seen eventually to coincide in 'absolute knowledge'. From the standpoint of the idea of 'the good', the philosopher-kings now have a perspective which allows them to see everything clearly, and that includes seeing the path from the shadowy cave up to the light as it really is, not just as it appears to the prisoners transiently climbing it. So from the final perspective of absolute knowledge the fully fledged philosopher can look back on the path she took and see it for what it truly is (and was).

One of the great complications, but also the fascination, of this work derives from the fact that it tries to integrate all three of these perspectives into the same literary text. As the text proceeds, Hegel points out, the 'we' which occurs in it has a systematically shifting reference. Sometimes it is 'we, for instance, Stoics, who are still struggling dialectically with the incompleteness and the contradictions involved in arguing out the particular position we hold at a certain moment'. The analysis is (purportedly) from the internal perspective of the Stoic involved in that discussion: what he thinks, how he sees the world, what problems he might see, how he might argue. Sometimes, however, 'we' refers proleptically not to a Stoic involved in discussion but to the Hegelian philosopher who has finished the whole course of dialectical discussion, has attained absolute knowledge, and from that point can comment on what is going on in the Stoic discussion from the outside, pointing out things that the Stoic participants themselves could not see.

*Phenomenology* is, then, a literary tour de force which is to be both an introduction to the system and the first part of it. It is an introduction because it describes the journey from common sense (where we are all initially assumed to be located) to absolute knowledge, presenting things from the point of view of the dialectical pilgrim who is passing gradually through a series of stages from one location to the other. It is a part of the system because it is also a commentary on the path to absolute knowledge from the point of view of that absolute knowledge.

Hegel thought he was not *merely* the chronicler of the effects of the end of the ancien régime in Central Europe, but also a philosopher. He had a rather traditionalistic conception of the task of philosophy: humans need orientation and meaning in their lives, ideally a full orientation, so philosophy must specify for us our location in the world as a whole and point out our direction within the all. Note that when he speaks of 'the world as a whole' he does not mean just the physical universe but also human society and culture. His philosophy, he thought, was the definitive theory of the meaning of everything. It was a form of 'absolute knowledge', a knowledge which humans have always striven to acquire in their art, their religion, and their philosophy. This 'absolute knowledge', Hegel claims, has in one sense always been present in human societies, albeit in a one-sided, distorted, and partially hidden form. Given the necessary relation of philosophy to the world, as expressed in his dictum about philosophy as its present grasped in concepts, the task of finding meaning could be discharged only if reality actually exhibited meaning, and exhibited it in the right way, that is, in a way which would allow humans to grasp it. Hegel holds that the joint impact of Protestantism and the French Revolution has transformed society in the first part of the nineteenth century so that for the first time, the 'meaning' of the world is visible. He was therefore, he thought, able for the first time to present 'absolute knowledge' in its full and appropriate guise.

For Hegel, the human need for orientation to which philosophy responds is a 'speculative' (i.e., a theoretical), not a practical need

(7.12–15/10–13). That is, philosophy's task finally is to seek meaning, attain understanding, or get a conceptual grip on the world, not to tell us what to do or issue injunctions, recommendations, or prohibitions of possible courses of action. Humans turn to philosophy when they wish to know what the world is like and to understand it, not when they are confronted with moral quandaries or ethically difficult decisions. As Hegel memorably says, if your problem is what to do, ask your rabbi, your lawyer, or a close friend; asking a philosopher about this is pointless (7.13–14/11–13; 7.27–28/22–23). It would be a bit like asking your dentist to recommend a novel (or, for that matter, a novelist to recommend a dentist): the dentist might be a cultured person or a close friend who knows your taste, but knowledge of the statics of human teeth is in itself no special qualification to judge literature. To say that philosophy is not practical but 'speculative' is not to say it will necessarily have no effect whatever on how people act; all sorts of things can influence how people actually decide to act. Some people flip coins; some observe the flight of birds. Most people will act in ways that will be influenced by the general understanding they have of the world. It is just that the effect on people's actions will be indirect and that it is not part of the contents of philosophy to issue 'oughts' or impose 'obligations'—it is only to understand these phenomena, as it tries to understand all human phenomena.

The absolute (speculative) knowledge which philosophy seeks is supposed to be complete and definitive, but not in the sense that it contains or implies every individual fact or law. Rather we try, as humans, to make sense of the world as a whole by using a variety of general concepts and categories. These might include such things as 'substance', 'living thing', 'cause', 'intention', 'perception', 'work of art', 'nation', 'virtue', 'law', 'god'. These are the items we use to make the world intelligible to ourselves. None of them, however, is in itself fully clear, so to orient ourselves in the world means to come to understand fully what these basic concepts mean, how they are used, and how they are interconnected with each other. Hegel thinks that this final task, specifying the connection, is especially important because it turns out that really to understand what any one of these categories means *is* to a large extent to see how it is related to all the others. This is his form of holism: understanding any of these basic concepts or categories correctly requires one to locate it precisely in a total system of all such concepts. So the set of categories must be both explicitly unified and also adequate for explaining and clarifying, in principle, everything. The absolute knowledge which humanity has been seeking and which Hegel finally, because of the historical circumstances in which he lived, is able to provide, is, then, a complete, consistent, interconnected set of concepts and categories covering all forms of meaningfulness—that is, all the ways of making sense of anything in the world and rendering anything in any way intelligible to us humans. The 'interconnections' between the concepts are argumentative, discursive, or 'logical' in character, and the 'knowledge' in question is mastery of these concepts in their interconnection and ability to use them to make sense of the world. Furthermore, a part of having the appropriate knowledge is being able to explain why past philosophers (as equally children of their time) were able to see only a part of the truth but not all of it, and the ability to explain why people in the nineteenth century were finally able to see the truth as a whole unveiled and in its proper form.

Think, then, of a group of people trying to come to clarity about how to understand, analyse, and explain their world, including (for Hegel) not just the abstract world of mathematics and logic, the natural world of physics, and the social and cultural world, but also human history. They will proceed in a variety of ways, but once they have done the preliminary work of looking about them, classifying the animal species they encounter, learning how to do long division, setting up some primitive code for regulating their social relations to each other, instituting forms of art and religion and so forth, they will turn to trying to see not just how individual aspects of their world are constituted but how it all hangs together. Hegel is convinced that this striving for totality or completeness and interconnection of knowledge is an ineluctable part of what it is to be human. To try to see and understand their world as a whole, humans may try out various tacks. Dances, pictures, myths, stories, prose cosmologies may be deployed. Eventually, they will hit on 'dialectics' of the kind practised by Socrates and Plato as a method of getting the comprehensive understanding they crave; that is, certain of them will make particular knowledge claims and propose definitions of terms, and others will ask critical questions about these claims. We will be especially keen to see if these claims are clear and comprehensible, but also whether they can be generalised and are compatible with other claims we know we wish to make. Plato's dialogues are so exceedingly vivid and full of apparently realistic detail—Aristophanes has the hiccups in the *Symposium* (185c–d) and has to have his turn to speak put off—that we might almost be tempted to think of them as something like transcripts of real discussions. But, of course, that is not the case. They represent idealised constructions of the ways in which arguments might go right (or wrong).

Now imagine, Hegel suggests, a form of dialectical argument that is *even more* idealised than the one we find in Plato. Imagine people in some historical context, who, given their circumstances, are maximally well-informed about their world, self-controlled, rational, tolerant, and persistent. And imagine that a group of such idealised figures were to conduct a completely free and open-ended discussion with no time limit and under optimal circumstances for conversation. Then the discussion will proceed in the progressive way in which some of the Platonic dialogues proceed. Proposals will be formulated, considered, developed, criticised, improved. Defective positions will be gradually discarded and replaced with better ones, not subject to the same criticisms as their predecessors.

Hegel holds, to be sure, that such a discussion, even in its most highly idealised form, would, if conducted at any time in the past, have come up against certain immovable limits and barriers which no amount of further empirical investigation, ratiocination, or dialectical discussion would be able to do away with. If you live, for instance, in a feudal society, you are never really going to be able to make rational sense of your social arrangements because they *are not* fully rational. Your political institutions are going to be encrusted with contingencies and irrelevancies and inextricably mixed with archaic forms of reasoning, biologistic fantasies (dynastic pedigrees that purportedly give a right to rule to the accidental offspring of certain families), religious mystifications (medieval Catholicism), and shapeless and incoherent works of art (legends about Arthur and the pursuit of the Holy Grail). Therefore, in such a society you are never going to be able to discover the full set of adequate categories, one that fully makes sense in itself and also makes sense of your world. They simply will not emerge at the end of a free ideal discussion. Given the holistic assumptions on which Hegel's position rests, this deficiency will not be an isolated blemish but will affect the meaning and adequacy of *all* the concepts and categories which people at that time use. So doing philosophy during the Middle Ages was a necessity—people can't help looking for meaning, and 'the total meaning of the world as a whole'—but it was also a necessary failure. The same is true of philosophy in antiquity because the ancient world was a slave-owning society. Such a society cannot,

Hegel claims, have a coherent concept of 'freedom' or even develop a proper legal definition of 'human being' (*homo*), because slaves would have to be classed either as 'human beings (and hence free)' or 'not human beings (and thus not responsible for any of their actions)' (7.31/26–27). Protestantism firmly establishes 'freedom' in modern Europe by its defence of the right of individual autonomous moral judgement, and the French Revolution makes it impossible to ignore the demand that even society and political institutions need to instantiate reason.[4]. The ideals of the French Revolution— *liberté, égalité, fraternité*—in a suitably institutionalised political form would be conjoined with post-Christian culture and sociability rooted in a post-Lutheran form of interiority, centred in particular in free individual conscience. In the nineteenth century, for the first time in history, human society was visibly, clearly, and intentionally oriented toward rationality, and this orientation was publicly acknowledged and, at least incipiently, institutionalised. When that happens, the way is open for an adequate form of philosophical reflection on the-world-that-is and our ways of making sense of it.

Hegel is sometimes seen as a hyperrationalist, and this is not completely wrong because he does ascribe to reason and the human understanding very extensive powers; at one point he even says of understanding and analysis that it is an 'absolute power' (3.36/18). That is, reason finally gives itself its own laws and criteria, and there is nothing apart from these relative to which it can be evaluated (or could be criticised). There are, 'in the long run' (which may be a very long run), no human powers stronger than reason and which could stand against it. It was, however, also a fundamental Hegelian tenet that the Reason which is all-powerful is *not* the subjective faculty of any individual human or the given social power of any particular group or historical society. Philosophy, as just mentioned, cannot give us a satisfactory world view, if the world will not lend itself to this. Philosophy itself cannot make the world be a comprehensible place if it is not, so its success in its enterprise of representing the world as rational depends on something outside itself, namely on the world itself—and that means, effectively, on history. In the long run society cannot resist the force of Reason, but this is something that is visible only in retrospect. We, at the end of the development which leads up to us, enjoy a full freedom which no previous society had and have conscious access to a Reason which we can see was operative even then but which they could only occasionally have glimpsed dimly and through a variety of badly distorting lenses. No amount of sheer ratiocinative power could have allowed Plato to construct an internally consistent satisfactory philosophy in a slave-owning society; nor could the collective efforts of the whole *studium generale* in Paris in 1300, because their society was fundamentally feudal. If you live in a society without freedom, there is *nothing you can do*. The aristocrat is 'more' free than the bondsman, but that is a comparative judgement, which, although not in any sense irrelevant—it is of extreme relevance for those involved in feudalism—or false, does not tell the most important part of what we can retrospectively see as the whole story, which is that no 'freedom' available at that historical period was more than a pale and anaemic anticipation of the freedom which everyone enjoys in the postrevolutionary world. That is not, of course, any consolation to the serfs, slaves, burgesses, aristocrats, kings, and emperors of the past, and was not intended to be. The idea that there could be such a thing as retrospective consolation is not one that Hegel entertains. We have no reason to think that they, our ancestors, would even have understood our ideas about freedom and our institutions, despite the fact that our modern freedom arose, in some sense, from their world (and its well-deserved demise). And even if *per impossibile* they had had cognitive access to the future, to what the end-point of their history would be (our world), they still had to live then, just as we have no choice but to live now. Hegel does on some occasions speak of his philosophy as 'the true theodicy'[5], but, as we shall see, this does not mean that it gives any past victim consolation, nor does it 'justify' anything either retrospectively or in the present. Hegel, to be sure, is trying to give a universal systematic overview of all human categories and thus needs to find a place for virtually everything, so one would expect discussion of 'justification' at various times. What should strike the reader as significant, however, is the extreme paucity of occurrences of any word that might directly mean 'justify/justification' (*rechtfertigen/Rechtfertigung*). It is almost as if Hegel were consciously avoiding this vocabulary.[6] The concept belongs originally to the domain of individual human actions to which there are alternatives and which are compared with some kind of normative code which is distinct from them. Then it can be extended in various ways: to the individual human action of holding a belief, then to beliefs themselves which are called 'justified' (meaning a person would be justified in holding them). Eventually, the use of the term could in principle be extended to the actions of what we now call 'nonnatural' agents such as corporations, governments, and states and to such things as codes of behaviour or systems of rules, which can themselves be construed as potentially justified or not relative to yet further, more general or more encompassing, sets of laws. To deploy the term 'justification' usefully requires in addition such notions as 'court', 'procedures', 'authority', 'law (rule)', and 'judgement'. In antecedently well-defined *local* contexts, for instance when dealing with the internal transactions in a chess club or the routine proceedings of a traffic court, these terms all make good sense, and there is nothing wrong with their use. However, to generalise from this and pursue 'justification' or the improvement of systems of 'justification' unrestrictedly and without an awareness of some limiting context which also gives the term concrete meaning is a form of conceptual cancer: an inherently subordinate mode of thinking is allowed to expand without limits into areas with which it can never hope to cope and in which it is not just a failure, but a destructive failure. The bureaucrat or clerk usurps the function of the philosopher.

It is a 'destructive' failure because a focus on 'justification' emphasises the fixity of authority, of rules, of procedures, of some administrative apparatus. But this is exactly wrong for philosophical or, as Hegel would also put it, 'rational' or 'speculative' purposes, that is, for asking questions that purport to concern the 'totality' of the world, how it hangs together as a whole, and how we should orient ourselves in it. The first thing (or rather the last thing) one is supposed to learn in philosophy, according to Hegel, is that there is no such fixity: all is movement and flux. The final image of 'the true' is not that of a series of entries in a bookkeeping system or even of some kind of orderly judicial procedure before the high tribunal of reason, but of a drunken bacchantic revel in which no one is sober (3.46/27). Such a revel is not *completely* without order of any kind, but the order it does exhibit is not practically justificatory. All individual forms of authority are dissolved into the universal flux of philosophical concepts, and that flux itself does not have the right format to serve as an authority relative to which justification can be demanded and given (in the sense in which people think they need such an authority and such a justification). Philosophy will give you a number of things: a sense of some order in that flux, whereby certain forms of authority arise out of others; an ability to survey the *whole* of that flux and locate every form of authority you will encounter in it; and a sense that this is really all one can reasonably expect to find. What it will not, and could not, give you is anything at all like the 'justification' or warrant for any individual action or belief. Many philosophers, and non-philosophers too, think or even demand that philosophy must provide 'firm foundations' for existing institutions *or* a free-floating sky-hook from which to hang to justify certain forms of acting (or radically de-legitimise others form of action) which is disconnected from existing institutions. Hegel rejects both of these demands. If you keep the relation between 'justification' and existing institutions tight, you will never get a context-free 'justification'. If you completely untighten the connection of 'justification' from particular, highly specific historical configurations and institutions, you are left with nothing, because the real content of 'justification' lies in the totality of these concrete connections. You may retain a highly abstract and general story about how things as whole in the world in general work and hang together; from such a story, however, nothing in particular about how any individual is warranted to act will follow.

Hegel makes great fun of the late seventeenth/early eighteenth-century philosopher Leibniz, who invented the term 'theodicy', as the author of what he takes to be one of the greatest absurdities in the long history of ludicrous philosophical misconceptions.[7] Leibniz thinks that God has before him an abstract space of possibilities and, within that, subspaces of possibilities that can be co-instantiated, that is, realised in the same possible world. From among these he chooses 'the best' and creates our world. We can discover that the world we live in is the best of all possible ones. Hegel compares this to a shopper who goes to the market with a prepared list of things to buy, or rather a preexisting list of the 'good properties' of the possible groceries he is seeking to purchase. The shopper then compares what is on offer in the market with the list and picks the best produce available. Hegel thinks that if anything like a God really did exist, the one thing that is clear is that his relation to the world could not conceivably be anything like this. Many contemporary philosophers have compounded the absurdity by trying to run a similar theory of possible worlds without a deity. The idea of a god in his study trying to decide what *would be* good, or at work on a list or code or protocol *before* creation, is a Bronze Age fantasy, no matter how sophisticated its elaboration.

Hegel believes one never starts with a set of abstract possibilities; one starts with what is the case. All there is, is what there is; reality is what is or what happens. Possibilities are always abstractions from that, not something that could be antecedently really imagined, even by an omnipotent deity. Part of what happens is that humans act, and in doing so they have, of course, various complex ethical and normative views which they bring to bear on their world and which they can (perfectly legitimately) bring to bear on anything they fancy. Nothing prohibits this, but it would be a mistake to attribute to it any special significance. The fact that modern secondary school teachers express moral horror at ancient slavery is not in any sense illegitimate; it just has no particular philosophical significance. That I or anyone else has this moral reaction is also a possible subject of speculative understanding, but that won't 'justify' anything. 'Justification' is inherently related to *actions* and the warrants for action, but in 2016 I could not even in principle act on an ancient society that has not existed for 2,000 years. Of course, in a completely different kind of case I may fight residual pockets of slavery and oppose practical attempts to reintroduce slavery in my own society, and then I will deploy all the moral and intellectual resources I can, including appeal to local authorities, contextually and institutionally specific local forms of argumentation, and whatever else I can think of or invent, but this is because I am arguing about potential actions that I might perform. I may also, if I wish—no one will stop me—look down on the Romans for being slaveholders, but given the absence of any action context in this case for me, that is just a shadow action, a cheap way of trying to feel good about myself.

Still, there is no doubt but that Hegel thinks his philosophy provides a 'theodicy' of kinds; he says so explicitly enough. However, theodicy in Hegel's sense is intended to provide not 'justification' but 'reconciliation', which is a completely different thing. When I am 'reconciled', I come to be 'warmly at peace' with someone (or something) which I previously saw as alien or hostile or offensive to me (7.27/22–23). This is a question of attitude (one might say), not of justification. In fact, it might almost be argued that I need reconciliation only if your action toward me was *not* justified. Peace and reconciliation committees operate not by showing that what *seemed* to be grievous wrongs were actually 'justified', but rather by showing a way to live in peace beyond the recognition that utterly unjustified harm has been inflicted. This is not to say that 'reconciliation' is *merely* a question of feeling in a certain way or that it is not possible to distinguish states of pseudo-reconciliation that are, for instance, dependent on deep illusions from instances of genuine reconciliation. Hegel's whole work, as it were, is one huge attempt to give a highly detailed but also highly contextual way of making exactly this distinction. It is also not, obviously, that being reconciled (or not) will have no effect whatever on human action, but its effect will be so highly mediated and dispersed that it will not be possible to connect it with any one specific course of action in the way 'justification' requires. Recall, finally, that for Hegel 'reconciliation' can be accomplished not just by philosophy but also by art or religion. Sculpting, exhibiting, and revering a statue of the Greek god Apollo, which represents him not as a jackal-headed monster but as a beautiful human being,[8] is not giving a 'justification' (in any interesting sense) of any particular form of social organisation

172

or politics, and certainly is not a 'justification' for a specific course of action, but it is an instance of 'reconciliation.'

To speak of some 'absolute justification' is to compare some individual act with a normative standard of some kind which is in principle completely distinct from it—otherwise it is circular. But where would a standard that is 'independent' of the-world-as-a-whole come from, and what could its standing be? I could use my own puny moral conceptions, and no one can stop me from doing this, but I am not foolish enough to take them to have any global or absolute standing. God wins his case by default because there is no independent court competent to rule on the 'justification' of the world. The point of philosophy is to show people why nothing is justified in any absolute sense but that it is possible to embrace the world 'in a warm peace' anyway. More cannot be shown.

Hegel's nonindividualism is another striking characteristic of his approach. Reason never occurs or is operative except through individuals—that is true—but it can also never be fully grasped from the point of view of the individual alone, and it certainly cannot be understood from the perspective of individual psychology. If one lives in a society like that of Europe in the nineteenth century, in which the dialectic does operate fully and successfully, one can even idealise this dialectic in a way that allows one to dispense with the idea that the 'dialectical discussion' is being conducted by two *distinct* humans at all. To the extent to which a philosophical discussion, say, the discussion of 'benevolence', becomes more fully rational, the individual personalities of the people involved in the discussion matter less and less. In the ideal case one thought and consideration will follow another in the same order, no matter who the discutants are. So actually it is as if the thought/concept itself were moving in discussion, developing itself, exhibiting its internal structure, even criticising itself by raising the obvious objections that arise, transforming itself. This won't happen unless humans are actually present discussing, but they, as potentially idiosyncratic, potentially irrational agents, are irrelevant to the structure of what is happening. That structure is, if one wishes to use this terminology, 'objective'. To take part in a philosophical discussion means not simply to be engaging in expressive behaviour but trying to be rational, to present one's position as rationally acceptable and therefore as potentially criticisable. This is true even if one does not know in advance 'what reason might require'. In fact, the most important part of a philosophical discussion is that, if it is properly conducted, as positions are discussed, criticised, and modified, at the same time the standards of rationality by which they are discussed, criticised, and modified themselves are clarified and improved. So no one in a real discussion can know antecedently to what she is committed by virtue of proposing a philosophical view. In the discussion, she finds out. All of this, however, can be construed as part of the inherent motion of the concepts involved. In the canonical form of Hegel's philosophic system, as expounded, say, in *The Science of Logic,* the dual perspective of the *Phenomenology* is no longer needed, nor would it be appropriate, and the concepts and positions are construed in such a way as to abstract from any particular agent who might propose them in discussion and are presented as objectively fully self-moving.

Hegel's nonindividualism has another aspect: individual psychology plays a remarkably subordinate role in his philosophy. For Hegel I am not essentially a biological individual or an individual with consciousness and other psychological powers or one who entertains propositions or has the capacity to reason; rather I am Spirit. 'Spirit' is a technical term that Hegel uses which refers neither exclusively to an individual nor to a group. He thinks this concept holds the key to understanding why his philosophy is different from all philosophies that went before. Previous philosophies were one of two types. One type was metaphysical. The metaphysician studied external 'objects' in the world and their properties and tried to explain everything in those terms. The kind of things which previous philosophers recognised as an 'object' got more and more sophisticated over the centuries, but their view was always some more or less complex development of the idea that an object was a (relatively) unchanging thing or substance that maintained its identity despite changes in its properties. The cat remains the same cat, even if her properties change (she loses her hair; she is in a fight and returns with a nicked ear; she gets pregnant and bears a litter of kittens). The other type of philosophy was basically epistemological and was focused on the individual human subject and its modalities, especially consciousness and knowledge. Philosophers of this type didn't study objects but human processes of knowing. The basic question is not What is there and how does it work? but What can we know and how do we know it? Hegel thought each of these kinds of philosophy was bound to end in a cul de sac. No metaphysician could ever really give an analysis of the basic phenomena of human subjectivity by studying what things there are in the world. There could be no metaphysics of consciousness, of the human subject, or of knowledge. The second type of philosophy gets nowhere because once one starts from and focuses exclusively on the individual human consciousness and its modes of operation, and treats this as if it was an autonomous domain to study, one will never get out again to the real world. One can never solve the basic problem of epistemology and show on the basis of some fact about or configuration of consciousness that an external world anything like what we imagine exists.

Spirit is supposed to provide a more all-encompassing concept either than the metaphysician's identity-maintaining substances or than the epistemologist's conscious subject. Spirit, 'the True', is, Hegel says, both substance and subject (2.23ff/9ff), more than both, but providing a space within which metaphysical and epistemological questions can be discussed, although always as subordinate and limited forms of enquiry. How are we to understand that?

Hegel ascribes to Spirit two properties. The first is

1. Spirit is an 'I' that is a 'we' and a 'we' that is an 'I' (3.145/110).

This does not mean that Spirit is something like a metaphysical group mind, but it is a theoretical way of describing certain human phenomena which do not lend themselves either to analysis in terms merely of individual psychology or to analysis in terms simply of the properties of groups. A good example of a spiritual phenomenon is a language, or in fact anything that at all depends on language. A language such as English or Turkish exists only as a collective social entity activated by individuals: 'I' speak this way to a large extent because 'we' speak this way (and vice versa). It is true that English would not exist if there had never been individual speakers who made use of it, but it is also true that the language preexists any individual speaker; every speaker finds it always already there. There is no path either from universal structures of rationality or from my individual consciousness and actions to a full understanding of the language as a social phenomenon. Universal structures won't explain the difference between English and Turkish, and no amount of introspection of the consciousness of any individual will give you a grasp of vocabulary items in the language which that individual does not happen (at some time) to know. In addition, you cannot understand me as an individual without understanding my beliefs, but they will be formulated in a language which is not (finally) my own individual creation, but a social phenomenon; that is, you can understand me only as a form of spirit, as an individuated part of an 'us'. Finally, 'I' can't understand myself except as part of a 'we' which I can alternately identify with and distinguish myself from. So in a sense even self-understanding is a 'spiritual' phenomenon.

The second property of Spirit is also unorthodox:

2. Spirit is a (social) formation that is always in the process of aspiring to making itself into (a better version of) itself. Hegel says again and again Spirit 'is' not anything; it is always 'becoming' something or rather 'making itself into something'.

The notion of 'becoming a better version of oneself' may not be merely empty and gestural but may be full of highly individuating content. You don't understand Athens in the fifth century unless you understand Perikles' Funeral Oration.[9] The Oration presents a very particular ideal of Athens as a place in which the idiosyncrasies of individuals were tolerated, political power was exercised by the citizens as a whole, and each citizen behaved like a 'lover' of the city. This does not mean that the Funeral Oration is a 'realistic' description of the way Athens was; it is a formulation (one particular formulation) of what (some) Athenians aspired for Athens to be. These are not, on the other hand, merely fanciful or invented aspirations, but have, Hegel thinks, some basis in the reality of Athenian life. There are much more primitive or rudimentary ways in which this attempt to make oneself into a better self can find expression. To stay with the example of language, even minimal kinds of language use depend on distinguishing between correct and incorrect usage, and to call some usage 'incorrect' is already to express a minimal aspiration toward eliminating or at least avoiding it. One might see in this the origins of what, when appropriately abstracted, is sometimes called 'normativity'.

Such a self-reproducing human community is both a substance and a subject. Fifth-century Athens is an instance of spirit because

it is organised to maintain its identity through change in its properties. Individuals are born and die, but, as long as the institutions
continue to function, they are born and die as Athenians. Athens is
a subject because its population can and does say 'we'; the city can
be said to know various things, such as what its own laws are, and
to act and react, for instance by declaring war on Sparta. It has specific institutions—assemblies, law courts, religious groupings, a
council (*boulé*)—whose job it is to be the real locus of such knowledge and such action and to try to ensure that the city lives up to
various aspirations, such as being stronger, more just, and better
prepared for various contingencies.

Let us return now to the members of the idealised group discussing 'meaningfulness' in a postrevolutionary society. What will
happen in their discussion? If all goes well, eventually it will pass
argumentatively through all the human forms of meaningfulness—
Hegel thinks they are all systematically interconnected, so that this
is inevitable—and the people engaged in the discussion will eventually converge on something which is stable and no longer subject to
disagreement or criticism. However, this 'stable thing' will not be a
single proposition but will rather be the whole process of argumentation through which they have just passed, which will lie spread
out ahead of them again. To return to the comparison with Plato,
for Hegel the dialectical ladder up from the cave does not terminate
at the top with a vision of the idea of 'the good', as if that was a
separate thing one could see, but, having arrived at the top, what
one sees is the whole trip up the path, successively reenacted eternally. What one comes to understand is that in a sense there is
nothing but the journey, and the whole process is an infinitely repeating circle. This circle exists only as we move through it; it is
nothing separate which we could say anything about 'in itself'—
what language would we use?—yet there is nothing arbitrary or

subjective about the steps on the path and the sequence in which they stand to each other.

There is, to be sure, in one sense a 'final' truth about the world for Hegel, but it is not a proposition; it is a form of conceptual and argumentative motion, a narrative or story, no part of which can be dispensed with or further abbreviated. The Truth is the System itself and Spirit passing around the stages that constitute it, infinitely. This story (and the actual movement of thought in which it is embedded) is teleological, so it moves in a certain sequence and direction and is directed in a certain way toward a certain end. That end is precisely that the story be told and the movement instantiated; so the movement is not just teleological but auto-teleological: its end is that it itself exists (which means that the movement which it is continues). In a way the whole of the universe can be seen as existing *in order that that take place,* and Hegel's whole philosophy is a specification of what else must happen (human societies must have abolished slavery, etc.) for this story to be coherently told. The final framework for meaning is this narrative motion, and finding out the final meaning of anything is just locating it in its appropriate position in this auto-teleological story/movement. *Ex hypothesi* anything you would care to mention has a place in the story—otherwise the system would be incomplete (which we are assuming for the sake of discussion is not the case).

When Hegel describes his own position as 'absolute idealism', this does not mean he thinks anyone ever has or has had an 'absolute' justification for anything. Rather, absolute idealism asserts, roughly, that anything/everything *can be idealised,* that is, comprehended as part of a systematic whole, which is the autotelic motion, the telling of the universal narrative story which was just described. This does not mean the external world does not exist or is some kind of mere simulacrum; that is a completely different kind of claim, and one that it would never enter Hegel's mind to make in his own name. Absolute idealism, as a form of speculation, comes precisely to the conclusion that 'absolute justification' (in any recognisable human sense of 'justification') does not exist.

Earlier I mentioned that moderns find it hard to follow Hegel into a way of looking at the world that eschews using concepts like 'justification', and I suggested that there might be something discreditable about this. We find it hard when living in a world that is as deeply unsatisfactory as ours is, to give up the feelings of vindictiveness or of pharisaic self-satisfaction which the use of the apparatus of 'justification' legitimises. If Hegel is right, and our world is as it is, then we are as we are able to be, and there is nothing inherently 'discreditable' about finding this hard. The question remains whether, having read the *Phenomenology* and observing the world around us, we do not find ourselves motivated to change it.

# Chapter Eight

# NIETZSCHE

Although Nietzsche would not perhaps always have been pleased to see it presented in this way, his basic project, as he recognises, is a variant of Christianity, a religion which he interprets, in turn, as a slightly debased form of Platonism ('Platonism for the common folk').[1] If Christianity purports to be a religion of universal, unconditional love, Nietzsche in his account of it puts emphasis on two other of its properties. First, Christianity has been peculiar in its commitment to what it calls 'the truth'. This, Nietzsche claims, is originally a moral demand for truth-telling, that is, an injunction that I not lie to anyone else; then this becomes a demand that I not lie even to myself, and finally an increasingly stringent demand actively to search out 'the truth' (*KSA* 5.395–401). Given that the 'truth' is usually uncomfortable for us, Nietzsche sees this first strand of Christianity as rooted in a form of asceticism—an active preference for that which is painful and rebarbative (*KSA* 5.339–367). The second important feature of Christianity is its cultivation of an ethos of introspection (*KSA* 5.408–411): it eventually comes to be the home of a very strict practice of psychological analysis and interpretation. The good life for the Christian is not one in which people merely perform external acts of a certain kind but one in which they act out of the motive of sheer love. As finite, nondivine creatures, we are never in this life going to be able to instantiate fully that absolute love, but it is important for our spiritual progress that we become as clearly as possible aware of our failings in this respect. It is, therefore, understandable that Christianity encourages an increasingly and relentlessly exacting and minute self-examination of our internal psychological states. Nietzsche, who sometimes liked to pose as a 'master psychologist',[2] is the heir of this aspect of Christianity, and when he describes himself as 'not a man but dynamite' (*KSA* 6.365), he is referring to the fact that the truths he propagates are particularly irritating, disruptive, and destructive, in one sense a veritable feast for the ascetic.

What is wrong with Christianity is that it has become massively implausible in the modern world. Or, to put it more exactly, it has destroyed itself; it is precisely those who are, in some sense, the most Christian who find themselves incapable of continuing to believe it. The reason for this, Nietzsche believes, lies in the true history of Christianity, the sources of its power and the origin of its constructs, which he has laid bare, most clearly perhaps in *Genealogy of Morality*. Its origins are in highly concentrated resentment; its continuing power lies in its ability to generate and focus hatred; and its characteristic habits and practices are expressions of a sadistic asceticism (toward self and others) gone out of control. Christian introspection and truth-telling will, if pursued consistently, confirm this. And what is the (at this point former) Christian like Nietzsche then to do, when he inevitably comes to understand this? Simple continuation of the usual practices and beliefs, once they have been seen through as devastatingly as this, does not seem to be possible

182

except perhaps for some few exceptional people who are absolute *virtuosi* of ascetic self-hatred and cognitive quick-footedness (say, Kierkegaard).

So although it is not completely false to say that Nietzsche thinks he has 'refuted' Christianity, this is also not really the way he would think about it. The reason for this is that Christianity is not primarily a sequence of propositions; rather it is a historically complex conjunction of habits, dispositions, beliefs, values, and practices which is directed at giving structure to human life and dealing with some of its less palatable aspects. So the question is less Is it true? than Does it work? Will rustling your rosary beads calm you down? Will communal singing, snake handling, and speaking in tongues cure your inner demons? Nietzsche thinks that it worked rather well for almost 2,000 years and that perhaps it still works for the odd anchorite, member of an isolated farming community, vagrant, deviant artist, infantilised adult, or religious eccentric.

I described Nietzsche's project as a 'variant' of Christianity. He would probably prefer to call it a form of 'overcoming' Christianity. Well, isn't Christianity itself all about overcoming? I suggest that we think about Nietzsche's 'overcoming' of Christianity along three dimensions, corresponding to the three dimensions of the Christian construction. Instead of 'universal love', Nietzsche aspires to 'unconditional affirmation'. Then he wishes to distance himself from the excessively ascetic Christian conception of truth and truth-telling. Finally, although one must admit that this is the least clearly articulated position of the three, he certainly wishes to break with the Christian ethos of introspection. Let me start the discussion with 'truth'.

Nietzsche thought there was something problematic about the facile way in which philosophers and ordinary people spoke about 'the truth'. Some people have taken to attributing to him rather spectacularly implausible views, such as that there is no such thing as the truth, there are no truths, or there are no facts; consequently, science is nothing but a huge delusion, and in the realm of beliefs anything goes. These views are so incoherent and yet remain so firmly rooted in the minds of some readers that it might be worthwhile to try to lay them to rest. There is a certain philosophical interpretation of 'truth, facts, science' (and for that matter 'knowledge') which eventually goes back to Plato, but after 2,000 years it has also deeply impregnated our 'common sense', which Nietzsche is keen to deny. However, to reject a philosophical theory of some concept or phenomenon is not necessarily to reject the concept or claim that the phenomenon does not exist; I can reject what I take to be a false or misguided theory of botany without thinking that flowers do not exist. I can also reject the phlogiston theory of burning without denying that burning takes place. This now common philosophical view which Nietzsche rejects is one that is deeply committed to a series of sharp distinctions—between 'truth' and '(mere) opinion', 'fact' and 'interpretation', 'science' and 'uncontrolled belief formation', and 'knowledge' and 'speculation'. It is also committed to the view that without continual surveillance of the border and sharp enforcement of these dichotomous distinctions, there can be nothing but cognitive chaos in our world. The structure of enquiry, constatation, hypothesis formation, confirmation, and evaluation that constitutes 'science' must in particular also be kept rigidly distinct from the domain of the emotions, all voluntative phenomena, and the 'interpretation' of results (e.g., in the light of human needs and interests). 'Truth' and 'the will' belong to different domains entirely, and only confusion can result from failing to keep the 'truth' insulated and hermetically closed off from all forms of volition and evaluation. Finally, the 'correspondence theory of truth' claims that

TRUTH US OPINION

truth is to be construed as the correspondence of a proposition with the facts of the world.

Nietzsche is not the only philosopher to find at least some elements of this analysis unconvincing, and he rejects it fully. 'Truth', he believes, is better understood as the pendant of a will-to-truth which operated under historical circumstances that could be analysed and, if it was so analysed, would be seen itself to have a history. 'Truth' did not grow on trees; it had to be discovered, and that meant there had to be a 'will-to-truth' which pursued and discovered the truth and which itself therefore deserved investigation. This will-to-truth developed historically in different ways. None of this in any way implied that 'truth' was just something made up by an arbitrarily operating form of human volition, although, as we shall see, it did perhaps mean that there was no interesting *philosophical* analysis that one could give of 'the concept of truth' in the abstract (such as the correspondence theory). Nietzsche was far from thinking that there were no such things as facts. On the contrary, he thought the acquisition of a 'sense for the facts' was one of the most precious, and the latest, of human achievements (*KSA* 6.247–248). Nevertheless, he also thought that, although it might be perfectly appropriate to distinguish 'fact' and 'interpretation' sharply in certain well-defined research contexts, this distinction could not sensibly be absolutised and construed in the fundamentalist way which some philosophers proposed. There were, of course, 'facts', but no 'facts' that were inherently and absolutely devoid of all interpretation. The idea of a bare, completely uninterpreted fact did not make sense. So the correspondence theory of truth is either false (if it presupposes the existence of uninterpreted facts) or tautological (if fact and interpretation can never be cleanly separated once and for all).

There are three issues here, different contexts in which 'truth' arises as a problem and in which it must be treated. First, there is the question about 'truths' (with a small 't'), that is, garden-variety statements about the world which are significantly strongly warranted and deserve to be affirmed. Do such statements exist, and are they distinct from nontruths, or is everything simply a matter of opinion, with no opinion having any priority over any other? The answer to this is, for Nietzsche, patently yes, they do exist. These truths include such statements about trivial matters as 'It is now raining (rather than sunny)'; 'Jane has just struck John a blow to the head (rather than the other way around)'; 'Tabitha prefers Parmesan to cat food (although it is not good for her)'; 'But this codex reads *est*, not *esset*'. They may also in principle include in some contexts such statements as 'The barometer has fallen'; 'This metal has a tensile strength of . . .'; 'This has a positive electrical charge'. One might also speak of 'the facts', although one must add sotto voce 'the facts *as appropriately interpreted*'. How much does the sun need to shine for the day to be 'sunny'? Is 'sunny'/'raining' really the only alternative? (Have you ever been to East Anglia?) What with perfect justice function as 'facts' in some contexts can be (and in some other contexts ought to be) unpacked so as to reveal the 'interpretations' with which they are associated. How much sun makes a day sunny? This does not imply that there is no sense in which the facts of the case exist or that one's cognitive relation to the world is completely indeterminate or random. That we don't know how much sun is required to call the day 'sunny' does not imply that one might just as well believe that Pontius Pilate composed *La Belle Hélène* as that Jacques Offenbach did. 'Interpretation', for a philologist trained in the nineteenth-century discipline, as Nietzsche was, does not mean simply making something up or complete laissez-faire. The philologist tries to develop well-judged interpretations, not to speak at random. What counts as a 'well-judged' interpretation is a complex matter, and there is probably no interesting *general* theory one can give which will allow one simply to decide in a mechanical way which of two interpretations is better. Again, context is all-important, and the contexts will contain local criteria by which such judgements can be made and also, in propitious circumstances, will be open to general reflection and criticism which may permit these local criteria to be improved. And, of course, one can discuss what 'improve' means in the specific context. None of this means that all interpretations are equally well-judged. So to say that the facts exist only as interpreted is a rejection of certain forms of naive realism; that is, it is a claim only that the form of determination of the facts is more complicated than everyday awareness (and certain philosophers who orient themselves too closely on it) recognises. Nietzsche celebrates 'a sense for the facts' (*KSA* 6.247–248) as one of the highest achievements of the human spirit, and equally it might seem appropriate to extend this to include a sense for the complexities of the modes by which we come to apprehend what 'the facts' are, which means the role which 'interpretation' plays.

That is the first of the three kinds of discussions of 'truth'. The second is what some philosophers, following Plato, might call the 'more strictly "philosophical" question of "Truth"': What is the definition of truth? Is it, for instance, the correspondence of proposition to reality? Or is it to be defined in terms of the internal coherence of a maximal set of beliefs? Or should we have a 'pragmatist' theory of truth? Or does Nietzsche perhaps hold none of these but have a new theory of his own?

Even a cursory reading of any one of the works of Nietzsche's maturity, particularly *Genealogy of Morality,* should suffice to indicate to the reader that Nietzsche does not propose to answer this question but rather wishes to destroy the complex of assumptions which one must make in order for the question to be at all a sensible one to raise. The usual approach assumes that associated with each linguistic item, such as 'temperance', 'knowledge', 'beauty', 'truth', there is a single abstract property which has an 'essence'. The proper way to do philosophy is to 'define' that essence in perfectly abstract terms (without, for instance, using examples). If one does not have such a definition, one does not at all have a grasp of the meaning of the term in question and could not expect to have any real knowledge of it, know how to use it properly, distinguish sensible from senseless uses of it, and so forth. In one of his later works (*The Twilight of Idols*) Nietzsche speaks of 'Egyptianism' as a characteristic vice of philosophers (*KSA* 6.74–75). The idea here is that philosophers begin to work by draining the blood and vitality from concepts and mummifying them. They do this particularly by extracting the concept in question from history and construing it as unchanging and abstract. The Platonic mode of operation described earlier, with its emphasis on definition, is an essential part of the preparation and mummification process. Euclidean figures and arithmetical truths have perhaps no history; virtually everything else does, and 'only that which has no history can be defined' (*KSA* 5.317). This does not mean, as Plato assumes, that no knowledge is possible. Perhaps to reject Plato means to admit that no 'certain knowledge' is possible, but then could it not be the case that this is the right conclusion to come to? And why, in any case, the obsession with 'certainty'? What does it even mean exactly? Still, a philosopher who does not follow Plato in his obsessive pursuit of definitions can sensibly think about and discuss such phenomena as 'temperance' or Christianity or 'truth', catching them as it were alive and on the wing without the help of Platonic taxidermy. The approach will have to be more historical. We can in fact tell many helpful and well-supported stories about how forms of truth-telling developed in human societies, how methods of enquiry and techniques of research for particular purposes came to be established, transformed, sometimes connected with other human endeavours, sometimes eventually forgotten. In fact humanity has accumulated quite a respectable amount of knowledge without ever succeeding in finding universally agreed formal 'definitions' of most of the major subjects of human interest. Do we have universally agreed definitions of 'law', 'morality', 'religion', even 'science'? If the Platonist insists that a definition-based form of certain knowledge is 'necessary', one should ask why. Nietzsche's suspicion is that the 'necessity' in question is a need which is rooted finally in the philosopher-king's 'need' to *claim* to have certain indubitable knowledge in order to justify his rule and crack the whip over the subject population in the ideal city.

This brings one immediately to the third complex of issues concerning truth, and the one that is of by far the greatest interest to Nietzsche. This is what we might call the 'ethics of truth'. Another part of the 'Platonist' view (modified for Christianity by Augustine) is that it requires no special explanation to understand why people seek the truth; it clearly has value in itself, and so one needs no distinct reason to look for it. Furthermore, knowing the truth is always inherently better than not knowing it. And finally, the search for truth is and ought to be unending and has no natural limits. Nietzsche does not accept the idea underlying this line of thought, namely that there is some one self-sufficient and self-contained concept of Truth that stands behind correct arithmetical calculation, good legal reasoning, careful observation of the natural world, the evaluation of portraits, political argumentation, and so on.

If one thinks about this seriously, it is not at all clear that it is always better for me to know the truth than not. Some moribund people want to know the truth about their conditions, but others really do not. In lots of cases, knowing how unlikely is success in some enterprise would have a harmfully dampening effect on one's level of effort or motivation. Even if knowing the truth is not actively bad for me, overwhelmingly many truths are of no conceivable interest or importance to me. A reasonable attitude toward them is indifference rather than a striving to push back the limits of knowledge. I need, then, a special reason or a special motive to undertake the wearisome task of trying to find out the truth about something. So the default position should not be 'Obviously he is sacrificing his health, sanity, and prospects and those of his family, friends, and associates in order to discover *this* particular truth; after all, it is a *truth* he is seeking', but 'Why is he doing this?'; 'Why is discovering this truth so important to him?'; 'What will-to-truth is moving him?' In particular, in the case of natural science, one won't have far to look to find the reason: No one likes to have malaria, say, so let's find out how it is spread. Might it be a good idea to count the number of sheep beforehand in order to be sure we have not forgotten one out there on the moor when we return at the end of the day? Wouldn't it be nice to be able to cross this river without having to swim it; how might we do that? Here it seems that the obvious usefulness of finding the truth is a sufficient motivation, but how is it useful to me to know that I am bound to die or that it is overwhelmingly unlikely that I shall attain a certain goal? Just to repeat, the approach described earlier represents a not insignificant challenge to many of the received conceptions, but nothing in it suggests—in fact quite the reverse—that there is no such thing as truth, that it is always irrelevant, or that astrology, haruspication, homeopathy, or sortition are as good as science.

So concepts of truth and truth-telling clearly have a different status for Nietzsche than they do in the original form of Christianity from which his philosophy is a derivative. What about the second

*better to forget than to forgive an insult*

component, the emphasis on focused and systematic psychological introspection as the key to revealing the truth about my real self, and thus the golden pathway to being able to lead a good life?

Christian-inspired introspection, whether it be that of Augustine or that of Rousseau, leads away from the surface of human life, the accidental tics, trivial habits, and routines, to what are claimed to be the depths, the hidden core, the 'reality' of the self. It is a movement from the superficial to the profound. Nietzsche, however, sometimes shows distinct signs of being allergic to 'profundity'. He praises precisely the pre-Christian superficiality of the Greeks (*KSA* 3.352); he admires people who do not so much forgive as simply forget insults they have suffered (*KSA* 5.273); *fare bella figura* made the Renaissance an especially agreeable time to live, not the speculation of Ficino or the introverted rumination of Northern European monks (and former monks). His *Ecce homo,* with its extensive discussion of his life by reference to his preferred diet, the landscapes he loves, and his favourite meteorological conditions, is about as far from Augustine's account of his life in *The Confessions* as it is possible to be (*KSA* 6.264–308).

Nietzsche's attack on the idea of 'profundity' extends to the associated ideal of authenticity. People's relation to themselves is, in reality, according to Nietzsche, one of construction. The idea behind the search for 'profundity' is that the further 'down' into ourselves we go, the more we will find our elemental 'real' self, and the demand for authenticity is the imperative that we express 'on the surface' in all our actions (and perhaps especially our speech) the real self beneath it all. The face we turn to the world should be the one that reveals our true self, not a mask. What if the further 'down' we go, the more we reach not any kind of primordial unified self but simply the realisation that any unity we might have resolves into bundles of disorganised and shifting, potentially (and actually)

191

conflicting impulses, that is, into a Typhonian mess that is not a self at all? There are two dimensions to Nietzsche's antipsychologism. First, if you conduct introspection systematically and relentlessly, you will eventually discover only a mass of constantly shifting, (at best) partially ordered impulses. The more you reflect, the more any kind of psychic unity or substantiality will dissolve in your hands. Second, masks and the cultivation of masks can be as important as the study of the face beneath the mask (if indeed there is a face beneath the mask).

As an opponent of the ideal of authenticity, Nietzsche is positively disposed to the wearing of masks. Any form of unity is, after all, the result of a conscious shaping of self, and thus a kind of mask. Perhaps Cato or Socrates were capable, by extraordinary acts of tenacious volition, of wearing always the same mask, and that was, to be sure, a sign of a certain kind of success, a success of the will, but it was also a sign of their limitation as philosophers because they needed to pretend that what was actually a constructed mask was their 'natural' physiognomy. The true philosopher knows that beneath any mask there may well lie not a natural face but another mask. In fact, beneath that mask there may be further masks, all the way down as far as we can reach. There is nothing necessarily wrong with that. In general the philosopher is not a person who wears no mask, but one who knows how to play with a number of masks, skilfully shifting from wearing one to wearing another, as circumstances demand. To be a philosopher is precisely *not* to be a person who never deviates from a single doctrine but to have a history of change (KSA 3.349–350). A philosopher is not someone who will 'get to the bottom of things once and for all' but someone who will be able to see the things in the world from a variety of different points of view or perspectives at the same time without getting confused.

MASK UNDER A MASK.

*do not stop evolving & become a petroglyph*

Perhaps, Nietzsche asks, it is a mistake even to assume that a philosopher has any 'final' or definitive opinions at all (*KSA* 5.231–232).

This positive valuation placed in *shifting* masks also puts paid to another variant of Egyptianism, the usual ethical ideal of the Western philosopher who uses her 'system' to transform living humans, starting with herself, into something like the stiff figures one finds in Egyptian painting: individuals frozen in uncomfortable, unnatural positions, fixed for all eternity. As Nietzsche himself describes this demand: someone who has once decided to be a Stoic should always in all circumstances invariably act as a Stoic (*KSA* 1.813), and this choice should impregnate even her smallest gestures. As a keen student and admirer of Montaigne, Nietzsche agrees with Montaigne's observation that in general it is beyond us to act always in the same way in all circumstances and remain always the same person one was. This is not really a viable human ideal, and what in principle is supposed to be so bad about acting according to circumstances? Why not adapt to the circumstances? Why should not skill in adapting be as highly valued as rigid consistency of belief and action in *all* circumstances? Humans try to be consistent; they also try to respond to changing circumstances. It is often not possible to do both at the same time. We often don't even know what would count as 'being consistent' or 'being responsive' in a given situation. One cannot simply do away with the difficulties which are part of what it is to be human by absolutising consistency (or by completely ignoring its claims).

So if one takes this strand of argument seriously, it is a mistake even to ask 'Who is the *real* Nietzsche?' or 'What are his *final* views?' Or rather, it is a mistake to ask these questions as if they were especially profound questions. They have a trivial answer: 'All of the opinions you can find in his work are "really" his', or he has a complex, exceedingly fiddly history of views which track in as much detail as possible the particular configurations of his life and thought within which each opinion was formed and had to be expressed. To look for either profundity or authenticity here is to have missed Nietzsche's point completely.

Nietzsche's views on truth and psychology are not, however, simple reversals of the Christian-Platonist views he rejects. After all, he does not exactly say 'Christians tried to be profound; how wonderful that the Greeks rejected profundity and chose to be superficial; let's Hellenise'. Rather what he says is that the Greeks were superficial, and this superficiality arose out of their profundity. So one does not simply reverse the polarities while allowing them to continue to define the discussion; rather one tries to undercut or relativise the apparent oppositions, or at any rate the received way of construing these oppositions. The same thing is true of Nietzsche's claims about affirmation. The official view, and one that a careless reader will almost surely attribute to Nietzsche after reading *Genealogy* (or indeed any works of the mature period), is that the world is to be divided up tidily into yea-sayers and nay-sayers, affirmers and deniers (of life), people who are essentially active and creative and those who are reactive and sullen. The Masters are the ultimate yea-sayers, and Nietzsche is encouraging us to identify with their universal affirmation. Only then can we recover our threatened vitality. This reading, however, flies directly in the face of the clear intention of the text. The point of the *Genealogy* is that historically, hatred and denial have become creative and that that is what has made us interesting and human. The superficially frisky, lupine Masters are actually self-satisfied bovines, incapable of producing genuine novelty. Masters and Slaves, affirmation and negation, active and passive are not best understood as antitheses that absolutely exclude each other. As the much overlooked but

*A PERSON CAN BE ACTIVE & CREATIVE OR REACTIVE & SULLEN*

194

particularly important section 12 of the first essay in *Genealogy* points out, the goal of the text is not to recommend a return to Stone Age forms of unbridled 'vitality', but something different. The virtues of the Masters and the virtues of the Slaves are opposed and engaged in a continual struggle with each other, but this means that they will both always be present, and they clearly depend on each other. No Masters without Slaves to look down on ('the pathos of distance') and no Slaves without Masters to react against. The internalisation of the distinction so that it no longer designates different social groups, but different internal psychological configurations and different ethical orientations, does not obliterate this mutual dependency. To be sure, in any given ethical configuration one of the two will have predominance over the other, but in no configuration will only one be present. There will be no pure Master morality (or pure Slave morality). It is precisely the inescapable struggle between the two that makes us human.

> *Man könnte sagen, daß er [der Kampf] inzwischen immer höher hinaufgetragen und eben damit immer tiefer, immer geistiger geworden sei: so daß es heute vielleicht kein entscheidenderes Anzeichen der 'höheren Natur' gibt, als zwiespältig in jenem Sinne und wirklich noch ein Kampfplatz für jene Gegensätze zu sein.(KSA 5.285–285)*

One might say that the struggle between the two has meanwhile been continually raised to a higher level and consequently has become increasingly profound and increasingly spiritual: so that nowadays there is perhaps no clearer sign of having a 'superior nature' than being split in two in this way and really being still a theatre of struggle for these two opposites.

Here the idea is not so much to undercut the opposition as to keep them both in play in an appropriate way.

195

One sometimes hears plaintive (disingenuous) criticisms of Nietzsche of two related kinds. One of them runs, 'Nietzsche was a trenchant critic of certain misconceptions and also forms of moral self-deception and spiritual narrowness, but he never actually went beyond mere criticism to present his own *positive,* constructive theory of how we ought to live our lives. *Schade.*' The other runs, 'Nietzsche is a purveyor of highly interesting but detached, fragmentary, and undeveloped *aperçus*. What a shame that he never succeeded in being more systematic; he failed completely to write a "system".' I think that these criticisms, in the form in which they are given here, are completely misguided. They suggest that Nietzsche was trying desperately to be Hegel but unfortunately failing, when in part the point of his work was that he was trying desperately *not* to be Hegel (or any similar systematic philosopher) but to engage intellectually with each situation as it came, without reducing it to a prepared category or a pregiven position in a discursive network. He thought that love of systems was a human weakness and that the stronger one's character, the less one would need and the less attracted one would be to a system. Nietzsche holds that if God were to exist, he would not, contrary to eighteenth-century views, be a master geometer with a universal system of the world. He would see each thing clearly as precisely that which it is and nothing else, and he would not need to use a concept to catch it and reduce it to something else he already knows. Humans are not gods, of course, and so they cannot attain this state, but that is a failing, not an advantage that they have, nor is it anything to be especially proud of or pleased with oneself for having produced.

So to the extent to which one does find something like a 'system' in Nietzsche, it is not at all surprising that it is the either repellent and clearly false or vacuous theory of the 'will-to-power'. It is repellent and false if 'will-to-power' is taken as something like a biological category; empty if it is interpreted sufficiently widely to include 'spiritual power'. That Nietzsche does fall into 'systematic' forms of thinking is a sign that he, too, is 'human, all-too-human', something he would readily admit to but not glory in. It does make a difference whether one sees systems as unfortunate necessities given who we are or as culminations devoutly to be aspired to. Nietzsche would have taken the preference for one or the other of these two possibilities as deeply indicative of the kind of person one is.[3]

This does not, of course, settle the issue about the value of Nietzsche's work. His criticisms might turn out to be less conclusive than one thought, his *aperçus* less stimulating and enlightening, or one might think he was wrong to wish not to have a system, or that he was right about this but failed to free himself sufficiently from his inner system-maker. These are all open questions, but questions one can ask about his work with any prospect of making progress only if one first sees correctly what he is trying to do and does not attribute to him, even tacitly, the reverse of his intentions.

One final aspect of Egyptianism is the predominance in philosophy of the prose treatise as the standard ideally appropriate literary form for presenting the unitary doctrine which is to constitute the guide to life. Philosophy has been practised in the past without being written down at all (Socrates 'der nichts schrieb' [*KSA* 7.12; 7.17]) or in the form of epic poetry (Parmenides, Lucretius) or symposiastic verse (Xenophanes, Solon), as dialogue which occasionally came close to drama (Plato, Lucian), in the form of letters (Epicurus), as a quasi-geometric system (Spinoza), as *aperçus* or aphorisms (La Rochefoucauld, Friedrich Schlegel). All of these diverse literary genres had to give way now in the post-Roman world to the treatise. Ideally, the treatise gives one the whole doctrine in a discursively organised and argumentatively developed form.

If the appropriate literary form for 'Egyptian' theorising is the treatise presenting a doctrine in a discursive form, then the rejection of the notion of a fixed 'doctrine' might be thought to have consequences for the literary form in which philosophy is expressed. Montaigne invented the essay in order to find a way of catching on the fly his rambling thoughts, but Nietzsche uses an even wider variety of diverse literary forms: in addition to the essay, the short epigram, the song, the dithyramb, and the aphorism, his work contains parodies of rhythmic religious prose (*Thus Spake Zarathustra*), parables, and commentaries on works of art (especially drama and music), as well as writings which, like *On the Genealogy of Morality*, have the form of academic treatises. This is part of his attempt to replace a view which holds that there is only one neutral and definitive way of looking at the world—a 'God's-eye view'—with a 'perspectivist' attitude which instead locates 'objectivity' in the deployment of as many different perspectives on a given subject as possible.

There is one final twist in the story of 'truth' in Nietzsche. He thinks that the pursuit of 'truth' need not be the all-encompassing human goal, and also he doesn't really think that truth and illusion are opposites in the way some older philosophers thought. What happens when I see through an illusion? The answer might seem to be clear. An illusion is a falsehood which I take to be a truth, and when I see through it, I realise this and give up the belief in question. Nietzsche is very concerned with this question but very dissatisfied with this answer. There can be illusions that are necessary for life, and giving them up may not be an option. For many philosophers this statement makes no sense. If an 'illusion' is necessary for life, then this can only be because it is in some sense an inherent part of our way of cognitively structuring the world, but if that is the case, in what sense can it be 'false'? We can come to see through

198

various beliefs as illusions, although that does not make it possible for us to give them up, such as the sun which continues to seem to us to rise each day even after we know it does not. Life is seeing through illusions which we then cannot get rid of. There is no stable point to this process of generation of illusion, seeing through illusion, attempted disillusionment, failure to detach oneself even from illusions one thinks one has seen through, generation of new and 'improved' illusions, and so on. To live is to participate in this process, to continue with it. We are desperate to get out, to stop the wheel, but that is not possible in this life. One of the most difficult lessons we need to learn is that this is the situation in which we as humans find ourselves. Nietzsche at any rate faced it. There is no way out; we must simply accept this unsatisfactory situation—that we can see through many illusions but cannot rid ourselves of them—and make the best we can of it, one way or another.

Truth & illusions are not opposites the all illusion of importance of our Life

# *Chapter Nine*

# LUKÁCS

Lukács had a very keen sense that 'philosophy' was not an autonomous discipline. Rather, the framework for the study of the human world was the manner in which human societies interacted historically with nature in various ways in an effort to sustain and reproduce themselves: people gather berries, dam up rivers to make it easier to catch fish, hunt game, burn down bits of forest or jungle to practise agriculture, eventually build factories, and so on. Right after immediate physical survival came social reproduction: people needed to ensure that their social arrangements remained more or less intact and that the next generation was ready to occupy the necessary social roles. In the course of this process of production and reproduction, humans developed various forms of knowledge and various ideational structures. These had a variety of uses. Some of them helped to increase production (soil science), some to keep track of resources (accounting), some to keep productive agents in their places (law) or train new ones (pedagogy). Forms of knowledge help to keep the society functioning in various ways. Since we have a pressing need for continuity in our economic and social relations, it is not surprising that our ideational products have a natural bias in favour of the legitimation of these arrangements. This, however, is not the only need we have. As societies become more complex and it becomes advantageous to be able to be responsive to a variety of different environments, they also tend to develop forms of knowledge that may permit a few favoured individuals or groups to get some cognitive distance from the immediate realities of their given situation and their inherited forms of interaction. Some forms of knowledge develop which contain a self-reflective and even critical potential. Philosophy generally aspires to be one of the more generalising and self-reflective parts of the cognitive and ideational apparatus of a society, but it has an uphill battle against both the sheer inertial weight of the past and the teleological shaping of existing cognitive tools to operate best when they are helping to grease the wheels of social reproduction.

'Critical potential', furthermore, is an especially tricky phenomenon to analyse. Forms of critical reasoning would not seem prima facie to be cogs in the mechanism of the self-justification of society which permits it to continue to reproduce itself effectively, but particularly highly developed societies are ones capable of subverting criticism and even of turning it in a backhanded way into a form of affirmation. We are all familiar with the ways in which advanced societies can turn even their own acknowledged scandals into forms of self-adulation: the Watergate scandal in the United States was widely said at the time, at least in US newspapers, to have demonstrated that 'the system works' because the culprit at the centre of it, President Nixon, who had had the monumental stupidity to tape-record some of his own more compromising conversations, was eventually forced to resign. It seems more reasonable to draw the reverse conclusion: see how inept one would have to be to be caught

out in such a regime. The 1960s and early 1970s saw the development of detailed analysis of some of the methods which advanced
societies used to 'co-opt' (as was then said) criticism, incorporating
it as part of the way the society affirmed and reproduced itself and
deflecting its effect as a force for serious or radical social change. To
permit or even encourage small-scale criticism or whistle-blowing
can, after all, be a way of making a given individual institution
(eventually) more effective and thus more difficult to delegitimize.
Even criticism of larger scope can be welcome, provided it is presented in the right way as 'internal'—that is, insofar as it appeals to
and tacitly endorses the recognised values that guide social reproduction and is seen to be in any case unavoidable. In Giuseppe Tomasi di Lampedusa's novel about nineteenth-century Sicily, *The
Leopard,* the son of a large landowner says 'For everything to remain the same [sometimes] everything has to change,' and at the end
of the brief Garibaldian moment which the novel presents as one
in which the world is turned upside down, the old landowners are
still in charge.[1] So it is difficult, if not impossible, to tell in a non-
contextual way whether a given form of critical thinking is really a
threat to the reproduction of a given social formation or rather an
integral part of an increasingly highly sophisticated apparatus of
legitimation.

Philosophy is, then, part of this social process of human interaction with nature and of the struggles over forms of social and economic organisation. Of course, it is an important constituent of
what it is to be human that we have the power to 'abstract', to focus
on some aspects of the world while ignoring others, and in principle
we can 'abstract' in an indefinite number of ways. I can tell the story
of nineteenth-century Europe as the history of the exotic flora that
was successively imported, ignoring the wider economic, social, and
historical context. Or I can tell merely the diplomatic story or just

describe a sequence of wars and battles. None of these ways of abstracting is per se utterly illegitimate; the question is which ones are more informative and more useful (in which contexts). Just, then, as I can treat philately, numismatics, or flower arranging as self-contained forms of practice and discourse, so I can in principle also treat 'philosophy' with no reference to anything outside itself, or with some minimal gesturing toward one or another of 'the results of contemporary science'. However, doing this seems especially inappropriate in that philosophy usually claims to be, in aspiration at least, a particularly general, particularly reflective and self-aware, and particularly self-critical enterprise. Philatelists can be satisfied with studying postage stamps for their own sake without asking too many questions about the basic conditions under which such a thing as a postal service exists; it seems much less satisfactory for philosophers, at least those who retain some relation to older ideals of self-understanding, to ignore how their questions arise, where their concepts come from. 'I'm a philatelist; I'm not interested in the internal organisation of the governments who issue the stamps' is at least a perfectly coherent position to hold. On the other hand, if I say 'I'm a philosopher; I'm not interested in why people ask *these* questions, why they find *these* answers so plausible, why *these* forms of argumentation suddenly come to have extremely wide use, why concepts of *this* form suddenly pop up seemingly everywhere, or indeed what becomes of my theories after I have proposed and elaborated them, how they are received, what effect they have on people', this somehow does not have the cadence of plausibility, unless it really were the case that philosophical concepts and theories came from nowhere and went nowhere. First, this seems clearly not to be true, and second, if it were true, it would immediately lead one to ask why in that case anyone should bother with philosophy at all.

In one way or another, through what are often long and oblique sequences of connections, some of them more discursive and argumentative, some more rhetorical, some finally perhaps almost merely associative or rooted in historical accidents of various kinds, philosophical theories are connected to the societies in which they arise and flourish. 'Philosophical problems'—the existence of the external world, the compatibility of freedom and determinism or of 'faith' and 'reason' or of duty and desire—are not in fact 'eternal human questions', despite anachronistic attempts to construe them as such, but are really in the final analysis social problems thrown up by history. Even if there are some problems all societies face, the specific way they will be formatted when they become objects of philosophical speculation will be highly variable, and it will be impossible, as it were, to 'extract' the timeless core of the problem without remainder from the specific form in which it arises. People in the Middle Ages obsessed about the relation between reason and revelation or reason and faith because they lived in a society which simply could not, for any number of reasons, conceivably have dispensed with a Church which preached a revealed religion based on faith. No one before the Stoics was interested in 'freedom versus determinism' in anything like the form this question took in the nineteenth century,[2] because ancient societies had a perfectly transparent, available notion of 'freedom': being a free person as opposed to a slave. And although deterministic conceptions (such as fate) existed, there was no notion of an exceptionless 'law of nature' in the sense in which that was developed in early modern science. 'It is your fate to be a slave', however, is not a contribution to the philosophical questions about freedom of the will and Laplacean determinism. The conflict of duty and desire becomes an obsession where an authoritarian state (or other structure) forces people to act against what they can see are their own deep desires. Thus it is no accident that interest in the conflict between duty and desire is such a staple of Prussian, and later National Socialist, academic and popular philosophy. When mechanisms of social manipulation become more subtle, more insidious, and more effective, people begin to worry not so much that their palpable desire might conflict with their duty but that their apparent desires might not arise from their own real, 'authentic' self.

To say that philosophy is not autonomous is a claim about the proper organisation of knowledge and then perhaps also about the way in which philosophy should be practised; it is not in itself a way of denying that philosophy has any cognitive content at all. Lukács believed that philosophy should be construed as part of society rather than as a disembodied activity which stood in no relation to existing social and economic relations, and he also believed that most of the basic philosophical problems that had haunted humanity for centuries had no solution in the terms in which they were usually formulated. That is, they had no possible, purely theoretical solution at all. They often *looked* like verbal or conceptual puzzles that ought to have solutions that were theoretical or conceptual, and they were treated as such by philosophers, but they were actually expressions of difficulties that arose in real life, and many real problems did not have merely conceptual answers. This did not, however, necessarily mean that philosophy completely lacked any kind of cognitive significance at all. Lukács wrote the essays which make up his *History and Class Consciousness* in one of the places and during one of the periods in history—the apocalyptic end phase of World War One in Central Europe—during which philosophy had a particularly vivid chance to show its cognitive relevance. These essays were some of his first publications after joining the newly formed Party of Communists in Hungary in 1918.

Empirical knowledge clearly sometimes does give us the power to resolve real problems: those on deck as the ship is going down may wish to know in which locker the life jackets are kept; that knowledge will not change the fact that the ship is going down, but it will help to keep the passengers afloat. What counts as 'the problem' is, of course, highly variable, depending on who is asking the question and in which context. For the captain, the problem may be how to keep the ship afloat for a few more minutes to allow the passengers and crew to escape; for the person on deck, it may be where the next lifeboat is (or, failing that, where the life jackets are kept); and for the marine engineer investigating the sinking, it may be how to avoid similar incidents in the future. In more general terms, the scientific knowledge which allowed humans to produce life jackets to start with, and the organisational knowledge that allowed them (after the *Titanic*, at any rate) to provide (and, ideally, distribute) one life jacket per passenger, were, however, both solutions to potential real problems. The person drowning, however, urgently needs a real life jacket, not a picture of a life jacket, not a definition of a life jacket, not even a theory of life jackets. In a society in which humans are constantly confronted in reality with duties which they cannot fulfil except at the cost of thwarting their own vital desires, any 'theoretical solution' to this 'basic problem of ethics' will be at best an elegant diagram of a life jacket. No amount of conceptual reinterpretation or theoretical fancy footwork will either make slavery or forced marriage disappear, if it really exists in the first place, or give us a humanly satisfactory way of tolerating it. The 'problem' of slavery in places in which it existed in the nineteenth century, for instance, was not a theoretical problem about how to reconcile freedom and necessity or duty and desire; it was a problem of a different kind, a practical and political problem. The problem would disappear (as the medieval problem of the reconciliation of 'faith' and 'reason' has disappeared) if the *social* world as a whole were transformed and became completely different. This does not imply that philosophical speculation is completely irrelevant to human concerns, only that the form relevance takes is not necessarily by providing solutions to what are defined at any given time as particular 'philosophical puzzles'.

Suppose I live in a society, for example any early modern society, which requires me regularly and systematically to do things that are violently incompatible with my fundamental desires. Philosophers have chosen one, or some variant or combination, of four ways of dealing with this:

1. Definition: this is a 'puzzle' arising from some conceptual problem which a well-trained philosopher will sort out for you. Perhaps people have misunderstood the way language works or have given incorrect definitions of central concepts or have failed to appreciate some argument for the compatibility of duty and desire which the philosopher can provide. The slave 'really' is 'free' if one understands 'freedom' correctly (e.g., as an inner attitude to the world). Or perhaps even free man are 'slaves', if one understand 'freedom/slavery' correctly: slaves of their passions, salaried wage-slaves, or slaves to the illusions of their time.

2. Metaphysics: maybe in this life duty and desire conflict, but there is another world, a metaphysical realm, which we will come to know after death, and in the afterlife we will lead in that realm God will reward those who do their duty in this world with commensurate, or even incommensurately large, rewards.

3. Unworkable empirical suggestions: for instance that by Schiller, the poet, dramatist, and philosopher to whose work Lukács devoted a lot of attention during his long life.[3] Schiller did not consider extreme cases like slavery but moderate cases of dissatisfaction with a life in which duty and inclination did not always coincide. He proposed that 'aesthetic education' could overcome this conflict: I

could learn through 'art' and aesthetic experience to cultivate and identify with those desires which would make me want to do what it was my duty to do. Lukács thought this indicated a serious engagement with the problem but overlooked the fact that a society in which the split between duty and desire was really fundamental and deeply rooted would never be able to institute a regime of aesthetic education of the appropriate kind on a large enough scale. To do so would be to undermine its own conditions of viability. So if such an aesthetic resolution were even possible, that would indicate that the problem was not much of a real problem to start with. Merely aesthetic 'resolutions' of what are in fact real social problems can even seem to succeed only at the cost of ignorance or distortion of reality or the propagation of large-scale illusions.

4. Honest recognition: one simply has to learn to live with the gap and potential conflict between duty and desire because it is a necessary and essential part of the human condition, and there is nothing anyone can do to change that.

Lukács clearly has particular respect for (4) but thinks that the supporters of this approach make a deep mistake in that they confuse what is absolutely impossible in *this,* our form of socioeconomic organisation, with what is impossible in *any* form of human life.

Lukács thinks that 'our' society—that is, the capitalist society we know, which began at the end of the eighteenth century and extends (in various modified forms) up to today—is an especially powerful generator of irresolvable philosophical puzzles because it is fundamentally nontransparent, an obscure breeding ground and incubator of murky conceptions and unclear forms; in addition it is based on a number of irreconcilable antagonisms. The reasons for this, he thinks, are deep-seated: we live in a society that is based on distribution of ownership of economic factors of production to private individuals, namely natural persons and corporations. These are forced to cooperate under conditions set by a legal framework which regulates them and which is absolutely essential for the operation of the economic system (and whose importance tends to be underestimated or denigrated by the agents who are its greatest beneficiaries). Nevertheless, the coordination imposed even by the most strenuous legal system still leaves the choice of exact employment of the private economic resources in question very much in the hands of the private owners. The form of organisation is antagonistic because each individual owner is encouraged to compete with the others, and each is to maximise the profits that accrue from the deployment of his or her own economic resources, even at the expense of other individual owners. The clearest expression of the nontransparency of this society is provided by the doctrine of the 'invisible hand', which was developed by Adam Smith as a way of formulating what is especially good about this form of economy. Such a society is set up, he claims, in such a way that the common good arises precisely from the fact that each individual actor pursues as energetically as possible his or her own private good. It is as if an 'invisible hand' took the actions of each and diverted the results to an end that no individual perhaps intended.[4]

Lukács, like Marx, has two objections to this. First, he thinks that the invisible hand does not invariably work as advertised. Smith had tacitly assumed that the 'common good' of the society in question meant no more than its material prosperity, but even in this impoverished sense, this is not the universal result of allowing private agents to use economic resources as they wish. Rather it is a description of something that happened under certain conditions in the past. It worked well enough (for some countries, especially Great

Britain) in the late eighteenth and early nineteenth centuries, but by the early twentieth century antagonistic competition was visibly not producing anything like a common good; rather it brought about wars, imperialism, and economic depressions. One might add to this that 'common good' meant 'the wealth of the *nation*', as Smith puts it, and the 'nation' in the form of its most well-off members may indeed become preternaturally better off without much improvement in the conditions of the majority of the population. Second, regardless of the issue of material prosperity, societies based on the 'invisible hand' necessarily fail to realise the highest possible human social good because they institutionalise a lack of full freedom.

For Lukács, 'freedom' is inherently a matter of degree, not a binary concept; that is, there can be no question of an absolute opposition between 'free' and 'not free', but rather one must consider what degree of freedom is exhibited by some agent in some situation. His claim is that the greater the power available (and expressed) in an action, the greater the freedom exhibited. Human action that is free to an especially high degree has two properties. First, it is an expression of a high level of development of human powers. To be free is to have the power to do *something*, and to be more free is to have greater powers to do *a greater variety of things*. The idea that 'freedom' is inherently a negative concept and refers to the absence of obstacles to particular possible courses of action is a mere shadow of the correct view, because what is a possible course of action in the first place, and also what can count as an obstacle, depend on the level of human power which has been developed. Power is the primary feature of any situation in which freedom is at issue; the existence of possible obstacles is only secondary. Second, an action is free to the extent to which the agents can see the outcome as what they intended and brought about by the action in question and to the extent to which they can 'affirm themselves' in that result. 'Affirmation of self' is almost a technical term, but its basic sense is that I recognise the action I have performed as 'my own' (or we recognise the action as 'our own'), and I approve of myself (or we approve of ourselves) because I (or we) have intentionally created something which is visibly worthwhile and deserves approbation and appreciation. If one construes 'freedom' in this way, that is, along these two dimensions, it seems an almost immediate corollary that collective action is in general going to be the primary locus of freedom, partly because in collective action more human powers can be mobilised and expressed than in individual action—this seems uncontroversial—but also because even individual self-affirmation can reach a higher level within the context of appropriately organised collective action. This is not even to mention the fact that virtually no individual action is conceivable, certainly in any society like ours, in which I do not massively depend on social institutions—the traffic police every time I use a vehicle to go anywhere, the postal service every time I receive or send a letter, the National Health Service every time I get ill—and in which I do not use socially produced artefacts (spectacles, books, electricity).

To be sure, to speak of 'free' collective action requires some notion of a collective 'subject' who could be the agent exercising this action. Such a collective subject would, Lukács thinks, have to be capable of having a minimally unitary form of consciousness with forms of desire, and intentions, coming together to form a single project or plan which all the humans who make up the collective subject could see as their own and identify with (at least to some extent). So a football team could be composed of people who shared a desire to play a certain kind of game at a high level of competence, perhaps even win a match or the UEFA Cup, who also knew that all the team members had a shared plan of action in dealing with the other team and collectively put this plan into action so as to win. In this case the team could see the winning of the match as an expression of their collective power and thus an instance of especially free action.

Lukács has an easy time showing that a society based on the invisible hand cannot ever exhibit a very high degree of freedom, if 'freedom' means what he takes it to mean, because the invisible hand means precisely that the individuals do not have the same desires or the same plan. Only as a joke could you say that economic competitors shared the 'same' desire: to outwit and get the better of the other person. If you are a seller, you do not share my desire to get the better of you (if I am a buyer); you wish to get the better of me. Furthermore, *ex hypothesi* the 'common good' that results from our interaction, if indeed such does result, was not intended by either of us. So there is no collective or common 'subject' who could recognise the action which realises the 'common good' (even if some action did realise such a 'good') as its 'own' action.

In a society like this, Lukács thinks, there will be significant limits to our ability to develop human powers because of the limitations on genuinely cooperative human action, and there will also be corresponding cognitive limits, rooted also in the economically necessary barriers to shared knowledge; it is generally better for me if my competitor does not know too much about my situation, preferences, and intentions. Lukács adds to Smith's account of the invisible hand Marx's class analysis. In the sphere of circulation there are distinct economic entities competing with each other purportedly in such a way as to realise the common good, but circulation presupposes production, and the basic fact about production is that it depends on the mutual relation between two antagonistic classes. One class consists of owners of capital (who are thus able to acquire control of means of production). The other class consists of atom-

ised individuals, torn from their original social context by the expro-
priation of their agricultural land (and similar phenomena) and
therefore forced to sell their labour power as their only resource in
order to survive; these are the proletarians.

In a society based on economic competition like that analysed by
Smith, in which the basic form of production is work in factories
owned by capitalists but kept in operation by a proletarian work-
force, all human relations, Lukács claims, will tend to become 'reified', and this includes forms of consciousness. In trying to explain
what he means by 'reification' Lukács refers to Marx's discussion of
'the fetishism of commodity production' in volume I of *Kapital*.[5]
Contemporary readers will also be reminded of Marx's account of
'alienation', most fully in his *Philosophic-Economic Manuscripts of
1844*,[6] although Lukács couldn't have had these in mind when
writing of *History and Class Consciousness* because the 1844 manuscripts had not yet been published at that time. As the term itself
suggests, 'reification' is the process by which something which is
not an object (such as a human subject or a social relation) is treated
as if it were an object, turned into an object, or conceptualised as
an object. This distinction between subjects and objects is and remains of the greatest importance for Lukács. The appropriate connection of these two into a proper unity is the final aspiration of his
political philosophy, but much of his work is devoted to analysing
the almost unsurveyably many ways in which this final unification
can fail, be prevented, or be blighted, especially by taking crude or
premature forms.

A subject is a centre of action and perception who views the
world from a particular perspective or point of view and who pursues plans; in particular it is capable of transforming itself (by
radically changing its beliefs, desires, plans) into something else.
I am a subject because I now do not have the power to read Polish,

but I could turn myself into someone with that power by pursuing a course of action which I might undertake. This would require me to form fixed intentions, make plans, and accumulate forms of knowledge which I now do not have, but in principle I could do that if I wished. Pursuing a fixed plan to learn Polish gives me a certain perspective on the world: I look around for Polish speakers to practise with, notice Polish newspapers, etc. An object is an entity that is merely acted on, pushed around by external forces, initiating nothing, and therefore without a perspective of its own. The three senses of 'reification' mentioned earlier—be treated as an object, be turned into an object, be conceptualised as an object—are connected in that to the extent to which a human subject is treated as an object, to that extent it may begin to act like a mere object, and to the extent to which I conceptualise what is in fact a human subject as an object, to that extent I may begin to treat it as an object; finally, to the extent to which I have been treated as an object and thus have become to some extent like one, to that extent I may begin to reify myself in thought. A similar analysis, Lukács thinks, can be carried out for a relation between two subjects or a social relationship. It, too, can be treated and conceptualised as if it were a simple relation between inanimate things.

It can happen, then, that I have been so universally and successfully treated for such a long time as if I were an automaton that I have actually begun to act as if I were a mere object. Even in this case, however, I am a human being who has been 'reified', not a literal cog-in-a-wheel (although it may then be easier for others, and also for myself, to think of me as if I were a mere thing). As Brecht put it in the 1930s,

*General, der Mensch ist brauchbar.*
*Er kann fliegen und er kann töten.*

214

*Er hat nur einen Fehler:*
*Er kann denken.*[7]

General, here we have a handy little gadget
called a 'man': he can fly a plane;
he can kill. He has only one defect:
he can think.

(Numerous high-tech corporations are, of course, now at work to develop drones, robots, and other automated weapons systems that do not have this defect.)

In a superficial sense, 'reification' and 'fetishism' seem to be opposites. In reification a human being (or a human social relationship) is taken to be a thing (or a relation between things); in fetishism an object which is in fact a mere thing—a stone; a piece of wood; a collection of feathers, bones, and pieces of metal—is treated as if it had the powers of an animate entity. Agent-like powers, that is, are ascribed to what is not an agent. The sacred stone can bring rain or cause the rain to stop, can bring on a plague, cause or cure sickness, even strike people dead; perhaps it can be angry, vindictive, helpful, fatigued, inattentive, or benevolent. When you enter its presence perhaps you should clap your hands to make sure it is awake.

The fetish cannot really bring on the rain, although, as anthropologists have pointed out, performing ceremonies to placate it can have all kinds of positive social effects, such as reinforcing a sense of solidarity in times of crisis. Most interesting for us are cases in which the fetish does seem to work. The man who violated the taboo by touching the fetish *does* soon come to a sticky end. In most cases this will be mere accident. However, even we, purportedly disabused and enlightened theoretical observers of this phenomenon, can see that there are cases in which something more than mere accident seems to be involved. There are, we might say, active social powers which do exist but are falsely ascribed to the stone or piece of wood. In a small society which is held together by strong common beliefs, especially 'religious' beliefs in the efficacy of the fetish, in which people are highly visible to each other, and in which mutual help is imperative for survival, visible thwarting of beliefs that are held to be associated with strong sanctions is not automatically a recipe for social success or even individual survival. A preternaturally strong person might get away with violation of a taboo, but not a normal person. It was said in the nineteenth century that if people *thought* you were bankrupt or a bad credit risk, then you *were* a walking bankrupt, because if they thought you were not creditworthy, they would not lend you money, even in cases which represented no more than the usual and virtually unavoidable ups and downs of business life. This would maximize the possibility that one of the recurring downs would be fatal to you, even if it need not have been (had people been willing to lend you the small sums, as they generally did lend to their neighbours in difficult times). The widespread idea that you were likely to default—and action appropriate to that belief—brought about the envisaged outcome. Similarly, if your friends and neighbours in a small, highly integrated society think you are accursed and highly likely to come to a bad end, your chances of ending badly are significantly increased, even though one cannot antecedently specify the exact mechanism through which this will occur.

So there are actually two slightly different ideas connected here:

1. The "power" which is attributed to the stone (to the extent to which it exists and is not just accident or pure illusion) is actually the power of the society as a whole.

2. The belief in the existence of this power is to some extent self-reinforcing. We bring it about ourselves that the fetish has what power it has by holding the beliefs and acting as we do.

However, although 'reification' might look to be the opposite of fetishism, in Lukács' discussion of capitalist society they are better understood as two complementary sides of the same process. Instead of endowing a nonpersonal object with personal powers, in alienation powers that are mine (or more importantly 'ours') are separated from us and experienced as 'alien powers' acting on us from the outside. The workers who produce our commodities are treated as mere things, reified, and the things they produce, commodities, are fetishized, because we attribute to them independent powers of action of the kind that only subjects have. Politicians are to 'obey' the dictates of the market, as if 'the market' were an independent dynast or potentate rather than simply, as Smith pointed out, the result of human action, which has no power other than that which we lend to it. To be sure, as long as production follows the laws of 'the invisible hand', it has a kind of autonomy because its motions are independent of the conscious control of any individual or group, but even this is an independence that we give to the system as a whole by acting as we do. Lukács thinks that we (now, i.e., post-1850) could, if we really wished, take back control of the process and deprive it of its pseudo-objectivity; we shall see shortly how he thinks this is possible. To use the terminology which Marx employed, the workers 'alienated' their own labour, congealing and embedding it in the commodity, where it looks back at them as if it were a foreign (alien) subject exercising power over them.

It is also important to note, as has often been done, that neither alienation nor reification (as understood by Marx and Lukács) is really essentially or in the first instance a psychological or merely theoretical category. In the first instance workers are 'alienated' not because they think of themselves in a certain way but because their work, the process of production, and the object produced which ought to be under their control—because it is the workers' own life activity—actually is *not* under their control but under that of the owner of the factory. Similarly, workers are reified because the work processes in fact treat them as things and thus contribute to an actual process of destruction of their initiative and subjectivity. Of course, if workers really are alienated and reified, it will be, as we say, 'natural' for them also to realise this, but whether or not they realise it and what consequences this has are matters for further investigation.

The reification of basic economic and social relations in society will, Lukács believes, necessarily lead to an increasing reification of forms of consciousness and forms of thought. Human action will be understood as interaction (under the pressure of external necessity) between isolated units whose perspectives on their own lives and actions can be ignored. There will be strong pressure to focus theoretical attention on individual facts rather than to look for the larger networks of meaning that give so much human action its orientation and inform human perspectives on the world.

A society like this generates paradoxes, contradictions, and antinomies of thought that cannot be resolved. These have, as it were, an objective and a subjective aspect. Take as an example the puzzle about how to overcome the antagonism between 'duty' and desire. First, 'social duty'—that is, what the society must require of its members in order to reproduce itself—has a rather clear content: the workers must accept starvation wages and massive coercion in the workplace so that the surplus value on which the society depends can be efficiently extracted from their labour power. How can they ever be expected actually to desire this rather than, say, to 'endure and learn to tolerate' it? It is the role of ideologies to try to make them actually desire what they must desire—work under alienated conditions—if the system as a whole is to survive and reproduce itself. Second, the fact that all forms of consciousness in the society are 'reified' will mean that even theorists will be increasingly unable even to understand the social world they live in, because even reified humans who are moved around on the checkerboard of the world market are not really mere tokens and can surprise one.

Philosophy, then, as it has generally been practised, is a nonautonomous pursuit which, for the specified reasons, is incapable, Lukács thinks, of dealing with the conceptual conflicts and contradictions that naturally arise in a capitalist society. At best it can note the gap between such things as duty and desire and recommend stoic toleration of the unbearable features of human life. As should be clear, this is not a kind of reductionism, nor one that renders 'philosophy' irrelevant, although it does require a change of focus and approach. From the fact that certain 'philosophical problems' have their roots in social problems it does not follow that we can destroy their hold on us simply by undertaking *unenlightened* social action. On the contrary, to abolish the social conditions that give rise to insoluble philosophical puzzles requires action that is informed by a correct understanding of human society and its history. For modern society this means understanding fetishism and reification. Such an understanding must, Lukács believes, have a significant philosophical component. For one thing it must be 'Marxist' (in Lukács' sense of that term). Lukács is clear that 'Marxism' does not refer to any specific set of doctrines but to a general approach to society which sees it not as a collection of individual facts but as a 'totality' comprised of human subjects acting and interacting.[8] 'Totality' is a philosophical concept, and so to the extent to which the members of the proletariat can act to realise their own interests *only if* they see their society as a totality, to that extent philosophy has a positive, cognitive, substantive role to play in the modern world.

A number of conditions, then, need to be satisfied if our society is to change in an appropriate way. First of all, human powers and in particular the forces of production in our society must be sufficiently developed to provide an appropriate level of economic surplus. Second, there must be a human agent who is in principle capable of bringing about the necessary change. Lukács holds that Marx has shown that such an agent exists in the form of the proletariat in an advanced capitalist society. This group is in principle capable of abolishing private ownership of the means of production and introducing a classless mode of economic production. However, Lukács follows Lenin in modifying Marx's relatively insouciant view that, as economic crises become more and more severe, it will become obvious to the workers what must be done. Rather, Lukács thinks, it is crucial to think in a focused way about the specific form which the consciousness of the members of the proletariat must take for it to act effectively. This is not something that will simply arise of itself out of the objective situation. Objective crises provide an opportunity, but whether or not that opportunity will be taken and, if it is, how exactly it will be grasped, are not foregone conclusions. The transition to a society which is classless (and in which the conceptual and theoretical antinomies that plagued capitalist society will disappear) will take place only if the proletariat has acquired the correct class consciousness and acts in accordance with it. The correct class consciousness would need to be philosophically correct—that is, Marxist in the sense described earlier (consciously centred on understanding the society as a 'totality'). This would mean that it would have to put the immediate details of any situation into an overall framework that connects it to the social system as a whole, and it will have to have drawn from a study of the system as a whole a correct analysis of where the real interests of the proletariat lie and how they can best be achieved. Lenin thought that proper class consciousness would not arise among the members of the working class during the normal course of events; they would at best be able to arrive at a subpolitical form of 'trades-union consciousness'. So if the transformation to a classless society was to succeed, there would need to be a party of professional politicians who had the appropriate philosophical knowledge, were able to transmit the right class consciousness to the members of the proletariat, and would serve as a vanguard for socially transformative political action. Lukács thought that at the end of World War One the time had come for philosophy to play a positive historical role by becoming the self-consciousness of the working class, organised behind such a vanguard political party.

There cannot be a single social subject under capitalism, because the society is split into classes with incompatible vital interests. No large-scale social project can satisfy the interests of both of these classes at the same time. A society composed exclusively of capitalists is impossible—who would actually work the factories? Perhaps at one time, say in the eighteenth century, capitalists had an important and even vital economic role to play, but now they are really mere parasites. A society composed exclusively of workers, however, is, in fact possible, and such a society, whatever other difficulties it might face, would lack the inherent contradictions of class. In a classless society there could in principle be a social 'we' which could organise social and economic life as a whole and see it all as a result of its own collective action, that is, as 'free'. Lukács speaks of such a society as one in which the proletariat recognises itself as the 'identical subject/object of history'. This means that there would be a collective subject, the proletariat, which knew that in knowing the social world (the 'object'), it was coming to know what was actually a subject: itself (and the intentional consequences of its own actions). Such a society would be characterised by complete social transparency.

One of the major criticisms levelled at *History and Class Consciousness* from the Left is precisely that Lukács can sometimes seem more interested in finding solutions to philosophical paradoxes than to questions concerning the basic survival and well-being of people in contemporary societies, but in a way, the interest of the book consists precisely in the claim that these two interests are not alternatives. Behind the writing of *History and Class Consciousness* lie a series of ethical concerns: Lukács believed, for example, that the strength of the Party was a *moral* strength (especially in the section entitled 'Rosa Luxemburg as a Marxist'). This means that it is composed of people who know a (or even 'the') fundamental truth about history and politics and have made the right choice. What does 'the right choice' mean here, and can Lukács give some sense to this notion?

In a text he wrote at about the same time as he was composing *History and Class Consciousness, Taktik und Ethik*,[9] Lukács makes the point that the modern world is in a state of suppressed civil war in which there is no 'neutral' position. The choice is either *for* the proletariat or *against* it, and to try to stay neutral is to choose to be against it. Members of each party are responsible for their choice, and that means also for the consequences of those choices. None of these choices is innocent. This distinction is intended to replace the distinction which is so close to the hearts of liberals, between the immediate agents who perform some action and those who (in one way or another) support the position of the immediate agents. This need not mean that no relevant moral distinction can be drawn between the person who actually places the bomb, the person who plans the attack, and those who in various other ways support the project in general, or even after the fact, but it means that these distinctions need not be the starting point—and are certainly not the definitive end points—of ethical thought. If the world is in a state of active civil war, one must choose sides, and no one should expect either side to be without guilt. It is an ethical demand that one realise this clearly and choose without trying to cover up one's complicity or hide it (even from oneself). The National Socialist view, of course, was not that each European society was (already, at least tacitly) in a state of civil war which pitted the workers against the capitalists, or, if it was, this situation was a creation of Marxists and other socialists who brought it about for their own purposes by propagating it. Rather, workers should see themselves as part of a national and racial community inherently at war (whether they knew it or not) with all other such communities for survival.

In a situation like this, how can one orient oneself? Lukács argues that if life in the proletarian vanguard party is the only form of life in which fully coherent social thought and action are at all possible because the 'standpoint of the proletariat' is the only one from which the society as a whole can even be seen, then it makes sense to try to stay in the Party even if this requires heroic sacrifice, not least the sacrifice of a comfortable individual conscience. If there is in fact no party which proleptically embodies, even if in a highly fallible way, the consciousness of the proletariat, then coherency is not possible, and the human fate is a fully tragic one; more or less any choice is as good as any other. We are, then, mere isolated, moral atoms swirling in a void, and each individual will simply be forced to make choices between incommensurate and contradictory goods and courses of action with no standards apart from shifting individual judgement. Suppose, then, I am confronted with a choice between A and B. If I choose A, I choose to live in a world in which nothing finally will ever make sense, action will be self-defeating and pointless, reason will be more or less useless, and people will lurch from one form of misery to another without hope of escape or improvement. If I choose B, I take a chance on constructing a world which has enough order in it for it to be a possible object of human cognition and foresight and in which human beings have at least a chance of improving their situation through rational collective action. To call a decision to take a chance on B—the choice in favour of the proletariat and its party—'irrational' or even 'arational' would be, Lukács thought, ludicrous. Of course, as an individual, one could always try to opt out of history; that was a decision people made, one that was historically understandable and had historical effects, but it was a decision arising from desperation and leading nowhere.[10]

One of the things that will strike, and perhaps disturb, contemporary readers of Lukács is the set of tacit assumptions he makes about the nature and structure of the human subject, the soul, mind, psyche, or personality. As his literary criticism shows, he was obsessed with a number of conceptions that might strike us as exceptionally Biedermeier and that blocked his access to much of modern high culture. His tacit ideal for a work of art was one that presented the interplay between rounded literary characters with fully developed and integrated lives.[11] He was especially keen on the notion of an 'organic' unitary personality. Few now are likely to find this conception either very plausible or very attractive. In addition, we are likely to think that to the extent to which we do find any kind of unity, either in literary characters or in real people, this should be construed as an imposed unitariness rather than as something 'natural'.

This might be taken to reflect badly on the very idea that the proletariat as a unified subject is to take control of its own fate, by virtue of abolishing the invisible hand and planning society and making society conform to its wishes. If the plausibility of this is supposed to depend on the strong analogy between a social subject and an individual subject, then are individual subjects even in the best of circumstances really always so full-bodied, so unified, and so harmonious? Is my individual mind, psyche, and consciousness always (or ever) especially unitary? Would it be an indubitably better thing if they were? Do I always (or ever) know my own mind?

Lukács, of course, would hold that *our* cultural obsession with nontransparency, indirection, modes of inner psychic conflict, and *Zerrissenheit* is a reflection of an unnatural state of society rather than an insight into the way things are, or at any rate the way things need to be. That is certainly a point that cannot be taken as having been established beyond the possibility of doubt.

*Chapter Ten*

# HEIDEGGER

Sleepwalkers are often said to be preternaturally surefooted, able to walk without hesitation in places where a fully awake human would be almost certain to stumble. In a reversal of this commonplace, Heidegger thought that all the readers of his first major work, *Being and Time* (1927), had, with the self-assurance of sleepwalkers, completely missed the main point of the book.[1] It was actually intended to be a 'metaphysics' of the most austere kind; however, his readers avoided the metaphysical 'question of being' which was at the centre of his discussion and were obsessed with one or another of the subordinate or merely preliminary, quasi-anthropological topics which the book treated: anxiety, guilt, authenticity, resoluteness, death, the modes of being-in-the-world, or the particular form of 'interpretation' he discusses. The published book is over 400 pages long, and whatever one might finally think of the plausibility of the theses it proposes or even the mode of argumentation, it is densely written and systematically highly organised. Why and how could so many readers have taken this thick, learned tome to be a kind of lowbrow self-help manual?

Of course, it would be easy to reply to this that Heidegger had only himself to blame if his intentions were not clear. He was a highly pro-active and skilful mystifier, and the text he published in 1927 as *Being and Time* was only a fragment of the originally envisaged full text; in fact it was only an incomplete fragment, albeit a large one, of part I of what was supposed to be a work in two parts (§8). If one needed to see the whole project before judging it—an assumption that does not seem unreasonable—Heidegger could have made judgement easier by publishing the conclusion of part I and all of part II. It eventually turned out, after decades of equivocation, which, however, left the strong impression in people's minds that part II was being 'withheld',[2] that it actually never existed, at any rate as a publishable text. So if the book, that is, the fragment of the book that was published in 1927, was widely misconstrued, there was some reason to think this might not be entirely the readers' fault. Heidegger takes a self-serving line here. He claims that contemporary interpretation of the work ignored its central contention, namely that it was necessary to ask the question of Being. However, he further claims that this purported fact actually *confirms* his view that humans are always concerned with this question, but always try to hide this concern from themselves. To understand this contorted claim requires a bit of an interpretative detour through the history of philosophy.

Heidegger was, as he repeatedly said, fundamentally a Christian negative theologian trying to destroy the pretensions of human reason so as to open space for a form of life that was 'more primordial' and different from the existing organised religious life in the West, and also from our post-Christian mode of existence.[3] What

one might call the 'enlightenment' or 'progressivist' view of culture
and history which emphasises the positive value of development,
elaboration, refinement, and sophistication is completely alien to
Heidegger. He sees history as a story of decline, and he has an obsession with 'origins' and with getting to that which is 'primordial',
which remained a characteristic of his writing during the whole of
his long life. These terms combine for him the sense of what is metaphysically fundamental, what is especially robust, and what is cognitively essential for any form of understanding. He avoided the
word 'ethics', but putting that aside for a moment, we might say
that terms like 'primordial' had a series of further ethical or at any
rate value-coloured associations: what is genuine, honest, authentic,
refreshingly unpretentious, and salutary.[4] Heidegger applied his general doctrine to himself: his origins remained, he claimed, decisive
for his development, and the goal of all his striving could not be
anything other than to return to that origin and understand and as-
similate it correctly. He had originally been in training to become a
Catholic priest but was eventually sent home from the seminary
because of poor health. He then completed his university studies as
a 'lay theologian' and began his academic teaching career in a university post for Catholic theology. The theological curriculum at
the time would have been of an especially desiccated and metaphysically top-heavy, late-scholastic kind which he later described as the
'system' of Catholicism; it was roughly what is known as 'Thomism'.
At a certain point in his thirties, Heidegger then had a rather spec-
tacular conversion to Lutheranism, identifying strongly with the
more irrationalist aspects of Luther's doctrine of 'faith'. The 'original' Christian message was like that of St. Paul in the 50s and early
60s of the first century: Christianity was a life of a faith that was a
scandal to the Jews and a 'folly' to the Greeks; it was the very opposite
of the life of wisdom, sober reflection, and calculated moderation.

Luther had notoriously called Reason a 'whore' who would do the bidding of anyone who paid her fee, and he thought it was necessary to break through the carapace of medieval philosophical dogma to get back to a more living and primordial Christian faith. Heidegger went him one better in that he claimed the rot had set in even earlier: the self-misunderstanding of Christianity had begun not in the shadows of the early Dark Ages but in the period between Paul and the Gospel according to John. If Paul in 55 CE says that Christianity is 'folly', the author of the Gospel of John can write in 100–110 CE that Jesus is the λογος, the rational principle of the Universe which Greek philosophers sought for so long. With the Gospel of John, Heidegger claimed, living Christian 'faith' came to be expressed in an utterly inappropriate rationalistic and metaphysical language derived from Greek philosophy. The Greek metaphysics with which Christianity was brought into contact in the late first century CE was itself a highly decadent, incipiently scholastic shell of a form of thought which six or seven centuries earlier (at the time of the so-called pre-Socratics) had been a vital intellectual tradition of thinkers engaged in trying to capture a unique and primordial kind of human experience.

Heidegger's original ideal, then, was to free Christian faith and the Christian form of life from Greek metaphysical categories so as to allow it to grow and flourish in a form more appropriate to itself than any of these categories would permit. However, since these same forms of metaphysical thinking had dominated all parts of human life and thought since antiquity, the only way really to free ourselves from them was to destroy them from within.

The one strand of Christian theology for which Heidegger feels some affinity is that of 'negative theology'. Negative theologians argue that everything in the world is completely dependent on a God, who is also utterly 'transcendent', that is, utterly beyond and different from anything that is in the world. As a consequence, normal human language, which is, after all, set up to speak about things in the world, has no application to God. So we can say (and hence know) nothing about God, except perhaps for some particularly thin negative assertions, such as that he is *not* identical to anything we might encounter in the world and does *not* have any of the properties we might apply to things in the world. In a certain way we might even say that God does not exist, given that 'exist' itself is defined as a mode or way of being in our world. Similarly, Heidegger thinks that everything-that-is is dependent not on the Christian God but on being (or perhaps one should write 'Being'), but that Being is neither itself a thing that is nor some abstract property shared by all-that-is. It cannot, he thinks, be a property, certainly not if one accepts the traditional way of construing such properties, namely as having a definite and specifiable position in a hierarchy of greater or lesser 'abstraction'. 'Red' is a property because it can be located *under* the more general property of 'colour' ('red' is a colour) and *above* the more specific varieties of 'crimson', 'scarlet', 'carmine', 'vermilion' ('scarlet' is a kind of red). It is this location which gives a property its specific content. However, in the case of Being, there is no more general property under which it can be ranged, so this form of analysis is not possible (§1).

The radical difference between that-which-is, that is, *anything-that-is*, and Being is what Heidegger later in his life took to calling 'the ontological difference',[5] and he thinks that the systematic ignoring of this difference has been one of the fundamental features, and basic errors, of Western philosophy. So normal human language, which refers in the first instance to things-that-are or events in our world, is inappropriate if extended to Being. This means that from the very beginning questions of language are central to Heidegger's project. His own retrospective assessment was that in his early work, including *Being and Time,* he thought he could break out of our usual ways of speaking and of disciplining speech into philosophical concepts and yet find another kind of potentially conceptual language that would be amenable to speaking of Being. So he tried to invent a whole new and, it must be admitted, completely outlandish set of concepts to make possible modes of expression that might allow us to ask and answer the question of Being more appropriately. There is a certain unclarity that comes to light here. Is the thesis that no normal, everyday language can apply to Being, that none of the existing philosophical vocabularies applies, or that no language at all could apply? In *Being and Time* Heidegger held that both everyday language and the received philosophical vocabulary that arises out of it needed to be discarded and replaced, but what he replaced it with was another, very different set of concepts and terms. They were different—'being-in-the-world', 'running forward to death', 'authenticity', 'resoluteness'—but they were still concepts (of a kind). Later he came to see this whole project in *Being and Time* as flawed and thought it was not possible to find a different form of conceptual language. He tried much later in his life to explore some forms of what he called 'poetic speaking' as a way of getting access to Being, but without any noticeable success.[6]

Why should we be at all interested in this 'question of Being'? Why isn't complete indifference and a hearty yawn the right reaction to this whole discussion? No one likes to see a pet research interest ignored, but it is a part of Heidegger's philosophical position that such claims to indifference are to be construed as merely feigned (and also, it turns out, as a kind of quasi-moral failing). What Heidegger calls 'forgetfulness of Being' is not mere inattention but an active power of wilfully enforced, purported disinterest.[7] It is only the exercise of this active power which makes it possible for us continually to ignore and overlook the ontological difference. If Heideggerian metaphysics is, as I am suggesting, a proposed successor discipline to the now defunct 'Christian theology', one can perhaps find some indication of the reason for this initially rather odd view in the history of religion.

For the monotheist, indifference to theological and religious beliefs tends to be construed as just another form of atheism because it is even more threatening to a monotheist that people could genuinely not care about religion than that they could have deviant beliefs. The monotheist at least has a category for proper, articulate atheists and can appeal to notions like wilful error, sin, and human obstinacy to account for them, so it would be convenient if indifference, too, could be brought under one of these categories. If I have sufficiently forceful theological beliefs, I can even maintain that there is and can be no 'innocent' lack of interest in religious questions. I can, for instance, claim that God has created humans with an inherent and ineluctable concern to know him and, therefore, to take an interest in religion. Christians of a certain kind, especially followers of Augustine, have a clear line on this: God made humans to know and love him, but Adam rebelled against this, and his sinful disposition has been inherited by all humans ever since. So claims of lack of interest are *really* especially dishonest and malicious forms of atheism and a rejection of God's manifest will. Feigned indifference is merely one partially camouflaged active decision to refuse to engage appropriately with God.

Similarly, Heidegger is of the opinion that humans cannot fail to be interested in 'the question of Being'—what it is and how it is different from beings—because in one way or another, humans must be construed to have given (at least tacitly) an answer to this question through their very mode of living. No human beings, Heidegger claims, can really be *completely* disinterested in how they are living, in their own mode of being. We cannot even imagine what a human life of true indifference to all aspects of the way it was led would look like. I am not indifferent if I make any, even the most minimal attempt to live in one way rather than another, and thus any way I do live can be seen as a way in which I am answering the question of Being. Purportedly, then, parallel to the religious case, claimed indifference is really a kind of wilful denial of the truth that one has an interest in the question of Being and has asked and answered the question. One would expect the discussion then to shift to whether or not it is appropriate to construe every form of human living as a way of (tacitly) answering the question of Being.

Heidegger's thesis would be exceedingly implausible if asking and answering the question of being was anything like giving a formal and explicit 'theory' of Being. Virtually no one has or has had such a 'theory', and if 'normal' human language is supposed not to apply to Being (as the negative theologian thinks it does not apply to God), then this is what one would expect. What about the claim that merely by living in a certain way (without necessarily *saying* anything) one can be seen, tacitly, to be giving an answer to theological questions (or then, in a parallel way, to 'the question of Being')?[8]

There is an important distinction here. On the one hand, one can try to resolve a life problem by giving an analysis, developing a theory, or proposing a set of concepts that will purportedly give one an understanding of the problem and provide a way of dealing with it. On the other hand, one can (sometimes) resolve a problem in life simply by living in a certain way. So if someone has a problem with, say, anxiety, to take an example that is close to Heidegger, I can present a theory about anxiety couched in a set of specifically psychological categories, and in various ways I can try to see how that could help to overcome the anxiety. However, I might also show that I actually understand how to live without anxiety simply by exercising that ability, by doing it. I simply live, or even learn to live, in a way that reduces my anxiety without having a theory. Heidegger tends to express this distinction as a difference between forms of 'understanding'. Some people simply know or understand how to live without anxiety. This is an understanding that expresses itself simply in its effective and successful exercise. It is different and distinct from any form of conceptual or theoretical understanding that one may or may not have in the relevant domain. Obviously these two forms of understanding are not exactly the same thing, but equally they are not completely unconnected, and there will be complex relations between them. People who live servile and insecure lives will tend, when and if they come to try to speak about their lives, to employ concepts like 'command', 'obedience', 'certain'. On the other hand, the suggestion made a few years ago that all school pupils be required to take instruction in neoclassical economics was intended to have the effect of changing the way they acted, making them more calculating (and thus also easier to predict). If these suggestions had been implemented, however, this formal instruction would probably also have eventually had some effect on the way the pupils actually began to relate to their own lives. Formal instruction does not necessarily have the effect intended— Catholic catechism classes do not necessarily produce pious Catholics. From this it does not follow they have no effect whatever; they do at any rate often produce something different from the equally unsuccessful Protestant catechism classes.

Heidegger's clear view is that these two forms—roughly understanding how to live and conceptualising how one lives—are mutually dependent in such a way as to make it impossible to say that one is basic and the other derivative. There is no breaking out of the circle in which these two phenomena coexist and affect each other, to find some absolute beginning. So medieval Christians have a certain way of living—they 'understand' how to live in a certain way—and they will use certain concepts and theories to give an account of that life, make it understandable to themselves. These two things are not exactly the same, but they are interdependent. If one looks at this phenomenon of mutual dependency of mode of existence and conceptualisation from the outside, say, as a modern scholar looking back on the Middle Ages, and tries to understand what is going on there, one sees a similar kind of circularity instantiated. I can understand how they lived only in terms that make sense to me, and that means attributing to them goals, desires, and attitudes that seem plausible to me and that can be made to fit into categories I have at my disposal. If I study them sufficiently long and intensely and with sufficient sympathy, I might, of course, find that my own ideas about what is a 'plausible' way of living begin to change. This circular relation of dependency does not make understanding impossible. If I immerse myself deeply and carefully in enough medieval literature, what 'I can make sense of' might itself change, so that gradually aspects of their life that looked very alien to me at the start begin to become comprehensible. Heidegger calls the circular structure instantiated here 'the hermeneutic circle' and thinks it is a basic characteristic of any human understanding (§§31–33). In the case in question one can see that there are a number of such circular structures in evidence. Some medieval woman has a way of living that is dependent on her understanding of, say, Christianity as a set of concepts and dogmas, but what that understanding is, is in some way limited by and dependent on what she can make sense of in her actual living. Equally what kind of life she will actually 'understand' how to live will be limited by and dependent on the concepts which Christianity provides to her. As I look back on her life, I too will be able to make sense of it only relative to the possibilities of living I in some way can understand and the concepts I can bring to bear. In both cases the hermeneutic circle is an inherently dynamic structure: it is to some extent true that she *is* a Christian, but she is also *trying to be* a (better) Christian (than she is), and her understanding of what that means and implies can change. The same is true for me; I am trying, and may succeed in my attempt, to get a 'better' understanding of her, but I do that by coming to see some possibilities that were possibilities for her as also possibilities for me. So to some extent as I interpret her I become more like her. If *per impossibile* I were to 'understand' her fully, it would be because I had become indistinguishable from her, and so no 'interpretation' would be needed; however, the circular motion has no absolute beginning and also, of course, no absolute end. There is no such thing as 'complete and perfect understanding' of Christianity (available to her or to me) nor complete and total understanding of her (available to her or to me) nor, finally, some 'complete understanding' I might ideally have of myself. Nevertheless 'understanding' is not so unstructured as to make it impossible to speak of a fuller or a less full understanding or a 'better' or a 'worse' understanding. It is just that the criteria for 'better' or 'worse' are highly contextual.

To be sure, I might want sometimes to speak, for instance, of a 'preconceptual' or 'pretheoretical' understanding that people have about how to treat those in need, but concepts like 'pretheoretical' will apply only contextually. That is, if I am speaking of nurses before the professionalization of this activity, I may say that they had a 'pretheoretical' understanding of how to do what needed to be done, but this simply means that they knew how to act before they were taught some specific doctrine that I consider to be appropriate in guiding action. This does not imply they had no thoughts before or were guided by no concepts at all in treating the sick.

Heidegger's emphasis here is precisely the reverse of that which one finds in Socrates. Socrates was keen to try to show the limitations of any form of human skill that was merely a theoretically unarticulated knack. In order really to know what one is doing, one needs to have a proper theory. In general Heidegger wishes to focus attention on ways in which inadequate theoretical or conceptual accounts can distort, blight, interfere with, or otherwise damage the way we conduct our lives or the way a false conceptualisation can *inhibit* tacit understanding.

Let us grant, then, for the sake of argument that we can assume that all humans ask 'the question of being' at least to the minimal extent that they are somehow concerned (one way or the other) with the way they 'are'—the way they exist, act, behave, fare in the world. This concern expresses itself in the way I conduct myself, so that the life I lead can be construed as a way of tacitly answering the question of what being is for me. Why should I then have an ingrained tendency to shy away from recognizing and acknowledging these facts (assuming they are in some sense facts)? The answer to this lies in another feature of Heidegger's account of what it is to live a human life.

A human being is an entity not so much of present fixed properties as of already existing obligations and commitments and of future projects and possibilities that are not yet realised. When Heidegger speaks of 'possibilities' as central constituents of what it is to be human, he does not mean by that positions in an abstract logical space. That is, he does not mean by 'possibility', say, the fact that it is possible that the cat is in the loft (as opposed to the possibility that she is in the kitchen, the garden, the sitting room, etc.). He (almost) always uses 'possibility' to mean 'specifically human possible ways of existing, acting, living, or "being-in-the-world"'. So a possibility is not 'that the cat be in the loft' but 'that I pick her up in order to get the book she is sleeping on' or 'that I go into the garden to watch her sniffing the air and chasing birds'. These examples are overt actions, and it is true that a 'possibility' for Heidegger is always embedded in a context of acting in the world. However, Heidegger uses 'the world' in a sense derived from Christian theology (*seculum*), and so it does not designate an actual space external to me. To say that some people live 'in the world' (in this Christian sense) is to say that they do not devote their life, for instance, to contemplation but, as we would also say, to 'mundane' concerns and interaction with other people who are equally engaged in everyday activities of various kinds. So 'the world' in the phrase 'my possibilities of acting or being in the world' does not refer to a topographic location—the loft, the garden, the kitchen—but rather to my existing set of everyday concerns and projects.

As a human being I am always already enmeshed in life, engaged in half-completed projects, bound by obligations I did not enter into with anything like full knowledge and to which I have never given full consent. There is an irreducible contingency and ungroundedness about most of my projects; I don't choose my relatives or place of birth, yet by the very fact of growing up within a situation basically structured by my social surroundings, I have acquired many of the projects that are most constitutive of me. I might like to *imagine* myself as a disembodied Enlightenment subject, completely freely and knowledgeably making a choice among the full field of possibilities and giving a convincing reason for every choice, but that is just a fantasy. To imagine myself *not* thus enmeshed is a profitless exercise of my imagination. The relation to my past is important, but in the context of the present discussion it is not as significant as the inherent human orientation toward future possible modes of action and experience. As a human being, I am always ahead of myself, pursuing projects in the world which have not yet been fully accomplished. I can, of course, look back at completed projects in the past, but as long as I am alive at all, I will also have projects still in the course of realisation and whose conclusion is outstanding.

Even on my deathbed I shall presumably be trying one final time to look around the room or listen to the whispers of the prospective chief mourners assembled around my bed. To have *no* outstanding projects is to have no future, that is, to be dead. In addition, my projects are not simply a mass of disjointed different things I am trying to do, but form connected strands: I take the train to get to the airport, in order to be able to catch the flight to Berlin, in order to buy the computer at Saturn on Alexanderplatz, so that I shall be able to finish the writing project, and so on.

Of course, various forms of the exercise of the imagination form an essential part of human life. I can imagine that I exist without any particular one of my projects, but if I try to imagine what it would be like for me to exist without any project at all, that is tantamount to imagining a 'me' without me. Actually to believe that I could exist without *any* project is a form of imaginative self-delusion.

Finally, and this is an important Heideggerian claim, all my projects are structured together into at least a tacit and aspirational unity or a single totality, some project about my life as a whole; this is presumably Heidegger's version of the subordination of everything to the singular idea of 'the good' in Plato. What this means, though, is that human life is necessarily incomplete. One could almost invert Lucretius' message. He claims that while we are still here, still alive, death is not, whereas when death is, we are no longer here; therefore it makes no sense to fear death. Heidegger claims that our life is essentially 'care', and a kind of care that can at the slightest provocation turn to anxiety, precisely because when death arrives it will always arrive at the wrong time, to thwart some project or at least render it incomplete (§§39–41). All our projects therefore are inherently fragile, which means all our living is fragile. To the extent to which they are all interconnected and eventually interrupted by death, they are all by their very nature incomplete and a failure. This

239

is what causes our desire to suppress the question of being. Radical nothingness is the opposite of Being, and we encounter such nothingness in certain experiences such as anxiety. Our own death, of course, is the final radical cancellation of all that we are, and facing our death is thus also facing our own possible nothingness. Concern about death thus is not mere concern about one or another of my possible individual ways of being but about my world as a whole, that is, about Being as a whole and as such. We always deal with anxiety and possible eventual death in one way or another, even if that way of dealing with them consists in trying to stop thinking about them. In dealing in one way or another with radical nothingness, anxiety, and death, we are also showing that we have *some* understanding of the opposite of nothingness, Being in itself and as a whole. In this sense we are asking and answering the question of Being as long as we continue to exist.

Even to raise explicitly the question of Being is at the same time to raise the question of my own death because it is to confront the fact that I am my projects for future possible ways of living. But becoming clearly aware of that unavoidably also focuses my attention on my death as the ultimate reason why those projects will remain unfulfilled. In a sense, then, all of Western philosophy is a reaction to anxiety in the face of death, although it is a reaction that tries to cover up the phenomenon. The form this reaction takes is what Heidegger calls the 'Falling' (or perhaps 'the Great Decadence', *das Verfallen* [§38]). Given my motivation to get away from thinking explicitly about Being, myself, and my possibilities— that is, finally, my death—I am tempted to understand myself in terms that bypass and short-circuit this whole complex and focus on something else which, purportedly, will not induce such conceptual and existential vertigo. That is, what I really am is a continual spiralling of possibilities, possible ways of being in the world, oriented toward my death. But how reassuring it would be if I were not that, but just one more thing with fixed and immutable properties, like the things I encounter in the world. The metaphor of the Falling then means falling out of the spiral of my possibilities into the fixed world in which those possibilities are realised (but to which those possibilities may never actually be reduced). There is an individual dimension to this Falling and a historical dimension. The philosophical analogue of this is that I try to use categories that actually apply to things in the world to describe and speak of myself, who, whatever else I am, am not anything in the world or at all like anything in the world. We wish and try desperately to interpret ourselves as standing firm and complete in our present with a set of properties, then moving through time toward a future, each segment of which is a new step forward from one fixed state of being-with-properties to another. Contrary to this, even to say 'what I am' at any given, fixed time must make essential reference not merely to my present state of being, because part of that state of being is a set of 'projects', things I care about and which are essentially connected with action in the future. So in one sense the future is not before us, but we are already there. Similarly the past is not 'behind' us but still with us as the *present* background against which alone our future and present have meaning. One immediate consequence of this is that we are never complete in our present but rather, as Heidegger says, always in front of ourselves out there in the world. We deal with the anxiety this induces by trying to construe ourselves as not out there in a future that will (at some point) end abruptly in death but rather as solid, present-centred beings that rest in themselves, just as chairs, billiard balls, and bits of masonry rest their being in a substantial present.

The historical dimension is the invention in Greek philosophy of the concept—or actually of the notion of an 'idea', meaning originally

a way in which things in the world appeared to be, then our way of
apprehending things in the world—and of conceptual thinking.
This was an important historical step in the process of falling. The
'concept' was invented as a fixed structure that would stand between humans and the world, give human cognition (and life) stability, and distance humans from too immediate a confrontation
with the question of Being (under the guise of answering that question). Rather than face directly, that is, the sheer brutal contingency
of the world, which at any moment can cease to exist (with my
death), the 'concept' gives me a soothing way of moderating that
contingency and focusing on some individual trait of the world,
some object. There is no anxiety-producing confusion assaulting me,
Being which can transform itself into nonbeing/death, but rather an
ordered structure of experience: 'Ah, that is a "mountain"; that is a
"river"; 'that is "thunder".' Each concept (and each object) is potentially in its predictable place, safe. Unfortunately this strategy did
not work, nor, given the nature of the human condition, could it
ever have worked completely. The repression of the anxiety which
is a constituent of human life is not ever fully successful, but what
Greek philosophy did was to initiate a long historical process which
has a certain internal logic that can be traced. This is a process of
gradual and cumulative degeneration in which the more philosophy
develops, the more complex the conceptual schemes it elaborates,
and the more elaborate the schemes, the further away they take us
from and occlude Being (and also my death). These philosophical
schemes eventually seep in even to everyday language, so that
now we speak without any special reflection about 'substances',
'subjects', 'essences', and 'causes', terms that originate in earlier
philosophical speculation. So by the twentieth century we were
caught in a web of concepts which are the latest and most calcified

residue of a project of understanding everything in the world in terms derived from, and at best appropriate to, objects, and which maximally cover up and make invisible the question of Being. This conceptual apparatus is one of the things that makes it difficult to come to an understanding of how to live which takes proper account of the question of Being.

So how can we get out of this situation? Eventually Heidegger thought that we could not do so by our own efforts. In an interview with *Spiegel* published after his death, he famously claimed that our situation was hopeless and that 'only a god could save us.'[9] *Sein und Zeit* was, however, written at a time when he still indulged in what he would later think were youthful fantasies of escape. Given that the two forms of understanding—conceptual understanding and an understanding that expresses and realises itself in the very act of living—are inherently connected and reinforce each other, changing one mode of understanding Being will require also changing the other, ideally at the same time. So there will be two (interconnected) dimensions to the attempt to exit from the current (according to Heidegger) ontologically unsatisfactory situation.

The first dimension refers to the attempt to find some mode of experiencing, or way of existing, that instantiates an understanding of Being which does not cover up the question. Heidegger thinks he has found this in what he calls 'authenticity'. It is a mode of choosing to pursue projects while refusing to ignore the fact that these are both in the final analysis ungrounded and necessarily connected to a single larger project which will come to an incomplete end with my death. 'Authenticity', then, does not refer to any specific concrete set of options or choices of action: to marry Regine (or not), to become a pastor of the Established Church (or not), to move to Berlin (or not). Rather it refers to the way the choice is made, my own attitude toward myself and my projects as I choose to pursue them. This is a way of living which does not make these choices and projects dependent on the illusion of being fully grounded or part of some larger project that could ever be fully completed.

The second dimension is the historical one, a 'destruction', in the original Latinate sense, an 'unbuilding or taking apart' of the history of philosophy, showing how, at each stage, the basic philosophical vocabulary has moved further and further away from one that would allow us to ask the question of Being. The first of these two dimensions was treated in the published (if incomplete) part I of *Being and Time;* the second was to have been done in the unwritten part II, so we don't know exactly how Heidegger would have proceeded concretely, unless we try to reconstruct what his treatment would have been by appealing to his many later writings on the history of philosophy.

The title of Heidegger's book *Being and Time* means philosophers have tried to resist recognising that Being is dependent on time because Being is revealed only to someone who *will-die*. Being is nothing for us save to the extent to which we have access to it, understand it, and deal with it, that is, have already tacitly dealt with it in one way or another. For humans that way is always one that is mediated by our essential nature as temporal beings. We are constituted through our projects, and these always extend into an open future which will, we know, eventually come to an end in death. In a backhanded kind of way even Western philosophy recognises the role of time in Being, in that one of the most usual traditional criteria for Being is 'that which *always is*'. Heidegger's response in a way is that there is nothing which 'always is'.

Heidegger doesn't seem to have had any particularly distinct political views at the time he wrote *Being and Time,* although, obviously, his violent rejection of the Enlightenment and all its works (and his origin as the son of a small-town artisan in a very rural region of southern Germany) made it unlikely that he would become a supporter of the radical Left. His politicisation seems to have taken place in the early 1930s. After a brief but highly visible period of political involvement as an active and publicly vocal National Socialist immediately after Hitler came to power, when he revelled in the title 'first Nazi rector of a German university', Heidegger found himself politically sidelined.[10] On reflection, he decided by the end of the 1930s that the official Party ideology was just an instance of the same kind of Western rationalism he had always opposed. He particularly objected to the attempt to base ethics and politics on science (namely the version of Darwinist biology which was used to justify racialist doctrines). According to one Gestapo report, made by a spy sent to observe his lectures, Heidegger had 'withdrawn into a private National Socialism of his own creation', a position, to judge by an interview he gave late in his life, he seems to have continued to hold until his death in 1976. In any case, after about 1939 or 1940 his philosophical views underwent a shift; at any rate there seems to have been at least a significant change of emphasis. The shift is from an early position which puts great emphasis on individual decisions to one focused on millennial historical shifts about which humans can do nothing. Although in some sense 'care' or 'concern' is at the centre of both the earlier and the later view, the kind of 'care' in question has changed. Individual engaged action is at the core of philosophy in the early period; the 'care' repeatedly invoked seems to be a matter of taking charge and forging ahead. The later philosophy devalues this and connects the appropriate human kind of 'care' with the virtue of a Zen-like 'letting-go' (*Gelassenheit*).[11] For the later Heidegger, humans must remain open and receptive to the calls which Being may make on us, and learn to take care of Being as a shepherd does his sheep. We need to become 'die Hirten des Seins'.[12] If the early model is activist and anarchic, the later position emphasises the need for humans to cultivate, take care of, and foster what is around them. Often there seems to be almost a proto-environmentalist tone to some of the later works.

*Being and Time* itself is written in a style that is very strongly exhortatory, but it doesn't seem to be advocating or denigrating any particular form of life or set of choices. Heidegger was often asked whether *Being and Time* was or implied an 'ethics', and he gave one of his usual slippery answers: that it was not an ethics, but that this did not imply that its content was ethically irrelevant. The best way to take this, I think, is as meaning something like the following: 'Ethics' is not a purely disinterested and speculative enterprise, but it is always 'addressed' to someone: 'You, child of God, do not do this'; 'As a rational agent you should avoid doing that'; 'Proletarians of the world, unite!' So before giving ethical advice, you should investigate *who* (if anyone) it was to whom you were proposing to give that advice. One of the strands of argument in *Being and Time* concerns whether or not a human being is an 'individual', a specific 'who'. Humans are born not as individuals but as anonymous members of crowds or groups, who all, we assume, have the possibility of becoming individuals. One becomes an individual by adopting an individuated attitude of care toward one's own life, and that means toward one's own life as a configuration of projects leading to death. To be 'authentic' is just to adopt such an attitude, and being authentic is a precondition to being a subject who is at all a potential addressee of moral discourse. So *Being and Time* describes one of the preconditions of ethics, namely the potential genesis and constitution of the ethical subject.

Given the understandable revulsion which National Socialism generates and Heidegger's close association with this movement, it is natural to look in *Being and Time* for the germs of what would motivate him or at any rate permit him, six years after the publication of the book, to become an active Nazi. Lukács in one of his later works (*Die Zerstörung der Vernunft*) takes the standard vulgar Marxist line that Heidegger's radical rejection of 'reason' meant that a move to the political Right was, eventually, almost inevitable.[13] Logical positivists, to the extent to which they bothered to take a position at all, tended to take a similar tack (although their notion of Reason was more tied to an interpretation of contemporary natural science than Lukács' was). Adorno wrote a small book about the authoritarianism and the aesthetic failings of Heidegger's style (*Jargon der Eigentlichkeit*), and he also pointed out that although there was a lot of discussion of 'time' and history in Heidegger's work, the only real topic is the passage of time in my own life and my relation to that.[14] There was no real history in *Being and Time*, that is, no study of social, political, and economic configurations of the past and how they changed, but it was a highly etiolated 'history of Being', a succession of studies of past *philosophies*. Finally, various people pointed out that Heidegger's persistent obsession with 'origins' could easily mutate into justification for a primitivism that was deeply unattractive. I think it fair to say that this discussion, although by no means useless, remains highly speculative, and often it comes close to making the mistake of looking for something like a single philosophical virus that caused fascism. This would be incorrect on two counts: first, because fascism was not caused by a philosophical mistake, and second, because there is no single philosophical view, as far as I can see, that all fascists held. It is true that National Socialism was overwhelmingly attractive to followers of the eighteenth-century philosopher Immanuel Kant and to devotees of Nietzsche and that it was anathema to Hegelians and logical positivists,[15] but what characteristic is it that Kantians and Nietzscheans have in common that they do not share with Hegelians and positivists?

Although Heidegger later claimed that *Being and Time* was a failure, he never repudiated it but continued to think it a necessary step on the road to philosophy. Or rather, to use one of his own favourite metaphors, he thought that philosophy itself *was* a path or way and that *Being and Time* was a set of steps along that way. The use of this metaphor becomes more extensive, the more sceptical Heidegger becomes about the possibilities of human action to change our relation to Being and the greater emphasis he comes to put on the need for us to wait with pastoral patience until Being 'reveals itself'. The Allies banned Heidegger from publishing and teaching immediately after the end of the war because of his National Socialist engagement, and the first collection of essays he published after the ban was lifted in the early 1950s was a volume entitled *Holzwege*. This does not mean 'forest paths', as the English translation will have it, as if we had here a soulmate of Eichendorff or Wordsworth enjoying himself in the fresh air, but, as Heidegger himself explains, the title refers to the paths in the dense forest which woodcutters cut to get the wood out. Such paths stop when they get to the stand of wood that is being extracted, which is otherwise inaccessible, so such paths usually, although not quite invariably, lead nowhere. In everyday German *auf dem Holzweg sein* means 'be on the *wrong* track, be on the highway to *nowhere*'. Heidegger himself was keen on making his work available in French, and the French title, *Chemins qui ne mènent nulle part,* gives the right tone. I think it would be wrong to identify Heidegger (and in general the philosopher) with the activist woodcutters who create the *Holzweg*. They knew, after all, what they were doing and where they were going: to that stand of trees over there that needs to be cut down. Heidegger is rather the relaxed shepherd wandering in the forest, wondering whether or not the path he happens to be on leads anywhere. If it is a *Holzweg*, the answer is: most likely it goes nowhere.

The more one studies Heidegger, the clearer it becomes that he was in almost equal measure a deft charlatan, an unreformable bully, and a supremely gifted modernist intellectual. He was probably the most influential philosopher of the twentieth century; certainly he was the most written about. This fact is unwelcome to many people because of their understandable revulsion at the very thought of a Nazi philosopher. None of his squirming and evasion and downright mendacity has ever made it in the least plausible to deny that he was a Nazi (albeit one who wished to be one on his own terms alone) and remained one until his death. The fact of his influence is particularly difficult even to see and appreciate in the English-speaking world of philosophy because that is virtually the only place where he has remained a marginal figure. Even if Heidegger had not been a Nazi, his contempt for forms of philosophy depending on appeals to mathematics, natural science, common sense, ordinary language, and all the other mainstays of Anglophone philosophising would have made his message hard to receive. Conceivably this position could change when the collapse of our ecology really begins to bite; there might be a revival of interest in Heidegger's later view, where the emphasis on 'care' as the human essence one finds articulated in *Being and Time* turns into an ethics of 'letting-things-be' (*Gelassenheit*) and taking care of the environment. But it seems more likely that the few survivors of the imminent catastrophe will have more pressing concerns than philosophical texts from the mid-twentieth century.

## Chapter Eleven

# WITTGENSTEIN

Many philosophers find it difficult to admit that they have changed their minds, but what could conceivably be wrong with that? As Keynes is said to have remarked, 'I change my mind when the facts alter; what do you do?' That, of course, is an excuse brought forward in order to give a retrospective explanation for a change of opinion on policy in the rapidly changing world of politics and economics, and, for those purposes, it has some force. It is perfectly reasonable to think that policy decisions ought to be considered dependent on an assessment of details of the real situation in the world; they will change. So there is nothing surprising about the need to change one's views when the facts change, and there need not be anything shameful or embarrassing when a theorist does this. However, the situation for philosophers is not quite parallel and not quite as easy as this. Some Marxists, to be sure, hold that philosophical activity always is, and must always remain, explicitly aware of the fact that it is closely connected with the actual world and so must change with changing circumstances, but they represent a minority. Most philosophers construe what they are doing as primarily related to structures that purportedly do not change over time or are invariants of some kind. There may be some details that are, as it were, sub-philosophical, beneath the notice of philosophy proper, such as questions of casuistry or applied ethics, and hence where making a mistake might be philosophically insignificant (although perhaps practically catastrophic); in addition, one might accept that at some level there were accidental, random, and unpredictable oscillations of political, economic, or social fact or new developments in religion, art, or science that could account for some changes of emphasis. Thus, like anyone else, philosophers, if they even condescend to make sufficiently low-level statements about the world at all rather than dealing only in generalities, may then fail to take account of some unexpected variable or be caught out by some inopportune fact.

In addition, philosophers sometimes change not merely individual beliefs but their 'position' as a whole; that is, they give up substantive theses or modify important structural features of the way they see the world. For some this issue does not arise because they enter the public realm with only a single work; Lucretius did not even do that, publishing nothing during his own lifetime and leaving his unfinished poem to be 'edited', as the ancients would say (i.e., published), after his death. If he had second thoughts, or if there were drafts containing 'other' positions, they never came to anyone's attention, not even, it would seem, in antiquity. The work itself might contain contradictions, 'tensions' between different elements, undeveloped passages that could be taken one or another way, but these do not necessarily represent changes of position.

Some philosophers' work, to be sure, is inherently or even intentionally internally fluid and open-ended: Montaigne and Nietzsche are examples that come to mind, and in some cases, such as in the dialogues of Plato, the presentation is so dialectical and so deeply structured by irony that the question of fixity of belief does not arise in exactly the same form in which it does for some later and more strictly dogmatic philosophers. Recall, nevertheless, how keen even Socrates is to emphasise that his 'hopes' for the future are fixed and firm. Still, by and large philosophers are widely assumed to be required to take relatively firm, considered, and unchanging positions on things. And if they do change that position, this raises the possibility that they have been merely accommodating to a present, either a philosophical present or a political present, that is now past, or that they have failed to be appropriately serious in their work, or—*horribile dictu*—that they have made a mistake in an area that was supposed to be adequately policed. This can be a position of potentially great embarrassment.

A philosopher who has written work that instantiates publicly what seem to be two clearly different positions, can, when confronted by someone who points out the change, take any one of a number of different tacks in trying to explain what has happened. In some cases, of course, the shift in position is itself a publicly documented event, as when Augustine has himself baptised a Christian or when Lukács joins the Party of Communists in Hungary. The very public nature of these acts deprives them of a certain kind of potential for impenetrable mysteriousness. There may be a clear conversion narrative that can be told and is perhaps expected, and there will be precedents and external forms for that. Augustine, an author much admired by Wittgenstein (and also by Heidegger), even devotes an important work, the *Confessions,* to the narrative of his (various) conversions and returns compulsively to the history of his own beliefs in a further work (*Retractationes*), published at the end of his life. The structured narrative of change of positions becomes itself an internal object of explicit philosophical scrutiny, perhaps even a part of the philosophical position eventually taken: no one can be born an Anabaptist; one must have been something else and have been converted, and the conversion story is integral to the position itself. The culmination of this development is perhaps Hegel's *Phenomenology*, where in a sense the narrative of past changes of position, which are also purportedly demonstrated to have been (retrospectively) 'rational', becomes, when correctly conducted, itself the full and completely adequate content of philosophical reflection.

Lukács was not committed, as Hegel was, either to the view that philosophy must be retrospective or to the idea that it is speculative rather than practical. However, his works before his public commitment to Marxism are now all automatically and straightforwardly covered by the etiquette 'pre-Marxist', and they can be discussed *sans états d'âme* under that rubric. Other works (e.g., the 'Blum-Theses', an outline Party programme from the late 1920s which Lukács composed) can be retrospectively characterised as 'appropriate for its time and situation'.[1] Furthermore, 'self-criticism' is a recognised category both in a certain form of organised Marxism and in Christianity, so discussion of previous positions, even errors, fits right in to established patterns, and in fact may be thought to strengthen the standing of the later position.

For philosophers outside the discipline of an even partially institutionalised, public creed, however, the choices are different. The two most influential twentieth-century philosophers, Heidegger and Wittgenstein, both born in the same year (1889), as dissimilar as they are in many respects, are like each other in that the work of each seems to fall into two distinct, historically separated periods, with a caesura in the 1930s. But then lots of things broke down in the 1930s. In each case the work after the break seems to represent not just a change of position but an almost direct reversal of the earlier position. Thus the early Heidegger, as represented by the works written up to the beginning of the 1930s, presents a conceptual analysis of the human situation, or what he sometimes calls a 'philosophical anthropology', seen from the point of view of the human individual (or, rather more exactly, of a biological entity that could potentially become a human individual through attaining the right attitude toward itself and its own death). From a sufficiently great distance (and if one squints sufficiently) *Being and Time* can be seen as a rebellious and deviant contribution to one of the three great established modes of philosophising. The first of these is old-style metaphysics: trying to look at the world by focusing on the objects in it, itemising them, describing what general properties they have, and discovering how they are related to each other. This is philosophy as an extension of science. The second approach emphasises regimentation and starts from some normatively stringent conception of correct thought and correct speech. In one way or another, the world has to be viewed through the lens of these patterns and structures, and, if that is done correctly, it will be seen to conform (except for certain accidental human deviancies, called 'errors', which can relatively easily be corrected with enough intelligence and application). Philosophy is to be continuous with mathematics and logic. The third form of philosophy puts human cognitive access to the world in the centre. Not 'What is there?' or 'What would it be consistent to say?', but 'How could/can/do we know?' For all its savage criticism of some earlier versions of this third mode—and particularly of the assumption that human knowledge is always primarily propositional knowledge and that one can sensibly speak of a human 'cognitive subject' as a distinct and basic entity which is congenital in the work of practitioners of this kind of philosophy—*Being and Time* is still discernibly a successor of works of this third type. Whatever the difficulties, obscurities, and perhaps even incoherences of Heidegger's later, post-1940 work, it does not belong to this third mode of philosophising at all. It distances itself from the conceptual analysis of propositional knowledge altogether and looks to hermetic forms of poetry for a basic orientation; it also seems not to treat individual human experience or any form of human cognitive processing as a privileged framework of any kind but tries to locate all human undertakings increasingly in the much wider context of what Heidegger calls 'the history of Being' and to see Being itself as the basic agent in history.

Wittgenstein's work also falls into two periods. His *Tractatus* (1921),[2] which is an instance of the second rather than the third of the three modes of philosophising I described, presents a view of language as an image or picture of a world of independent facts, all of which can be expressed in a relatively simple propositional form; the meaning of a proposition is its reference to one of these hard-edged 'facts'. Whatever is not such a 'fact'—important as it might nevertheless be—is not a possible object of discussion. Wittgenstein published virtually nothing else during his lifetime, but by the 1930s he had established a cult following among a large group of students and young philosophers. Shortly after his death, in 1951, some of his students published the *Philosophical Investigations,* a text he had been working on for several years. In this text Wittgenstein clearly and explicitly rejects as completely wrong his own earlier view that the essential nature of language is to be a picture or model of a world. He also rejects the metaphysics of facts which, according to the *Tractatus,* constitutes the structure of the world. Instead, he construes language use not as the holding up of a mirror to the world but as a (collection of different) form(s) of social action. It is not impossible for us to 'represent' the world, to try to give a picture of it, but that function is a special and peculiar one which requires certain highly distinctive conditions to be satisfied for it to be possible; the descriptive proposition is not the paradigm of linguistic meaning. Meaning is neither a purely formal or logical property of propositions, nor is it some kind of associated psychological phenomenon that has its locus in the privacy of the individual's mind. Meaning depends on and can only be understood by reference to a set of complicated social practices that are much more than 'merely' linguistic. So far, so Hegelian, one might think, but this aspect of the Hegelian philosophy had been more or less completely lost after 1848 (except among some Marxists). So the fact is that Wittgenstein is to some extent reinventing the wheel, but that is not an argument either for or against the correctness of this view.

The *Tractatus* was in intention a highly conventional, purportedly apodictic philosophical treatise. In its preface Wittgenstein claimed that the truth of the statements which the book contained was 'unantastbar und definitiv' ('untouchable and definitive'). In the preface to the *Philosophical Investigations* he then asserts with deeply refreshing honesty that the position he proposed in the previous work was wrong.

How, though, was the *Tractatus* wrong? The work is intended to show that 'anything that can be said at all, can be said clearly'. The *Philosophical Investigations,* however, are an investigation of the unbounded multiplicity of ways in which one can say things that cannot be said 'clearly'. The idea of 'clarity' with which the *Tractatus* operated turns out to be itself completely confused: at the same time too rigid and too indeterminate. The criticism of certain widespread conceptions of 'clarity' and of some associated notions ('determinateness', 'precision' [§88], 'unambiguousness') is one of the most interesting and powerful parts of the later book, which argues on a wide front against a whole range of other prejudices about the necessary univocity and determinateness of language.

Certain forms of clarity, as it had customarily been conceived by philosophers, cannot be necessary because they are not possible. No 'picture' of the world ever could be absolutely clear and sharp (§§71–88), at any rate not in the way philosophers have construed sharpness and clarity. We can only ever hope to 'represent' the world in ways that are shot through with ambiguity and indeterminacy. Habitual social behaviour of a kind that is inherently variable and inherently unpredictable is all that gives even the most austerely referential statements any kind of connection to reality.

The Renaissance discovered the infinite ambiguity of language, the fact that any statement can be interpreted in a variety of different ways. The third book of Rabelais illustrates this in an extreme way, when it describes how Panurge tried to get advice about a practical problem: Should he marry or not? He consults all the authorities he can find but is shown to be sufficiently quick-witted and clever to turn any advice he receives which does not conform to his antecedent desires into something that is grist for his mill. When the experts in question (e.g., the dead poet Vergil, consulted via the *sortes vergilianae* [a sort of medieval *I-Ging*], the Sybil, and others) tell him in no uncertain terms that his wife will beat him, rob him, and cuckold him, Panurge develops increasingly complex interpretations of the 'meaning' of what the experts say and interprets their advice as meaning she will be a careful, loving, faithful, and honest wife.[3] After the advent of Christianity this indeterminateness of meaning becomes a staple of fairy tales. No one can *ever* couch a wish with such precision as to prevent the Devil from fully granting it as literally formulated and requested but in such a way as essentially to thwart it.[4] No matter how many further qualifications and explanations are added, there is still always room for more than one reading, and the process of adding has no natural end and can run on indefinitely. As epicycles of interpretation become more elaborate, perhaps they become less plausible; this may be correct, but then meaning would come to depend on the 'plausibility' of a certain reading or interpretation. 'Plausibility', however, was thought to belong to a totally different domain of discourse from the strict analysis of cognitive meaning. It was a matter for rhetoric rather than for semantics; at least that was the view most philosophers took. So although the 'meaning' of 'The cat is on the mat', 'This solution has turned blue' or 'It is raining' *seems* to be so simple that the statement itself wears its meaning on its sleeve, not requiring any further interpretation, that would not be the case. The basic paradigm and also the point of departure for further thinking about meaning, about *all* meaning, is the situation of Panurge confronted with a verse from Vergil which he must 'interpret', a situation in which ('obviously', one would be tempted to say) a number of different interpretations are perfectly possible and no one interpretation is absolutely mandated with unmistakable clarity by 'the text itself'.

Hobbes recognised the problem here, that of the openness and potential indeterminacy of all linguistic meaning and the potential variability of the ways in which humans might interpret any sign. His solution was the appeal to the power of the sovereign, who can make words mean what he wants by enforcing a certain reading of them. He enforces his own reading by acting: if you 'interpret' a law in your own way and act on this, he has the power really to make you regret it. Hobbes' view does put the correct emphasis on conformity in *action*. If the sovereign makes a law that anyone walking on the grass outside the castle will be subject to capital punishment, does this leave open the possibility that 'capital punishment' here means simply 'major, important, significant punishment' rather than, say 'the death penalty'? Or does it mean specifically decapitation (rather than hanging, impalement, smothering in thick blankets, lethal injection, lapidation, electrocution)? Hobbes holds that the sovereign could prevent any interpretation but one from establishing itself by himself acting in a certain way. If he wished it to be clear that 'capital punishment' meant specifically 'decapitation' (rather than merely any old form of execution), then he could have the head of any executioner removed who hanged the criminal rather than decapitating him or her. Now, of course, sovereigns will not generally do this job themselves but will have someone else, such as another executioner, do it for them. How exactly does the sovereign instruct these other executioners in the precise nature of their duties? Do they need further instruction through coercive punishment? There are presumably also an indefinite number of further potential executioners at the sovereign's disposal, and they are, *ex hypothesi,* completely overawing, but what use are they in a concrete case if the sovereign cannot make his or her wishes precisely clear? 'Brexit means Brexit', as we have all recently seen, is a foolish thing to say if one is genuinely trying to make any progress at all in understanding or indeed trying to explain something, although it can have some effect as a rhetorical club to brandish in order to rally support among the faithful or to belabour the heads of opponents.

At a certain point 'explanation' (and its enforcement with club or scimitar) must stop. This will be at the point at which people simply respond or react with what they take to be spontaneous or routinized or unreflective forms of behaviour; that is, they react, as we say, *without thinking.* These spontaneous forms of behaviour are taken for granted, not explained or even discussed (in the given context); they are not created ex nihilo by the sovereign, but presupposed and taken for granted as 'natural' and not requiring, or perhaps even admitting, discursive comment. These routines can and do change. Anyone who has moved from a country where traffic moves on the right of the road, such as France, to one in which it moves on the left, such as Japan (or vice versa), is familiar with the surprising number of 'natural' reactions that one was not even aware of exhibiting—such as automatically looking to the left (or right) before crossing a street—and that need to be adjusted to the new environment. Of course, one gradually changes them once one has even become aware of them, and even changes them so much that if a French driver returns to Continental Europe after living for a decade in Japan, it may take a day or so to reestablish the old habits. This does not mean that under particular circumstances, particular forms of human reaction might not be explicitly thematised and examined, and even subjected to new norms and changed, but this will always be a case of focusing on a very specific reaction against the background of a massive stock of other reactions that are taken so much for granted they are effectively invisible.

What gives us the illusion of fixity is that most thought and most language use is not the formulation of absolutely clear propositions about hard facts but routine, regular participation in a variety of what the later Wittgenstein calls 'language games'. Suppose a first builder is passing out stores to a second builder, and there are two kinds of objects in the yard: rough-hewn wooden planks made of pine and large round polished pieces of granite. If the second builder shouts out 'Timber', he is being completely clear: he does not want the other to give him one of the large round stones but one of the wooden planks. If he says 'Stone', he wants a piece of the granite. 'Timber' does not formulate or assert a proposition or have a truth-value. It is not even a full sentence with subject-predicate form. However, it is clear enough, and as precise and unambiguous as needed. To say that this speech-event is 'clear' means that both of the builders can use it effectively to help them to do what they need to do. The set of possible human uses, needs, and actions is completely open-ended—there are virtually no determinate limits to it—and thus there are no given determinate limits to what is, or could be, 'clear'. That 'Timber' is 'clear' is the case because of the language game they are playing. If they had short wooden planks (for window frames) and long wooden planks (for floors) in their store, *and* if each of these was used for a different relevant purpose, so that the second builder might reasonably want one rather than the other, then 'Timber' would no longer be clear and specific. Does he want short planks or long planks?

Language is essentially action, an activity of speaking and part of the way people get things done. From the fact that saying 'Timber' is not asserting a proposition that has truth-value, it does not follow that it cannot be evaluated in various ways. It can, for example, be said to be unwise (to mark this boundary the builder needs large stones rather than wooden planks because planks would soon rot in the rain and snow) or immoral ( this storehouse actually belongs to someone else, and they are clearing it out illegally) or even just mistaken (he meant to say 'Stone' but misspoke himself). In making all these judgements I am, of course, adopting a position *outside* that of the language game they are playing (but, if Wittgenstein is correct, *inside* one or another other, more extensive language game). There can be games that consist in evaluating other games: two football teams compete, perhaps initially without any umpires, but in the more usual case there are umpires and overarching sporting organisations that comment on the play between the two teams and evaluate it; in certain cases they may even legislate for it and regulate it. Whether one counts these governing bodies as 'part of' the original game, as if the umpires were themselves participants, or as members of a separate corporation playing a separate game (the game of regulating football) is a question that has no answer. The reason is that language games themselves, like virtually everything else, have no absolutely clear, precise, or fixed boundaries. We may try to impose those, but that is doing something to the world, not discovering a boundary that was already there. Whether or not the interaction takes place correctly is a sociological fact; that is, it is something that in the first instance the participants in the action and then the wider community will determine according to whatever evaluative processes they decide to use. There is no way to specify either what the limits of that wider community are or what they will decide to allow or disallow.

If human life in society is (among other things) a matter of participating in various language games, and if some of these games may have the observation and regulation of other games as their content and goal, the question immediately arises about the relations of the various language games in a society. Platonically inclined philosophers will look for the possibility of organising these in a hierarchy under a single super–language game (which may be, say, 'logic' or 'philosophy' or, for some older-style theorists, 'theology'), but this seems precisely what Wittgenstein wants to deny. He thinks this is impossible and in any case would be inadvisable because it would impose fixity where flexibility is a virtue. To some extent he seems to claim that all language games are embedded in something he calls 'our form of life', but he is completely unclear about what this is. It seems most likely that a form of life consists of a certain number of natural and social features that are the preconditions for language games. One is tempted to say 'If our form of life is a precondition for language games, there must be limits to it, and therefore we must be able to study them and learn about the limits of possible language games', but there is no evidence that Wittgenstein would have accepted this. 'Form of life', too, seems to be characterised by a highly fruitful indeterminacy. Who is the 'we' presupposed in speaking of 'our'? Which 'we', under what circumstances? What does 'could' in 'could recognise as a part of our form of life' mean? A form of life in any case is not itself a separate and distinct object of study, or if it is, it is an indirect and highly empirical study, and it is certainly not possible to deduce anything significant from purported knowledge of our form of life about how our language games must be constituted. And whatever a form of life turns out to be, the whole point of introducing it is to *deny* the existence of a super–language game. A form of life, whatever it is, is certainly not itself a language game.

It is perfectly natural for us, after 2,000 years of post-Platonic indoctrination, to assume that every word we use has a meaning and that this meaning is like a set of invisible railway tracks extending into the future which guides how the word can be used (§218). But there are no such railway tracks; there are only social habits and social decisions. If they change—and they can change without any difficulty and need no one's warrant to do so—the meaning changes. This does not mean that every change is completely irrational or unmotivated, but the reasons may well be social or psychological and not, as it were, strictly cognitive, and they are certainly not necessarily connected to some inherent meaning the word has by itself. Even when the reasons are in some sense cognitive, it does not seem that the inherent meaning of some word determines future usage. We have good reasons to deny that a whale is a fish; one might even say these were good cognitive reasons in that they were connected with what our biology tells us is most important. But the decision to call a whale a fish, or to deny that it is a fish, is not a merely semantic decision, not one mandated by the 'very meaning' of the terms used. It would also be wrong to think this means that the meaning of our words is *now* completely fixed and clear but *could* change. That meanings change is true, but trivial. Of course we *could* begin to use the word 'rabbit' to refer to a certain species of bird, but so what? The point seems rather to be this: if we did begin to use a certain word differently or in a differently constituted language game, this would retrospectively show that the meaning never was as clear as we thought it was. 'Timber' in its appropriate context is clear enough, but, even then, how do we know that it refers to the material 'wood' rather than to the shape of a plank (rather than the round shape of the stone), or to 'rough-hewn thing' rather than 'polished thing'? If suddenly we add to our stock of rough pine planks a quantity of well-planed oak planks, there is nothing in the antecedent usage which requires us to call the oak planks 'Timber' (because they are made of wood) rather than 'Stone' (because they are 'polished' rather than rough-hewn). There is *no fact* of meaning apart from social usage, and even such usage is incapable of giving the distinctness, precision, and lack of ambiguity we all crave and which philosophers in the past purported to analyse. The implications of this, Wittgenstein realised, were tremendous. For one thing, if there is no final precision and clarity, there can be no final 'justification' for actions or beliefs. If I don't know what a belief really means in the final analysis, any justification of it must be local, relative, and deeply praxis-dependent.

If words don't have inherent sharp and clear definition, and if the appearance of sharpness is no more than an appearance, then to the extent to which clarity, precision, and determinateness exist (which is less than we assume), they are always artefacts brought into being by highly structured social institutions (dictionaries, law courts, school systems), and these institutions and practices which exert a palpable constrictive force on language users and their actions are fragile and variable and could never in principle engender absolute precision. Such institutions in turn can exist only if there are lots of shared and tacitly accepted, although in principle variable, forms of unreflective human response. Whether or not, then, the world is composed of hard, sharply defined 'propositions', we couldn't ever formulate them in a way that was absolutely unambiguous because it will always depend on a relation of human reactions which may change in unpredictable ways, and we cannot theoretically factor these out because they (if we consider all of them at the same time) are necessarily beyond formulation. Not that any *one* by itself could not be tied down, but they form an unsurveyable and indefinitely extended mass that cannot be grasped at one go.

It is not insignificant that the *Tractatus* was a series of numbered and subnumbered propositions, according to a complicated system that purportedly indicated the relative 'logical weight' of each one. This external structuration modelled on that of a mathematics textbook seemed appropriate for the view of the world that was presented in the book: a unified world of facts expressed in a highly formalised language. There is to be a *single* system. *Philosophical Investigations,* on the other hand, is closer in literary form to Montaigne or to Nietzsche in that it is composed of a series of texts of various kinds, including short essays that stand by themselves, short discussions that seem to represent a 'continuation' of the discussions being conducted in the sections around them, small interludes of apparent *monologue intérieur,* quasi-dramatic encounters between (imaginary) interlocutors who raise objections, lists, aphorisms, discussions of diagrams or figures, and more. Most of the components of the *Philosophical Investigations* are, at under two pages each, generally significantly shorter than essays by Montaigne, although longer than the 'aphorism' which was an established literary genre in German in the eighteenth, nineteenth and early twentieth centuries. Wittgenstein calls them 'remarks' (*Bemerkungen*) and says they represent his characteristic way of thinking.

We might wonder whether this structure, so different from the obsessively organised *Tractatus,* was intended to reflect the new flexibility and freedom of Wittgenstein's views about philosophy as analysing the variety of human ways of sense-making and understanding meaning. Just as there can be an open and changing set of different language games with no antecedently fixed limit (§23), so the form which philosophic reflection takes can be more open and fluid and need not be some fixed propositional form. However, as Wittgenstein himself makes clear in the preface, this fluidity and fragmentariness turn out not to have been intentional and part of a conscious programme. He states that he continued to want to produce a finished book as a unitary structure of the conventional sort. He thinks, that is, that his inability to transform his texts into a 'whole where one thought flows from another' was a failure rather than a discovery of a different way of thinking about things and viewing the world, or 'success' in a different enterprise. He floats the idea that the disparate nature of the 'remarks' that make up the book might be connected not just with what he was able to accomplish but with the nature of the project itself ('dies hing mit der Natur der Untersuchung selbst zusammen': 'Vorwort'), but rather than pursuing that thought in any way, he immediately lets it drop and falls back into what looks like the more conventional view.

In the *Philosophical Investigations* Wittgenstein presents at least two slightly different, although perhaps not incompatible conceptions of the task of philosophy. The first is that philosophy is a voyage through a conceptual domain, a 'domain of thoughts' (*Gedankengebiet*), during which the philosopher makes a number of different sketches of the landscape, which he then modifies, revises, cuts back, and puts together to form an image/picture (*Bild*) of this landscape. This makes it seem as if Wittgenstein thought that 'the landscape' was already out there, just waiting to be criss-crossed by an explorer eager to map it out. Presumably, though, he does not mean that all the various landscape sketches, the accounts of different language games which the book contains, are or even could be seamlessly integrated into a single unified picture, because he then writes that the book is 'really just an album'. An album, however, is not in general something with unified representational content but rather is more like a scrapbook held together by one or more external purposes. I might have put together an 'album' of the year I lived in Berlin, with photos, but also with maps, sketches, newspaper clippings, concert programmes, even tickets, S-Bahn timetables, old DDR transit visas, and (if I had been that way inclined), pressed flowers, bits of the hair of favourite people, menus, the labels from bottles of wine, fingerprints of colleagues who seemed suspicious, and specimens of their handwriting. Each of these things has a different function, and they are held together only by the complete contingency that they caught my attention and appealed to one of my predilections (or hatreds) at a certain time in a certain place. In this sense the album may give a 'picture or image' of life in West Berlin in 1982–1983, but it is not at all like the unitary picture of the world as a whole (or of some part of that world) which many philosophers tried to produce.

A second conception of philosophy one finds in the *Philosophical Investigations* replaces the bearded cosmic mapmaker or pimply adolescent computer modeller with the idea of the philosopher as engaged in a skilled activity, in particular as 'therapist'. 'Philosophical' problems arise when language takes a day off to get drunk (*wenn die Sprache feiert*). In everyday life we distinguish solids, liquids, and gases, and despite some marginal phenomena (such as marmalade), we don't usually have much difficulty making this distinction. If I can pick it up with my fingers, it is a solid; if I need a glass or cup, it is a liquid; if I smell it, it is a gas. If someone were to ask whether an electron is a solid, a liquid, or a gas, this would be a typical 'philosophical' question—that is, one in which I am using language ('liquid', etc.) in a context which is very different from that of the language game in which it 'naturally' functions. Thinking too long or too hard about this 'question' might give me a mental cramp. The philosophical therapist can perhaps treat that cramp by explaining that I have abstracted a certain form of words (solid, liquid, gas) from the location in which it makes good sense: the study of things I can touch, scoop up, sniff out. I make a mistake by trying to impose the use of that same form of words in a completely different context, say, of a laboratory with Bunsen burners, electrical coils, measuring devices of various kinds, mechanical hands to reach into chambers where the temperature is far below zero, and with theorists standing at blackboards covered with equations. It is the shift from one language game to another that makes the question about how to classify an electron unanswerable (and generates the mental cramp). Once you understand where the terms used to formulate the question really belong, you see that they have no application in the purported 'philosophical' examples, and the question or problem disappears. The philosopher as therapist causes these problems to dissolve by pointing out their origin in a misapplication of terms in a context that is inappropriate for them. He or she does this on a case-by-case basis; there would be no other way, given the nature of the difficulties he or she is trying to treat. Each case may be slightly different. The 'album' which Wittgenstein presents may be a kind of dossier of previous cures: perhaps one can learn from studying it, but that learning does not consist in generalising because each case in the album is different.

So on this second view about philosophy, the goal is not to get an 'image' (*Bild*) of the landscape but to learn to get around in (a variety of) landscapes. The model of a 'solution' is (§§153ff.) '*Jetzt weiß ich weiter*'—Now I know how to go on—which, despite the use of the apparently cognitivist term 'know', actually means not that I have a theory but merely that I can confidently and successfully go on; I know how-to-do it. To do this might require any number of things, some of them being connected with having the right kind of theory but others being of a different status altogether, such as learning to attend to certain features of the world. Being musical does not mean knowing which keys have three flats, but is chiefly a question of being able to hear when the singer is flat, the rhythm is off, and the players are not quite together, and perhaps being able to sing on key and in time oneself, and that is a question of complicated forms of attention, discrimination, and cultivated talent, not of conceptual mastery of a theory.

This does raise the question whether it is really correct that all philosophical questions are questions about the misuse of language. In two of his more memorable phrases Wittgenstein writes, 'Die Philosophie ist ein Kampf gegen die Verhexung unseres Verstandes durch die Mittel der Sprache verhext' [Philosophy is a struggle against the bewitchment of our understanding by the instruments of language' (§109)] and 'Was ist Dein Ziel in der Philosophie? Der Fliege den Ausweg aus dem Fliegenglas zeigen' [What is your goal in philosophy? To show the fly the way out of the fly-bottle' (§309)]. Does this attribute to language an independence or autonomy from society that Wittgenstein himself in other places is at pains to deny? To be sure, perhaps we are bewitched by language, but 'language' is not necessarily a locus of some *independent* confusion. Will *all* (really, *all*) be well if we get our language correctly policed? Will even all-that-philosophers-can-treat be well? Is Lukács wrong to think there could be some problems that were better understood not as linguistic misapprehensions but as structural difficulties or contradictions in our social practices, including our language games, themselves? If there were such, would one be able to get out of the bewitchment by means of linguistic therapy alone?

Wittgenstein's later way of trying to write philosophy attaches it to and focuses it on a kind of dismal everydayness. Contrary to Plato, everyday life is cognitively confusing, a dark cave from which we try to escape to attain the light, but that we can rise through thought or theoretical activity to a better, superhuman state. It is also not the case, say, that rural simplicity was healthy and regenerative: the small Austrian village where Wittgenstein worked as a teacher was a breeding ground of exquisite sadism, as he soon realised and admitted. Nor did 'nature' provide access to an organic order which was destroyed by abstraction and would reemerge if those abstractions were undone. Everyday speech and life were not particularly wholesome. There is nothing redemptive or even salubrious about being in the builders' yard shouting for timber. Trying to escape from it, though, through traditional philosophical activity will only add to our own confusion.

Earlier I mentioned the strange phenomenon that Wittgenstein seems to think there is a 'conceptual territory' that is simply given and can be criss-crossed and explored without considering the possibility that it could be changed, internally restructured, expanded, or constricted. At one point Wittgenstein makes the remark about his friend and colleague Frank Ramsey that Ramsey is a 'bourgeois thinker'.[5] This, I think, means that Ramsey thought all conceptual space was like that. But in saying this, Wittgenstein is clearly intending to distinguish his own attitude from that of Ramsey. Wittgenstein was not a bourgeois but a religious thinker, or rather one kind of religious thinker. There was only the order there was—to that extent the bourgeois thinkers were right—and philosophy left everything as it is. But there was another side to reality, which was mysterious, transcendental, 'beyond' our world; this 'other side' was not part of the order, but still it was there. God was not part of the world but was universally present, although in no way visible. The question, then, is whether 'bourgeois' and 'religious' are the only possibilities. Is it really out of the question to think that a philosopher might be an inventor or a constructor of something new, perhaps a conceptual inventor like Hobbes ('the state') or the inventor of a new language (as Heidegger sometimes aspired to be)? The dichotomy 'bourgeois/religious' would also exclude thinking of the philosopher as revolutionary (Lukács) or as a utopian speculator (Plato).

To return to the issue with which this chapter began, it is striking that the basic change in philosophical orientation between the *Tractatus* and the *Philosophical Investigations* was not accompanied by any other important change in Wittgenstein's form of life. He was a highly sensitive and aesthetically gifted man with wide cultural interests, but the complete and radical transformation of his philosophical position did not cause him to change his mind about music, architecture, ethics, literature, politics, or, for that matter, anything else. He also had continuing religious and spiritual interests, although not of a denominational kind, but his attitude toward his own life, or his own spiritual concerns, does not seem in any way to have changed. Partly this is just the detachment which is a result of construing 'philosophy' as a relatively self-contained technical subject. In Wittgenstein's own terms (in his early *Tractatus*), 'Ethics and aesthetics are transcendent' (6.421)—there is nothing you can say about them. The later view in the *Philosophical Investigations* maintains that philosophy 'leaves everything as it is' (§124).

This may be one of the reasons it was relatively easy for Wittgenstein to change his mind and admit that he had been wrong. Being wrong in matters of philosophy doesn't really change anything in

271

ethics, politics, or matters of the spirit. If Augustine was wrong, he would, after death, find himself down in hell with the Donatists; being on the wrong side for Lukács wouldn't just mean ending up in the gulag but would entail losing his connection, via the Party, to any form of meaning at all. Could Nietzsche have lived his life as a satisfied, if not exactly 'happy' *rentier* if he had believed he had a duty to obey the commands of his Creator, as expressed in Scripture? In contrast, for Wittgenstein philosophy has become an entirely academic affair. Or, in fact, even less than that, if Max Weber is right and the 'proper' academic is someone who thinks 'the salvation of his soul depends on making *this* conjecture in *this* place of a corrupt manuscript, or on the correctness of *this* equation as a solution to *this* problem'.[6] Wittgenstein was concerned with the salvation of his soul; he had a deep cultural commitment to the continuance of the eighteenth- and nineteenth-century Viennese musical tradition, and he had lots of interesting things to say about these topics, but, as far as one can tell, he did not think they had anything to do with his philosophical work. Even in the preface to the *Tractatus* he writes, 'We see that [the problems of philosophy] . . . are solved in this work but that just shows how little the solution of those problems signifies. [*Vorwort*]'. Perhaps this is a sign that he has taken the notion of a '(philosophical) problem' too narrowly, as he certainly has in the early work, but even later he never seems to give up this view.

One can, of course, turn this around and wonder whether the thick patina of depression that hangs over Wittgenstein's work is not itself partly an expression of the loss he suffered when he came to the opinion that philosophy has no alternative but to become just an academic subject, and one of even less significance than physics or philology.

This perhaps underestimates a certain existentialist strand that can also be found in Wittgenstein's work. Philosophy can become a kind of life obsession, and then one can make the salvation of one's soul depend on getting the philosophically 'correct' answer, or at least avoiding clear philosophical error. For certain people, having this obsession may not even be a 'choice' in any interesting sense, but a fate. 'Philosophy' in this sense would seem to lose its claim to universal human relevance.

*Chapter Twelve*

# ADORNO

The world inhabited by post-Hegelian philosophers is full of reversals, inversions, and metatheses (of various kinds). Hegel says of philosophy itself that it is 'common sense turned upside down' and that the French Revolution exhibited the spectacle of a world trying to walk on its own head—trying to organise politics and society according to reason, not the conjunction of mere accident and might.[1] Marx, in turn, says of Hegel's dialectic that it is illuminating, but it is standing on its head and needs to be put back on its feet right side up.[2] One of the weirder chapters of the *Phenomenology* concerns a world view in which people are unclear as to what is positive and what is negative, what is a force and what is the thing propelled along by that force.[3] Loss of control can lead to vertigo and madness. We first encounter Büchner's deranged poet Lenz walking through the mountains in the rain and mist: 'He had not a care in the world; he was just sorry he could not walk on his head.'[4] However, for those on earth who try to walk on their heads, the heavens are an abyss under their feet.[5] Whichever way was 'right side up' by

274

the 1940s, there was a politically established social formation that presented itself, correctly or not, as the polar opposite of Hegel's 'bourgeois' state: the Soviet Union. Heidegger wrote, with what Adorno would have taken to be characteristic peasant crudeness, that 'metaphysically speaking', the United States and the Soviet Union were 'the same thing'.[6] And although Adorno detested Heidegger and everything he stood for politically, socially, and philosophically, he did not, finally, completely disagree with him about this, although, of course, his self-respect required him to phrase his views in a more subtle and sophisticated way. Adorno could even appeal to an established Hegelian figure: the simple reversal of one structure into its mirror image was *not* a model of advanced human progress. Putting the Bolsheviks into the Winter Palace and the Romanovs against the wall was not necessarily much better than the reverse. Adorno was never at all attracted by Soviet-style socialism and does not ever seem to have felt the need to demonstrate this publicly in any very detailed way.

Heidegger, of course, had no direct experience of life either in the United States or in the Soviet Union, so his views are to that extent based on second-hand reports and his own theoretical constructions. With Adorno the situation was different. In Germany he had been classified, according to the Nürnberg Racial Laws, as a 'half-Jew' because his father came from a family that had in the nineteenth century been Jewish, but his mother was a Catholic from a Corsican emigrant family in Frankfurt, and Adorno himself had been baptised, brought up, and even confirmed as a Roman Catholic. However, his marriage to a 'full Jew' automatically caused him to be himself reclassified as a 'full Jew', which made it impossible for him even to consider staying in Germany. In the late 1930s he and his wife emigrated to the United States. *Minima Moralia* is the response to the fundamental shock that Adorno received, the trauma from which he never really recovered: the direct encounter with the American way of life. It became increasingly clear that his emigration had saved him from certain death, but it had landed him in an infernal region of a different kind which he would not have been able to imagine had he not seen it for himself. War, massacre, political and economic collapse, even genocide was, after all, the stuff of history—Adorno knew this—but the utter spiritlessness of life in the New World and the complete absence there of anything he could recognize as 'culture' was something else, and he became keen not to let his great and justifiable relief about his escape from Hitler dull his aesthetic, moral, and intellectual sensibilities or blind him to the horrors of life in southern California. Heidegger and Adorno were not the only two strange bedfellows when it came to their judgements about the United States. Bertolt Brecht, also on the run from the Nazis, held Adorno personally, intellectually, and politically in a kind of amused contempt, but when he, too, found himself washed up on the shores of the Pacific, the one thing on which they did agree was their opinion of their place of exile:

*Nachdenkend, wie ich höre, über die Hölle*
*Fand mein Bruder Shelley, sie sei ein Ort*
*Gleichend ungefähr der Stadt London. Ich*
*Der ich nicht in London lebe, sondern in Los Angeles*
*Finde, nachdenken über die Hölle, sie muß*
*Noch mehr Los Angeles gleichen.*[7]

Thinking about hell, I'm told, my brother Shelley, decided
that it was a place rather like the city of London. I,
who don't live in London but in Los Angeles, have decided,
when I think about hell, that it has a greater resemblance to Los
    Angeles.

Brecht had been to some extent imaginatively prepared for what he encountered, in that 'America' had played some role in his imaginative life before his arrival there,[8] but that was not true of Adorno. *Minima Moralia* is a kind of prose version of Brecht's poem, motivated by initial disbelief, then by the same shock and horror: How could a human population have turned what might have been a moderately attractive natural environment into such an abomination and built a society so wholly devoted to deceit, corruption, and human self-degradation, a huge 'mortuary' of the human spirit?

*Minima Moralia* is the beginning of Adorno's attempt to keep equidistant from both behemoths, Hollywood and Magnitogorsk, and to try to resist their respective subtle or clumsy embraces in the only way he felt he could, by engaging in social criticism. Since he was not living in Magnitogorsk and had never even visited the Soviet Union, direct critical analysis of Soviet society of the kind he could give of American society, based on immediate experience, was not possible.

The appeal to immediate, individual, subjective experience might seem slightly unusual in a philosopher who, like Hegel and Marx, puts so much emphasis on institutions, large-scale structures, and historical developments. The reason is, partly, I think, that Adorno sees that simply reversing Hegel seems to have done little good in the medium term. Whatever increases in freedom and release of cultural energies there might have been in the Soviet Union in the 1920s, and Adorno was in fact never at all impressed by these, they had certainly disappeared by the late 1930s. So perhaps the answer was not standing Hegel upside down but turning him inside out? Hegel's *Phenomenology* is a kind of *Bildungsweg*, describing a path by which an individual can, as it were, move forward by looking back. By understanding my (and that means also 'our') past, and fully and consciously assimilating it, I move ever closer to being able to 'embrace' it (and 'our' present) warmly, be 'reconciled' to it. Becoming more 'me' means being reconciled increasingly to 'us' and affirming the rationality of our institutional life. To be sure, from another point of view the *Bildungsweg* is a perpetual *Leidensweg,* a Way of the Cross, each stage of which is a process of bitter disappointment: Stoicism doesn't work; scepticism doesn't work; the Enlightenment doesn't work; the French Revolution ends in the Terror. Anyone who reads Hegel's *Rechtsphilosophie* learns that the generation of a dishonoured, impoverished class—what Marx will call the 'proletariat'—is a great 'unsolved problem' of modern times.[9] One can think of Adorno as objecting that he has followed the whole of Hegel's argument but missed the last step: that rational comprehension of universal disappointment implies warm affirmation of everything (or, perhaps of 'everything as depicted in Hegel's System').[10] Hegel is clear about this: he claims that his System has exhaustively developed and deployed *all* forms of rationality and meaningfulness. What is more, he has shown that each one of us— Adorno, Carnap, Heidegger, Trotsky, Pétain (and you and I)—has been made possible as the rational individual we each (more or less) are through the process he sketches in *Phenomenology* and that speculation about some 'other' possible paths through history are just so much codswallop—infantile projections of one sort or another with no cognitive standing. *If* that is the case, Hegel claims, and you run through the path to Absolute Knowledge correctly, you will see that you can have no rational grounds for rejecting the whole process. The only alternative to embracing and affirming the whole thing (including oneself as one of the results of the process) is radical scepticism.[11] Of course, he admits, you can step out of the realm of rationality altogether, sit down by yourself in sceptical silence, and not say anything, and in that case you become an irrelevancy. But 'not saying anything' was never an option for the voluble Adorno. If systematic rationality means affirming Treblinka, the gulag, or Beverly Hills, then so much the worse for systematic rationality.

The ideal Hegelian individuals at the end of their *Bildungsprozeß* find all contradictions resolved in affirming themselves, their/our history and our present. But what if there is a contradiction, which the System itself cannot resolve? What if, having the past I have, I find I *cannot* make the required step to affirmation? Hegel would have had to claim that this was a sign that one had not understood the System. But suppose one gives every indication of having understood, and furthermore never stops talking in a way that clearly instantiates the kind of rationality a Hegelian would have to recognise, and yet does this in such a way as systematically to read what Hegel sees as an elevation of the individual to universality as oppression of the individual by the universal? Humans can bite the hand that feeds them; there is nothing irrational about that, although it may be unattractive. I can acknowledge that what, in one way, was a great benefit or cultural achievement was, at the same time, based on the unbridled oppression of others (and also required of all of us significant amounts of self-oppression). All who now live in Britain—not to mention the United States—are still benefitting from the horrors of the Atlantic slave trade. It produced profits that helped build the cities, hospitals, concert halls, libraries which we all enjoy, and thus it is part of what made us who we are. Understanding that in no way disbars me from rejecting the slave trade. Furthermore, to live effectively in a society that profited from the slave trade also required increased forms of self-oppression even from the white, free population, who would be subject to various restrictions on their ability to act spontaneously; this oppression was nothing compared with what was inflicted on the slaves, but it was not nonexistent. In fairness, Hegel himself did not think the fact that we are who we are because of past slavery in any way pre-cluded us from rejecting the slave trade absolutely and practically combating it *in the present*. I could reject it effectively in the present because it belonged to a past which we had historically overcome in the process of becoming who we (now) are. But what if we think we were mistaken to think that we had fully overcome this past, or if it arises again to haunt us?

What Adorno does is, roughly, to construe *himself* as the culmi-nation of the *Bildungsweg* of Western culture. Rather than allowing himself to be talked out of his reactions, perceptions, and 'subjec-tive experiences' by the Hegelian who tries to denigrate and relativize them by putting them in the context of the Big Picture of Systematic Rationality, Adorno stands by them and develops them (rationally), thereby, he hopes, throwing doubt on the universality of Hegel's final affirmative stance toward the world. This turned Hegel inside out because it accepted that his holistic analysis of the larger facts of our world—the social institutions, legal systems, economic order, religious formations—*was* appropriate for understanding them. However, rather than affirming that individual reactions, desires, and perceptions were to be subsumed under or 'sublated' in a dialectical understanding of these larger structures, it was denied that this larger understanding in any way caused me to revise or relativize my nega-tive reactions to (oppressive) institutions or to make my peace with these institutions. *Minima Moralia* illustrates the way in which the reactions of highly educated individuals do not conform, as Hegel would have to argue they would, to the structural demands made by present social institutions and do not incline them to embrace these institutions. In his later work *Negative Dialektik* Adorno goes further and writes a whole treatise on the *non*identity of particular and concept.

To show that my immediate experience gives the lie to the claim that I should be reconciled with my social world is *not* to claim that my immediate perceptions and reactions, or indeed any individual's, are pure, absolute, or in any sense stand independently of the social context in which they are generated. Of course, if you wish to grasp life in its immediacy, you need to look at the experience of the individual in the context of the 'external powers' that influence and structure it. Society (and history) constitute, if one wishes to speak in that way, the conditions of possibility of the experience which any individual has. Seeing the conditions that are necessary for my reactions, however, does not invalidate them but is the only thing that will really permit me to understand them and to cultivate and deploy them correctly.

There does at first glance seem to be something slightly repellent about Adorno's stance, as the representative of the highest aspirations and vocation of spirit *in partibus infidelium*. Both Brecht and Lukács, for their own differing reasons, thought that Adorno was a deeply unserious character and philosopher. Lukács, whose father was a very wealthy Budapest banker and who therefore came from a background as privileged as Adorno's own, spent the war in extreme poverty (and great political danger) as a foreign Communist in Moscow. He once described Adorno as residing in the five-star Grand Hotel Abyss, enjoying the luxury of a comfortable seat on the balcony, where the view of the poor starving outside was just one more aesthetic spectacle that added an extra *frisson* to the experience. *Minima Moralia* would be the book in which Adorno complained about the poor service in this hotel.

Brecht wanted to write a satirical novel about a group of people he called the 'Tui', intellectuals who got everything backward. Chief among these were the members of the so-called Frankfurt School to which Adorno himself belonged. The facts, Brecht thought, were simple. Hitler and his associates were Chicago-style gangsters, and the capitalist form of economic organisation was basically large-scale larceny. Rather than recognise this, the Tui intellectuals discussed Goethe, atonal music, and Voss' translation of Homer and reflected on why there were no proper door handles in the United States, whether you could tell how beautiful a woman was by listening to her voice on the telephone, whether a garden should or should not have a wall around it, and what it meant to have house guests. The Frankfurt School was funded by a wealthy German speculator who imported grain from Argentina to Europe. A man with what was called at the time a 'social conscience', he wanted someone to study the causes of the economic crisis in Europe. As Brecht pithily put it, he could have saved his money because the answer is simple: he (and those like him) was the cause.

It is true that Adorno was never at a loss for a plausible, or at any rate highly articulated reason for doing and thinking what he actually did and thought. The general thesis of *Minima Moralia* is that society is, as Hegel and Lukács say, a totality, but that it is a 'false' totality, not one in which everything fits together so as to be for the best. It is so powerful and so insidious that its falsity infects everything, every person, every desire, every gesture. 'Nothing is harmless anymore' (§5). This unrelentingly negative global view is associated with what seem to be repeated bouts of special pleading in favour of whatever position Adorno himself happens to occupy. However, the conjunction '*nothing* is innocent' with repeated references to the *advantages* of being . . . exactly like Teddie Wiesengrund (Adorno's original name) does strike a false note, as do the discussions of the uniquely intolerable (actually rather insignificant) indignities to which Teddie Wiesengrund has been subjected.

Adorno's response to this in *Minima Moralia* (for, of course, he *had* a response) was an aphorism: 'The splinter in your eye is the best magnifying glass' (§29). He makes no attempt to deny that he is *both* an excellently placed observer *and* damaged goods, and that these two traits are connected. This comes not long after a section, in fact the very first section of the main text of *Minima Moralia*, which gives a defence of the cognitive advantages of having a conventionally privileged position of wealth, standing, and influence in society, like that which Proust had and that which Adorno knew he had enjoyed before his emigration. If privilege brings no moral superiority, it also need not be associated with any special moral dissoluteness or cognitive weakness, and it might well allow one to see certain things more clearly than others did. On the other hand the émigré, as Adorno tells us in the preface, is always damaged in one way or another. But even such damage can be turned to cognitive advantage. It was not merely a 'rationalisation' for him to hold as he did that refugees who checked their critical faculties at their port of entry deserved his contempt, or at best his grudging sympathy: they were suffering from something like a form of Stockholm syndrome. Just as the *kapos* in concentration camps mimicked as best they could the uniforms of the SS guards, so emigrants who 'assimilated' to the American cults of boosterism, positive thinking, and 'success' and tried to adapt to the prevailing iron incuriosity about anything outside the narrow American form of life, were giving up a part of themselves that might well be valuable, blinding themselves deliberately, and proleptically overidentifying with potential aggressors in order to forestall actual aggression.

Like Augustine, who believed that human salvation made its appearance in the world at a certain historical time and that everything was different thereafter, Adorno thinks that 'truth' itself has a 'temporal index' or a 'temporal kernel'. If one wants 'truth' to have any serious relation to ethics, political philosophy, or human action, one needs to accept this. 'Positivist' conceptions of truth, as Adorno called them, construe 'truth' as finally a matter of observable fact, and they depend on the idea that the methods employed by the natural sciences have some kind of distinct priority in determining what 'truth' is, although various positivists disagreed radically on what exactly these 'methods' were and how exactly the application of them was connected with the pursuit of 'truth'. Adorno thinks that if one takes this tack, and makes the employment of the methods of the natural science the only canon of truth, one must abandon ethics, politics, history, society, religion, the human soul, and art to the outer darkness of 'irrationality' and thus open the doors to superstitions (like astrology and forms of the occult [§151]) and even to the most disreputable politics, because then no political position is alethetically worse than any other: they are all equally outside the domain in which true positions can be distinguished from false ones.

What one needs is a more encompassing notion of 'truth', like Hegel's. 'Truth', for Hegel, is in the first instance a structural property of a world, when all its parts fit together rationally and harmoniously—although the 'harmony' was sometimes of an exceptionally astringent kind—and then (derivatively) a property of corresponding human attitudes toward such a world which properly engage with it and satisfy the fullest possible criteria of internal rationality. 'Truth' is a matter of degree, not a categorical property, because things can fit together more or less rationally and harmoniously. Another way to put the same thing is that something can be said to be 'true' to the extent to which it cannot be (rationally) criticised. This doesn't mean the mere 'correctness' of individual empirical propositions can be ignored as irrelevant—quite the reverse, because if they are not correct, they clearly do not satisfy rational standards and can be criticised. But it does mean that being compatible with the existing 'facts' is not a sufficient requirement for 'truth'. One must always ask oneself whether what one has to deal with in a given situation is really a matter that can at all be properly formatted as a question of 'fact' at all; many things that *look* like matters of simple fact are really much more complex. In addition, many things which can be rationally discussed and about which it makes good sense to try to be discriminating cannot be reduced to questions of empirical 'correctness'.

If 'truth' has a temporal index, then it might well be that there was a time when it was appropriate for philosophers to make positive constructive suggestions for social change, that is, when certain progressive theories were 'true', but that that time is past. In the late eighteenth century the philosophers of the emerging bourgeoisie had an actual historical chance to realise some of their projects. It made sense for them to make positive proposals. Now, however, that is, in the period after World War One, society is so corrupt and has developed such a capacity—an almost infinite capacity—for turning what are intended as positive and constructive suggestions to its own benefit and the possibilities of successful constructive engagement are so limited that relentless negativism is the only reasonable attitude for a person of sense and discernment. This does not so much mean negative action—throwing bombs—as detaching oneself as completely as possible from the realm of direct action and analysing the weaknesses current society reveals. In the contemporary period philosophy can only be social criticism, and that criticism can only be negative, not 'constructive'. It would be a major mistake to try to work out any positive suggestions for reform or to present any positive ideals. Adorno later connects this central claim with the old Hebraic prohibition of 'graven images'.[12] Just as the ancient children of Israel after their return from exile in Babylon were prohibited from sculpting an image of their god and had to learn to deal with a visual empty space,[13] so we should avoid any positive specification of some good state to which we are enjoined to aspire. We should particularly avoid positive utopias. The reason for this is a danger which Adorno articulates and takes to be the main danger that confronts us at this moment, namely the totalitarian realisation of what are, in their origin, utopian projects. We live in a social system that is virtually all-encompassing, all-powerful, and also all-flexible. Such a social system can take over and adapt to its own purposes *any* positive proposal that one might make. We have special experience of the way such systems can turn even highly critical proposals for 'reform', to the extent to which they have even minimal positive content, into ways of strengthening its hold on populations. Utopian projects in fact end up making the society more closed and oppressive. Philosophy then must be relentlessly negative, formulate no positive ideals, and avoid making proposals for active social transformation.

Adorno announces the subject of *Minima Moralia* as the attempt to reconnect philosophy with what used to be its central and most important topic, 'What is the right life for a human being to live' ('Zueignung'/Dedication)? This topic, he says, has come to be neglected or ignored or is radically 'privatised' and construed as a matter merely of individual lifestyle, private passion, or mere consumer choice. In contrast to the complex dialectical fireworks that accompany or even constitute the essential part of many of his discussions, Adorno does give a clear, if to many disappointing answer to this question: 'There is no right life that can be led at the moment because society is "false" and so organised as to make leading such a life impossible' (§18).

*Minima Moralia* tries to show that our world is a constant catastrophe (§65) and that the basic reason for this is the discrepancy between what is and what could be.[14] In the past, humans had limited resources and powers, so suffering was simply an expected part of human life, perhaps to be railed or struggled against, perhaps to be accepted. This might be sad, but there was nothing toxic about this situation. The old philosophical story about desire and the satisfaction of desire (fulfilment) arose in such a world of necessary suffering. I would like to live on indefinitely, but I cannot satisfy this desire because I shall die one day soon; I am hungry and desire to eat, but I cannot fulfil this desire because the harvest was poor, our rudimentary transport system has broken down, or the masters are consuming all the grain. I may grow angry and band together with my fellows to burn down the master's house, but a jacquerie is not necessarily a general solution to the problem of poverty.

Now, Adorno claims, this old story should receive a new twist, or rather two new twists. First, to the abstract discussion of 'desire' and 'fulfilment' we must add a discussion of real collective human powers and their relation to the use which is actually being made of those powers. Collectively we now actually have the power to turn the world into paradise, and yet what we have produced is what Adorno saw through the window of a car travelling through the American landscape (§28). We *could* (in principle) end human want and poverty, but we choose not to. Think of Lucretius' way of asking his basic question: Life *could* in principle be 'worthy of the gods' (*dis dignam vitam degere nil impedit* [III.322]), yet foolish people turn it into hell on earth by worrying about life after death and practicing despicable rites of propitiation for gods who do not care at all (III.1023). It is the *discrepancy* between the two that is the problem, and the opportunity, for philosophy. *Minima Moralia* documents the split between powers and their realisation through analysis of a plethora of individual examples, showing how even in the apparently most trivial phenomena one finds traces of the catastrophe which is modern life and of the way in which every attempt to extract oneself from it has only made things worse.

The second twist is that in the old story there was not much disagreement about desires. Of course, in most societies we know of there was some elementary awareness of the fact that some desires were perverted, excessive, unhealthy, or what have you. Even Plato in the *Republic* talks about a city of pigs. However this was, in the past, a relatively limited and easily surveyable set of phenomena, and no one thought that starving agricultural workers were not perfectly right to desire what they desired. The situation in the modern world is different in that we generate artificial, excessive, and false desires and needs on an industrial scale, so much indeed that it really is sometimes not antecedently clear what is a real desire and what is not. To move outside the realm of what Adorno himself directly experienced, we can understand a desire for a typewriter if one has to produce long texts that must be easily readable, and one can endorse it as sensible and real, but what about the desire for the latest electronic gadget? What is more, one can even argue that our economy is based on the continued production of false desires and would collapse without it.

Adorno believes we cannot remedy this situation merely by thinking. We might, then, immediately conclude that thought is futile, and in a sense that is right. However, we can trace the causes of this cataclysm and its effects, and perhaps there is a kind of limited and bitter—even perverse but none the less real—individual happiness to be derived from the success of the project of understanding them. In fact, perhaps one of the few pleasures left is to understand our own unhappiness. So the only sensible course for us is to try to continue to live to the extent to which we can manage it, as 'subjects'—as active centres of feeling, thought, and action, rather than merely as cogs turned by other cogs in the social mechanism. Society works to suppress as much as possible exactly such activity; the social system requires us to be unaware of our true individual and collective powers and to be deceived about our real desires. It is just barely possible that some accident of history has permitted some of us to acquire and retain the capacity for thinking and reacting to the world, and, if so, we must continue to indulge in it as much and as long as we can. Even if the intellectual activity open to us is restricted to the observation of the way in which the Hegelian dialectic realises itself in everyday life, we must pursue this chance. It is in fact even a minor act of resistance. One should, on the other hand, also be under no illusions either about the final significance or success of such resistance, about the price which individuals must pay for cultivating it, or, for that matter, about its own purity and innocence. This is minimal, if not nil.

There are a number of objections that immediately come to mind here. The first is perhaps about the very idea of thoroughgoing universal negativism. It is tempting to think that negative criticism is somehow parasitic on *some* positive conception of how things could be for the better. This can seem plausible, if one focuses on antecedently highly structured decision situations in which failure to act in a particular way is tantamount to acting (positively) in some determinate other way. If someone explains to me that they have planted a bomb on a certain airplane which will explode unless I perform some action, such as flipping a switch, then it makes some sense to say that my failing to flip that switch has killed the people who die when the airplane crashes. Of course, I need to know about the connection between the switch and the bomb for this to be the case, but in the example I am assumed to know reliably about this connection. We will be perhaps especially tempted to say I have done something positive here if the action I must perform to prevent catastrophe is itself trivial, easy to do, and without serious cost to me. However, this argument from negative (failure to act) to positive (mass murder) seems plausible (to the extent to which it does) only because of the highly determinate framework conditions that have been imposed on the example artificially: the bomber sets up the situation so that I have morally 'no choice'. Without that framework, or if I am permitted to envisage another framework— having the power to inform the captain of the flight and tell him to neutralise the bomb—my failure to throw the switch is not necessarily equivalent to the act of killing all the passengers. It is one of Adorno's contentions that society always tries to make an indeterminate world determinate. That is part of what societies do, and it is not in itself a bad thing. However, our society is set up so as to reduce uncertainty and indeterminateness by ruthlessly suppressing alternatives (and that means even the human capacity to envisage alternatives). Another aspect of this is that our societies try to ensure that nothing new ever happens in them, that no novelty can emerge. The best way to do this turns out to be by the constant generation of pseudo-novelty: there is always a new film in the cinemas (but the plot, characters, and style always follow one of a small group of existing recognisable patterns). The future is supposed to be an infinite repetition of the present, just as the past cannot be construed as genuinely different but is a mere stage on the way to a present that is destined always to stay the same (§150).

The transformation of high industrial productivity and great intellectual effort into a massive attempt to allow nothing to change (except to let existing things get bigger) was the ultimate perversion of the human spirit—intelligence disconnected from ethics (one might say); intelligence turned into an anti-ethics. Still, the idea that this could be a potentially stable state is nothing more than a nightmare. Our prospects would be an unlimited continuation of the present based on manic and rigid reproduction of pseudo-change. Fascism is the final mobilisation of fear of indeterminacy. That is why people who have an obsession with 'absolute clarity', mistrust ambiguity, insist on a clear separation between races, have no sense of humour, or dislike atonal music have what Adorno called an 'authoritarian personality' which predisposes them to support right-wing political movements.[15]

To engage in strictly negative criticism is to deny the present while also rejecting the temptation to appeal to one of the pregiven sets of pseudo-alternatives which the society permits. There is nothing inherently irrational about claiming to know that this is false or wrong without being able to say what would be right: we don't know what the possibilities are. Let us not be too quick to close anything off or to alight on some completely determinate course of action. Our power to do this is limited (for various reasons, including because the society makes it difficult for us), but what else do we have?

This brings us to the second objection: Can one really isolate oneself completely from the realm of action? And then, if this were to be possible, would it be a good idea? The answer to the first question is obviously no, of course one cannot live a life of complete isolation. That is why Adorno says that 'nothing' is harmless anymore (§5). As far as the second question is concerned, Adorno maintains that we do not know a priori that action (any action) is always better than failure to act. Sometimes simply not doing anything is (by far) the best one can do.

When Franz Kafka said 'Mexico is everywhere', this was not a remark expressing a Trump-like prejudice against a certain place in North America or its inhabitants. 'Mexico' is being used here as a metonym for 'a place of random oppression and inconceivable cruelty', and he meant that no place had a monopoly on perversion, oppression, and degeneracy. What particular place plays this symbolic role changes historically. Thus, in the Christian Apocalypse 'Babylon' does not refer in the first instance to a city in Mesopotamia (and the 'Whore of Babylon' is not an Iraqi sex worker) but is used to mean a place of maximal and infamous impiety and decadence, and when Protestants speak of 'Rome', they are not always strictly referring to the city on the Tiber. In the early modern period 'Constantinople' (i.e., Islam) sometimes played a similar role; Hobbes probably did not know much about it, but he thought he knew a priori that it must be the most despotic place he could think of. So for Kafka, who lived for the last part of his life in one of the successor states to the Habsburg Empire, 'Mexico', land of the culturally inscrutable but bloodthirsty Aztecs, played the role of 'Babylon', 'Rome', or 'Constantinople'. When he says 'Everywhere is Mexico' he certainly did not mean that human sacrifice by priests wielding obsidian knives (with subsequent cannibalism) was rife in the suburbs of Prague in the early part of the twentieth century. Nor did he necessarily mean that his fellow-citizens were well on the path to dedicating their own version of the Great Pyramid of Tenochtitlan on the Hradčany. Rather it meant that we have little reason to congratulate ourselves on *not* being Babylon, Rome, or Constantinople. The Christians who railed against Babylon themselves constructed the Church of Rome, whose record of tender toleration of schismatics, doctrinal deviants, and unbelievers was nothing to be proud of. The men of the Reformation burned as many heretics as Catholics did and were deeply implicated in the construction of a disenchanted world view which encouraged us to treat our environment simply as material to be exploited, one of the consequences of which is the ecological catastrophe we now face. Hobbes at least knew that the vaunted *libertas* of the city of Lucca was no greater than what one could enjoy under the 'Great Turk' (as Hobbes calls him).[16] Look at Prague closely and, if you can, with the detached and unprejudiced eyes with which you look at Mexico, and you will see the horror beneath the veneer of familiarity.

This might be thought to take us back close to our original question at the very beginning of the book: 'Is it better to be satisfied in Santa Barbara (or Palos Verdes, Malibu, San Francisco, or Orange County); or to be dissatisfied in Limoges, Colchester, Benevento, Zwolle, Zagreb, or Leipzig?' It will come as no surprise to the reader that Adorno would reject this question as ill-formed, not merely because it is Eurocentric—something that would not actually have been of concern to him but which might bother us—rather, because he would hold, adopting, mutatis mutandis, Kafka's remark to our own changed circumstances, that 'in the modern world, although you may not realise it yet, there is no cure and no escape: everywhere is California'.

# CONCLUSION

## The End and the Future

In his *Lectures on the Philosophy of Fine Art* Hegel states that there was a period in human history *before* art; people certainly had predilections for certain rhythmic patterns and there were perhaps even some primitive decorative practices, but they were not sufficiently developed, sufficiently important, or sufficiently connected with other forms of meaningful activity for us to call them 'art' in the full and proper sense. Similarly, Hegel claims, we now (i.e., in the early nineteenth century) live in a period '*after*' art.[1] This does not mean, he hastens to add, that art does not exist any more. Past art is still admired and important, and contemporary art is still produced and appreciated—it may even develop further and become more 'perfect' than the art of the past; it may occupy a dignified niche in human society and human life. However, it has lost what once was its 'highest vocation': it is no longer the place where people find their highest needs satisfied and their highest interests articulated. We admire the archaic torso of Apollo—we may even, with Rilke, think it enjoins us to change our lives—but we do not bend the knee.

Setting aside Hegel's own views, we might ask whether the same kind of analysis does not apply to philosophy. There was a time 'before', when there were various different human practices: giving advice, criticising other people, investigating the environment, telling stories. Some people are better at one or another of these activities than others are, although people can disagree on who exactly is better than whom and why. Gradually, it may happen that people begin to get reflective and systematic and to cultivate assiduously one or another of these ways of acting, and eventually some of these activities may become entangled with others: we tell stories about the gods, and part of that is advice or even commands that we think they give to us. 'Philosophy' designates a particular configuration into which some of these practices entered and in which they remained for a rather long time. It did not exist forever but arose at a certain time, although, given the inherent looseness of human language, there can be reasoned disagreement about exactly when that is. I began this story with Socrates and his practice of using ratiocination (consisting of dialectical questioning and response) to seek self-knowledge and also a knowledge of what human life was best, and I focused on the moment when he had to defend this practice against claims that it was incompatible with traditional religion and led to the corruption of young citizens. The post-Socratic complex of logic (of a kind: the study of ratiocination), theology, ethics, and political philosophy came over the centuries to seem to have a natural unity, but it could, in principle, dissolve back into the successors of its original constituent elements, or even, if it remains more or less intact, it could, for one reason or another, stop being important and lose the centrality it once aspired to have and laid a claim to. We can certainly envisage such a possibility, and arguably that is the situation in which we find ourselves now. Like studying Greek sculpture in late nineteenth-century Paris, we may go through the motions of arguing for or against utilitarianism, examining the implications of a proposition in logic, analysing ambiguities in the use of some concept, or running for the hundredth time through the 'proofs of God's existence', but the soul and spirit are not appropriately edified and elevated by this, and its only social function is pedagogical. This may, of course, be a good development, part of the 'sobering up' we needed.[2] We might in retrospect also claim that philosophy never did articulate the deepest human interests; that was always a myth.

Still there has been enough overlap between the functions and continuity in the change of roles and concerns that one can pick out an identifiable configuration called 'philosophy' that lasted from the Peloponnesian War to the failure of the movements for reform in the second half of the twentieth century (often called 'the sixties' or '1968'). Or we can date it more precisely, from some time after 399 BCE, when Socrates was executed, to some time shortly before 1976, when Heidegger finally died (and the spurt of increase in economic productivity that was released by World War Two finally came to an end). In a sense Socrates was not a philosopher; at least it is not at all clear he would have called himself that or that anyone during his lifetime would have referred to him in that way. The first occurrence of the terms 'philosophy' and 'philosopher' are in Plato, although there is a story that they were invented by the earlier thinker Pythagoras, who, however, has the disadvantage of probably not having existed. Even if Pythagoras did not exist, though, we know that a group of people called 'the Pythagoreans' did, and so perhaps they did invent the word before Plato.[3] We don't know what the 'real' Socrates, as opposed to the character in Plato's dialogues, would have called himself, or indeed whether he would have called himself anything at all. Perhaps he called himself a 'sophist', as did Aristophanes (and also various other ancient writers who did not stand in the Platonic tradition).[4] Once the word 'philosophy' exists, perhaps invented by Plato, its use can be extended backwards, especially if there is a strong retrospective reason to distinguish what Socrates was doing from what others like him did. Talking to Socrates was not 'doing philosophy'—it was just talking to Socrates. Philosophy arises when people, after Socrates' death, try to reenact their memory of him, arguing as they think he would have, taking a keen interest in whether and in what ways the argument was like and in what ways it was unlike what they can remember of him. The sublimated eroticism of this performance is part of its attraction. To say that Socrates was not himself a philosopher, though, should be no more paradoxical than saying that Lord Sandwich never ate a 'sandwich', because to eat a sandwich is not to have a piece of meat between two thin slices of bread but to eat that thing which Lord Sandwich used always to have.[5] Or to claim that Jesus was not a Christian, a self-evident truth. And if even part of being a pious Muslim means trying to imitate the exemplary life of the Prophet, then the Prophet himself was not a Muslim in that sense because he was not imitating his own life but living it. The activity gets its identity, consistency, and substance only from its status as a repetition / variation of what it takes (correctly or not ) to be its own past.

If happy eras are blank pages in history,[6] the connection of philosophy with periods of political and social distress, dislocation, civil conflict, and especially political or military failure also seems clear. Plato invents various fantasies about the 'young Socrates', but the first real glimpse we get of him is standing in the cold outside his tent during the Athenian military campaign in Thrace in the middle of a war that was going to end in the most complete of failures for Athens. If Socrates had died during the retreats at Amphipolis or Delium, *or* if Athens had won what we call the Peloponnesian War, there might well have been nothing like what we know as 'philos-ophy'. Speaking about a 'beginning' of philosophy is, then, always somewhat arbitrary, and the same is true of its end or death. Just because nothing much seems to have happened since the 1970s doesn't mean that the dying embers of the subject might not flare up into life again under the right circumstances. Some physicists, after all, claim that there has been no significant progress in physics since the 1970s, but it would be very rash to declare the further de-velopment of that subject definitively over.[7]

In fact, philosophers have proposed two different kinds of the-ories about how, in what circumstances, and why philosophy arises. What motivates people to ask philosophical questions, and what kinds of answers do they look for? The first line of approach, initiated by Plato,[8] is that it is a positive theoretical response to amazement, surprise, admiration, or wonder at something that is seemingly incomprehensible but impressive. The second approach also has an origin in antiquity, but it is most closely associated with Hegel and various of his followers. This approach emphasises that philosophy is a reaction to negative aspects of our general ex-perience of the world: to apparently irreconcilable practical conflict, severe suffering, real loss, experienced deprivation or weakness. I don't start philosophising when the cherry tree blossoms in May but when the government demands that I do something I find deeply and unconscionably repugnant, when loved ones die in random vio-lence, when I confront the radical failure of my plans or my own death, or when my society as a whole seems bent on visibly self-destructive action. In a situation like this, I either look for a reason to accept the failure and inadequacy as inevitable, and therefore something I must simply learn to bear, or I try to understand why what seems to be an experience of pain, frustration, and failure is (really) not any such thing. Then there might be a kind of division of labour in which philosophy provides the 'reason' for accepting failure, limitation, and deprivation, and religion, especially monotheistic religion, provides a compensatory and fantastic consolation.

There is in principle a third approach, historically a minority view common only among some followers of Hegel (including Marx and John Dewey), which emphasises not the unchanging nature of the universe and the world we live in—as an object of wonder or something we must learn to tolerate—but as an inherently humanly malleable domain and which construes philosophy as a way of seeking to change the world so as to make it more satisfactory.

One implication of adopting the second or the third approach is that in a fully satisfactory society, one in which even my death has become not a complete and unmitigated trauma but, say, a positively integrated culmination of life, philosophy would be superfluous and would thus not exist. Or perhaps it might survive as a bit of historical folklore or theatrical spectacle, like the 'reenactments' of battles from the English Civil Wars which certain small towns sponsor. This does not imply that in deeply unsatisfactory societies philosophy will inevitably arise or maintain itself. Its existence will also depend on any number of further factors. In particular, for philosophy to exist, deeply rooted dissatisfaction with the state of our world must be experienced by some people who are living a life in which their basic physical needs are satisfied, are capable of focusing developed intellectual and cognitive powers on their situation, and do not think the situation is so self-evidently hopeless that there is no point in thinking about it. So we cannot assume that as our world falls apart now in ecological catastrophe, there will necessarily be any renewal of philosophical activity.

Philosophy presupposes a certain minimum of optimism; it is a comic, not a tragic genre of writing. Just as Western philosophy was coming to an end in 1960, the poet Paul Celan was awarded the

Georg-Büchner-Prize of the city of Darmstadt. In accepting the prize, Celan gave a speech in which he described poetry as 'that form of speech which declared that mortality and futility were infinite' (*diese Unendlichsprechung von lauter Sterblichkeit und Umsonst*'). In an earlier version of the same claim, he added that poetry 'remains mindful of its own finitude'.[9] The phrase Celan uses (*Unendlichsprechung*) has a post-theological and post-ecclesiological coloration. *Heiligsprechung* is the process in the Catholic Church through which a person is declared, after death, to have been 'holy' and thus officially promulgated as a recognised saint whose intercession may be invoked by the faithful. Poetry makes the official announcement that our world is one of death and futility and proclaims that there are no limits to the extent to which this is true. Poetry can perhaps tolerate this truth, but it might not be so clear that philosophy, committed as it always has been to an almost dementedly sunny view of the world as a place where things in the final analysis make sense, can be equally tolerant and itself survive.

Perhaps it is just an outdated romantic illusion to expect some kind of originality in philosophy, to expect that philosophers will be inventing new concepts, new ways of thinking and arguing. Something like philosophy can continue as an exercise in running through traditional thoughts and forms of argument in pedagogical or propaedeutic contexts. We don't expect originality in subjects like anatomy, apart perhaps from some originality in the mode of presentation; nevertheless we think it of great importance that potential health workers have a firm grounding in it. The schools of philosophers in Athens were not closed until the sixth century, although nothing we would recognise as original thought had taken place in them for several centuries. Such institutions, especially if they are surrounded by an aura of prestige (whether warranted or not), can maintain themselves by a kind of inertia for a surprisingly long time. This is the current state of philosophy in the universities. And, of course, there will be an informal place for thinking about the logical and linguistic puzzles that have come to obsess some. This is a harmless occupation, like Scrabble or solving crosswords, and there is no reason to think it will not continue, even if as a private pastime. One should not assume that 'philosophy' as we know it is indispensable for human life, or even that it is necessary or advantageous for high cultural achievement. France produced no philosophers of note to speak of in the nineteenth century, but is none the worse for that: it had Flaubert, Mallarmé, Cezanne, Berlioz, Rimbaud, and dozens of other remarkable artists, scientists, and scholars. Philosophy may connect in various ways with deep-seated human needs, but it is a highly peculiar social and cultural configuration which requires a highly specific set of conditions to flourish. These conditions, whatever they are, do not seem to have existed during the past forty years.

Just as there were precursors and outliers to philosophy—students of correct speech, observers of nature, experts in healthy living, and ethical authorities before the time of Socrates—and just as it is difficult to say exactly why some sage who lived before Socrates is 'not quite' a philosopher, so there is no reason for there not to be successors who will share some of the traits of philosophy, provided the species survives. The highly bureaucratised society we live in now will continue to need, as long as the coming ecological catastrophe is not yet fully upon us, experts in rules and rule-following, and there will be niches to be occupied in various technical and scientific subjects, although it would be naive to give too much weight to the actual role of philosophic concerns in science because they turn out generally to be of significantly more importance to philosophers than to actual scientists. There will certainly still be people who try to tell others what they ought to do and cite reasons for this. Among the inhabitants of these niches, there may survive some successors of philosophy for a while.

The twelve authors whose works are discussed here do not form a natural group or an invisible *collegium* or tribunal. They do not stand on the peaks of time and talk to each other, nor do they look down at us from some place beyond the heavens with eyes full of grim or benevolent satisfaction or of stern admonition. Their writings have been preserved for us by the merest of accidents, and it is the contingencies of history that have moved the tectonic plates of our world into a position from which it is possible for us to read what they wrote and find some of it comprehensible, relevant, and enlightening. For people in the historical situation in which we find ourselves, however, these works do reward study.

As this book has tried to show, the questions which humans ask change, depending on the historical and social circumstances. Which questions count as 'philosophical'—rather than administrative, scientific, or religious, or simply uninteresting, pointless, obtuse—also changes. Most of the questions which philosophers asked in the past were never convincingly answered, although for one reason or another (usually as a result of unpredictable social change) some simply disappeared. So there is no reason to expect us to have any better luck with our questions than all previous generations had with theirs. There are, however, questions that do not go away, even if we know we cannot adequately answer them.

*Ils dirent . . . qu'ils avoyent aperçeu qu'il y avoit parmy nous des hommes pleins et gorgez de toutes sortes de commoditez, et que leurs moitiez estoient mendians à leurs portes, décharnez de faim et de pauvreté; et trouvoient estrange comme ces moitiez icy necessiteuses pouvoient souffrir une telle injustice, qu'ils ne prinsent les autres à la gorge, ou missent le feu à leurs maisons.*

They said . . . that they had observed among us people satiated and gorged on all kinds of commodities, and yet their fellows were beggars at their door, wasted away with hunger and poverty, and they found it odd that these impoverished fellows were able to tolerate such an injustice, and did not grab the others by the throat or set fire to their houses.

—MONTAIGNE, "Of Cannibals"

# NOTES

### Preface

1. Paul Veyne, *Dans l'éternité je ne m'ennuierai pas* (Albin Michel, 2014), pp. 65f.
2. Jean Paul, *Ideen-Gewimmel*, edited by T. Wirtz and Kurt Wölfel (Die Andere Bibliothek, 2013), p. 26.

### Introduction

1. Haydn Symphony no. 45 in f-sharp minor (1772).
2. See R. Dodds, *The Greeks and the Irrational* (University of California Press, 1951); M. Detienne, *Les maîtres de la vérité dans la Grèce archaïque* (Maspero, 1967); Friedrich Nietzsche, *Kritische Studienausgabe*, edited by Mazzino Montinari and Giorgio Colli (Walter de Gruyter, 1967), vol. 7, pp. 460–498, 515–530, 538–559.
3. Apart from anything else, there are now technical reasons for being highly suspicious of the very idea of a 'closed system of knowledge' in the way that was traditionally construed. See Ernest Nagel and James R. Newman, *Gödel's Proof* (1958; NYU Press, 2001).

4. John Dewey, *Reconstruction in Philosophy* (Holt, 1920), and *The Question for Certainty* (Minton, Balch, 1929); Michel Foucault, 'La function politique de l'intellectuel', in *Dits et écrits* (Gallimard, 1994), vol. 3, pp. 109–114.

# 1. Socrates

1. A convenient bilingual text ('Bruta animalia ratione uti') is available in Plutarch, *Moralia*, edited and translated by William Helmbold (Loeb Classical Library, 1957), vol. XII.
2. The numbers here are so-called 'Stephanus-numbers' referring to the standard sixteenth-century edition of Plato by Henri Estienne ('Stephanus' in Latin). They are usually reproduced in modern editions of Plato's work either in square brackets in the text or in the margins
3. Gilbert Ryle, *The Concept of Mind* (Routledge, 1949).
4. See Plato's *Meno* and *Theaetetus*.
5. Specifying *exactly* what Socrates claims not to know turns out to be more difficult than it looks, and one rather quickly runs into numerous paradoxes, but that Socrates in *some* sense is denying that he knows even most of what 'everyone' knows seems clear.
6. See also Michel Tournier, *Vendredi* (Gallimard, 1969), chapter 2.
7. Socrates, *Apology*, 29–30. Note that the choice of lives at the end of *Republic* (617–621) is clearly of types of lives as totalities.
8. Karl Marx, *Kapital I*, in *Marx-Engels-Werke* (Dietz, 1968), vol. 23, pp. 192–200.
9. Σχολή (scholé), the word from which our 'school' eventually derives, originally meant 'leisure'. See also Josef Pieper, *Muße und Kult* (Kösel, 1948). Roman authors are keen to praise virtues of *otium*. See, for instance, Cicero, *De Officiis* Book II and *De re publica*, Book I; Seneca, *De brevitate vitae*, XIV.1 (see also *Epistulae morales*, 72.3, without use of the word *otium*).
10. Max Weber, *Wirtschaft und Gesellschaft* (Mohr, 1972), pp. 11–14.
11. Friedrich Nietzsche, *Götzendämmerung: 'Das Problem des Sokrates'*, in *Kritische Studienausgabe*, edited by Mazzino Montinari and Giorgio

Colli (Walter de Gruyter, 1967), vol. 7, p. 21 ('verkehrte Welt'); p. 25 ('quere Entwicklung'); p. 48 ('Fanatiker').

12. In *Les caves du Vatican* (Gallimard, 1914) André Gide tried to represent a fully gratuitous act. Whether the complexity of the novel is an indication of how rare such events are, or of how difficult it is for us to represent them, or indeed whether this distinction itself is one that can be maintained in the final analysis, are all open questions.

13. Plato, *Euthyphro*, 2–16.

14. Euripides, *Hippolytus*.

15. The Buddha; Lucretius, *passim* (*vide infra*) ; Friedrich Schlegel, *Lucinde: Idylle über den Müßiggang*; Paul Laforge, *Le droit à la paresse* (1883; Édition Mille-et-une nuits, 2000).

16. The Buddha, Lucretius *passim (vide infra)*, Fr. Schlegel *Lucinde : Idylle über den Müßiggang*; Paul Laforge *Le droit á la paresse* [1883] (Édition Mille-et-une nuits, 2000).

17. Jakob Burkhardt, *Griechische Kulturgeschichte* (Spemann, 1900).

18. Lewis Carroll, *Alice's Adventures in Wonderland*, chapter 3.

19. This is a slight exaggeration because Socrates/Plato in other places countenances the possibility that I may simply be preternaturally lucky or may have divine aid, which explains my success.

20. This is partly obscured in translations which render the Greek word νόμος as 'law', which is not incorrect but fails to take account of the fact that the word originally meant something like 'usage' or 'custom', and so it requires great delicacy to hazard a guess at what exactly it means in each context. Think of 'law' in these early Greek contexts as like 'the law of the jungle'; Kipling may have amused himself with the fantasy that this was some kind of legal code with individual provisions that could be specified, like the clauses of a statute, but that is fantasy.

21. G. W. F. Hegel, *Vorlesungen über die Philosophie der Weltgeschichte* (Suhrkamp, 1970), vol. 12, pp. 329–330.

22. Hesiod, *Theogony*, edited by M. L. West (Oxford University Press, 1966), pp. 251f, 384.

23. Pindar, *Pythia*, I.15ff.

24. Sigmund Freud, *Gesammelte Werke* (1969), vol. VII, pp. 225ff.

25. Plutarch, 'On the E at Delphi', in *Moralia*. vol. V.

## 2. Plato

1. Friedrich Nietzsche, 'Das Problem des Socrates,' in *Götzendämmerung*.
2. Friedrich Nietzsche, *Kritische Studienausgabe*, edited by Mazzino Montinari and Giorgio Colli (Walter de Gruyter, 1967), vol. 7, pp. 224–225.
3. Michael Cook, *Commanding Right and Forbidding Wrong in Islamic Thought* (Cambridge University Press, 2000).
4. David Wiggins demonstrates the falsity of this assumption in 'The Claim of Need' in his *Needs, Values, Truth* (Oxford University Press, 1998).
5. See also Émile Durkheim, *La division du travail social*.
6. See, for instance, W. Von Humboldt, *Über die Grenzen der Wirksamkeit des Staates* (Reclam, 1986); see also Friedrich Hölderlin, *Hyperion*; Friedrich Schiller, *Über die ästhetische Erziehung*.
7. Plato, *Republic*, 419.
8. Plato, *Lysis*, 207–208.
9. The most influential modern version of this is probably that defended by G. E. Moore in his *Principia ethica* (Cambridge University Press, 1903).
10. Or actually also 'good *for what*.' See pp. 67–70.

## 3. Lucretius

1. The story of the finding of this manuscript is told in an engaging way in S. Greenblatt's *The Swerve* (Norton, 2011).
2. St. Jerome, *Chronicon*, in *Eusebius Werke*, edited by Rudolf Helm (Akademie Verlag, 1956), vol. 7, p. 149.
3. See Hermann Diels and Walther Kranz, eds., *Fragmente der Vor-Sokratiker* (Weidmann, 1996), vol. 1; G. S. Kirk, J. E. Raven, and M. Schofield, eds., *The Pre-Socratic Philosophers* (Cambridge University Press, 2007).
4. For a generous selection of writings by Epicurus and others in the Epicurean tradition, see A. A. Long and D. N. Sedley, eds., *The Hellenistic Philosophers*, 2 vols. (Cambridge University Press, 1987).

5. Aristotle, *Metaphysica*, 984a11–16.
6. Conveniently reprinted in G. W. F. Hegel, *Werke in zwanzig Bänden,* edited by Eva Moldenhauer and Karl Markus Michel (Suhrkamp, 1970), vol. I, p. 243. Proposed other authors of this text, apart from Hegel, include Schelling and Hölderlin.
7. It is true that Epicureans sometimes gave the impression that they were not interested in the *details* of cosmological speculation; one detailed hypothesis might be right, or perhaps another. Provided the atomistic framework was not called into question, it did not really matter which one was correct. It would certainly be a mistake to get very upset trying to figure out which one way true. This, however, is not to say that the ethics prescribes cosmology, as seems to have been envisaged in the *Systemfragment*. See further the end of this chapter.
8. Diels and Kranz, *Fragmente der Vorsokratiker,* Fr. 15.
9. Max Weber, *Wirtschaft und Gesellschaft* (Mohr, 1972), pp. 327–344, 360–363.
10. But see Augustine, Chapter 4.
11. Herodotus, *Histories,* I.136–138.
12. The idea that there is a common sense morality which formulates the demands of minimal social intercourse and is, as it were, independent of particular religious or ideological formulations plays a certain role in the thought of Lenin (for instance, in *State and Revolution* [International Publishers, 1943] and of Trotsky [*Their Morals and Ours*, Pathfinder Press, 1973]).
13. This theory was widely held in antiquity. Richard Raatzsch pointed out to me that this is less straightforward as an account of the origin of belief in gods than it might first seem, because the account seems to presuppose that one has the idea of a god, to whom the thunder is attributed, but the point was to account for the origin of that idea.
14. See Diels and Kranz, *Fragmente der Vorsokratiker,* vol. 1, pp. 132–138.
15. See Ludwig Feuerbach, *Das Wesen des Christentums* (Reclam, 1984).
16. See D. A. Russell, ed., *Libellus de Sublimitate: Dionysio Longino,* Oxford Classical Texts (Oxford University Press, 1968), chapter VIII.9.
17. In his collection *Ein Hungerkünstler* (Verlag die Schmiede, 1924).
18. *Si quis dixerit, per ipsa novae Legis sacramenta ex opere operato non conferri gratiam. . . . Anathema sit.* Canon 8 of session of Council of Trent (1547) in Heinrich Denzinger and Adolf Schönmetzer, *Enchiridion*

*symbolorum definitionum et declarationum de rebus fidei et morum* (Herder, 1965), p. 382.

19. I was once told by my teacher Sidney Morgenbesser that reflection on this point was part of what alienated him eventually from Reconstructionist Judaism (which he defined as 'equal parts of Dewey and Moses').

## 4. Augustine

1. For a series of particularly implausible interpretations, see, for instance, *The City of God,* X.25, but because of his acceptance of the doctrine of prefiguration, virtually any of his readings of the Old Testament will seem far-fetched to someone without his theological beliefs. See E. Auerbach, 'Figura', in *Gesammelte Aufsätze zur romanischen Philologie* (Franke, 1967). See also Dante's 'Letter to Can Grande', in *Danti Alagheri Epistulae,* edited by Paget Toynbee (Oxford University Press, 1920), p. 173.

2. Rabelais, *Gargantua et Pantagruel* (Pléiade, 1994).

3. Friedrich Nietzsche, *Kritische Studienausgabe*, edited by Mazzino Montinari and Giorgio Colli (Walter de Gruyter, 1967), vol. 1, pp. 533–549; vol. 7, pp. 83, 133–134.

4. Ibid., vol. 1, pp. 875–890; vol. 7, pp. 442–448.

5. *Confessions passim.*

6. Heidegger quotes this in *Being and Time,* §9.

7. Gospel of John 1:12: 'ἔδωκεν αὐτοῖς ἐξουσίαν τέκνα θεοῦ γενέσθαι.' It is admittedly less clear that this is a real change of human nature if one takes ἐξουσία nontraditionally to mean 'license, warrant, permission'. Vulgate has *potestas,* which perhaps suggests more strongly change of nature than mere authorisation.

8. St. Jerome, *Letters,* xxii, 30.

## 5. Montaigne

1. As Nietzsche puts it, 'Sokrates ist der ideale "Naseweise": ein Ausdruck der mit dem nötigen Zartsinn aufgefasst werden muß', which gets both

sides of the equation right: an endearing smart-aleck. Friedrich Nietzsche, *Kritische Studienausgabe*, edited by Mazzino Montinari and Giorgio Colli (Walter de Gruyter, 1967), vol. 7, p. 17.

2. Michel de Montaigne, *Les essais,* edited by Jean Balsamo, Catherine Magnien-Simonin, and Michel Magnien, Bibliothèque de la Pléiade (Gallimard, 2007), III.2; *The Complete Essays of Montaigne,* translated by Donald M. Frame (Stanford University Press, 1958), p. 610. Subsequent citations of page numbers in the translation will be preceded by 'F'.

3. Pyrrho is a particular presence in II.12; see also the beginning of II.29.

4. *Meno,* 71–72.

5. See G. Kerferd, *The Sophistic Movement* (Cambridge University Press, 1981).

6. See Diogenes Laertius, *Lives of Eminent Philosophers,* edited by Tiziano Dorandi (Cambridge University Press, 2013), pp. 420ff.

7. For Jesus as a Cynic philosopher, see B. Lang, *Jesus der Hund* (Beck, 2010).

8. See also the antimonastic utopia, the Abbé Thélème in Rabelais's *Gargantua et Pantagruel.*

9. At II.12/F418 Montaigne specifically seems to move from the traditional vocabulary to what I am claiming is his 'new' vocabulary. He moves from speaking of *connoissance de soy* and *raison* to various versions of idioms using *s'entendre* within the space of a few lines.

## 6. Hobbes

1. Think of Uncle Tom.

2. Perhaps this is a slight exaggeration, but the absence of explicit resistance is ethically a crude measure, and one sees in Hobbes' work the authoritarian consequences of making it central.

3. See René Spitz, 'Hospitalism', *Psychoanalytic Study of the Child* 1 (1945): 53–74.

4. Peter Kropotkin, *Mutual Aid* (Heinemann, 1902).

5. This view is challenged by David Constan in his 'Clemency as a Virtue', in *Classical Philology* 100, no. 4 (October 2005): 337ff.

6. Plutarch, *Vitae Caesaris*, 54.
7. Michel de Montaigne, *Les essais,* edited by Jean Balsamo, Catherine Magnien-Simonin, and Michel Magnien, Bibliothèque de la Pléiade (Gallimard, 2007), II.32; *The Complete Essays of Montaigne,* translated by Donald M. Frame (Stanford University Press, 1958), pp. 547–549.
8. John Maynard Keynes, *General Theory of Employment, Interest, and Money* (Cambridge University Press, 1936), chapter 12.

## 7. Hegel

1. G. W. F. Hegel, *Grundlinien zur Philosophie des Rechts,* in *Werke in zwanzig Bänden* (Suhrkamp, 1986), vol. 7, pp. 26–28.
2. Actually he seems to have sent the manuscript to his publisher three days before the battle but worried it would be lost in the post.
3. See Hans Friedrich Fulda, *Das Problem einer Einleitung in Hegels Wissenschaft der Logik* (Klostermann, 1975).
4. *Hegel: Werke in zwanzig Bänden.* Edited by Eva Moldenhauer and Karl Markus Michel. Suhrkamp,1970, vol. 12, p 529ff.
5. *Hegel: Werke in zwanzig Bänden.* Edited by Eva Moldenhauer and Karl Markus Michel. Suhrkamp,1970, vol. 20, p. 455.
6. One passage which seems to point in a different direction from the one indicated here is vol. 7, p. 27. However a closer inspection with attention to the context and to Hegel's exact phrasing here will dispel that first impression. This is a passage in a 'Preface' and we know that in Prefaces and Introductions, Hegel consciously felt he was speaking 'outside' the system, and could allow himself a more popular and less than fully 'scientific' mode of expression. Also the term he uses '*Eigensinn*'(Nisbet: 'obstinacy') is certainly not a term of unmitigated approval. Looking for 'justification' is a Protestant obstinacy, which, to be sure, does honour to human beings (but that does not mean it is the final word in philosophy).
7. *Hegel: Werke in zwanzig Bänden.* Edited by Eva Moldenhauer and Karl Markus Michel. Suhrkamp, 1970, vol. 20, pp. 236–255.

8. *Hegel: Werke in zwanzig Bänden.* Edited by Eva Moldenhauer and Karl Markus Michel. Suhrkamp,1970, vol. 13, p. 21.
9. Thucydides, *Historiae* II.35ff.

## 8. Nietzsche

1. Friedrich Nietzsche, *Kritische Studienausgabe,* edited by Mazzino Montinari and Giorgio Colli (Walter de Gruyter, 1967), vol. 5, p. 12. In an early manuscript he described his own position as 'umgedrehter Platonismus' (Platonism turned around [vol. 7, p. 199]). Citations from the work of Nietzsche will take the form *KSA* 1.100, that is *Friedrich Nietzsche: Kritische Studienausgabe.* Edited by Giorgio Colli and Maurizio Montinari. Walter de Gruyter, 1967, volume 1, page 100.
2. Ibid., vol. 6 p. 307; also vol. 6, p. 147 (Dostoyevsky, he says, is the only psychologist from whom he could learn anything).
3. Johann Gottlieb Fichte, 'Erste Einleitung in die Wissenschaftslehre' (1797; Meiner, 1961), section 5, p. 21: 'Was für eine Philosophie man wähle, hängt sonach davon ab, was man für ein Mensch ist: denn ein philosophisches System ist nicht ein toter Hausrat, den man ablegen oder annehmen könnte, wie es uns beliebte, sondern es ist beseelt durch die Seele des Menschen, der es hat.' [What kind of philosophy one chooses depends on what kind of person one is, because a philosophical system is not a dead appliance lying around the house which one can pick up or put down as one likes, but rather is animated by the soul of the person who adopts it.]

## 9. Lukács

1. Giuseppe Tomasi di Lampedusa, *The Leopard,* translated by Archibald Colquhoun (Collins, 1960), p. 40.
2. See Michael Frede, *A Free Will: Origins of the Notion in Ancient Thought* (University of California Press, 2011).
3. Friedrich Schiller, *Die ästhetische Erziehung des Menschen in einer Reihe von Briefen / On the Aesthetic Education of Man in a Series of*

*Letters,* edited by Elizabeth M. Wilkinson and L. A. Willoughby (Oxford University Press, 1967).

4. Adam Smith, *The Wealth of Nations* (1776), book I, chapter 7.
5. Karl Marx, *Marx-Engels-Werke* (Dietz, 1968), vol. 23, pp. 85ff.
6. Ibid., supplement 1, pp. 467–588.
7. Bertolt Brecht, *Die Gedichte in einem Band* (Suhrkamp, 1981), p. 638.
8. György Lukács, *History and Class Consciousness: Studies in Marxist Dialectics,* translated by Rodney Livingstone (Merlin Press, 1971), pp. 171–175, 199.
9. Printed before *History and Class Consciousness* in the Aisthesis edition, pp. 45ff.
10. See *Taktik und Ethik (supra).*
11. His term for this was 'realism'; see his *Essays über den Realismus* (Luchterhand, 1971).

# 10. Heidegger

1. Martin Heidegger, "Brief über den Humanismus" (Klostermann, 1947).
2. 'Zurückgehalten', as he puts it in 'Brief über den Humanismus'.
3. Karl Löwith, who had been Heidegger's *Assistent* during the late 1920s and early 1930s, reported to me this self-characterisation as 'a Christian negative theologian' in conversation in Heidelberg in 1971–1972.
4. One might contrast this general approach with that of Nietzsche, e.g. at *KSA* I.806–807.
5. Martin Heidegger, *Wegmarken* (Klostermann, 1975), pp. 334ff.
6. See, for instance, his interpretations of Hölderlin in *Erläuterungen zu Hölderlins Dichtung* (Klostermann, 1963), or his interpretations of Trakl in *Unterwegs zur Sprache* (Neske, 1959).
7. Heidegger, 'Brief über den Humanismus'.
8. See Meister Eckhart, 'Martha und Maria'.
9. Heidegger in *Der Spiegel,* 31 May 1976.
10. Some documents from this period are collected by Guido Schneeberger in his *Nachlese zu Heidegger* (Selbstverlag, 1962). Recently some notebooks (1,300 pages of them) from the period between 1931 and 1975 have been published under the name *Die schwarzen Hefte* (a name

Heidegger himself gave to them and which refers to the colour of the binding of the notebooks) (Klostermann, 2014).
11. Martin Heidegger, *Gelassenheit* (Neske, 1959).
12. Heidegger, 'Brief über den Humanismus'.
13. György Lukács, *Die Zerstörung der Vernunft* (Luchterhand, 1954).
14. Theodor Adorno, *Jargon der Eigentlichkeit* (Suhrkamp, 1964).
15. Hans Sluga, *Heidegger's Crisis* (Harvard University Press, 1993).

## 11. Wittgenstein

1. Extracts from these are printed in the volume *Geschichte und Klassenbewußtein* (Aisthesis, 2013), pp. 699ff.
2. *Tractatus logico-philosophicus* (Suhrkamp, 1969), originally in Ostwalds, *Annalen der Naturphilosophie*, 1921; now most conveniently *Schriften I*.
3. *Vide supra*, Chapter 4.
4. See the film *Bedazzled* (1967).
5. Ludwig Wittgenstein, *Vermischte Bemerkungen* (Suhrkamp, 1977), p. 40. The remark seems to have been made in about 1931.
6. Max Weber, 'Wissenschaft als Beruf', in *Gesammelte Aufsätze zur Wissenschaftslehre* (Mohr, 1973), p. 589.

## 12. Adorno

1. G. W. F. Hegel, *Werke in zwanzig Bänden* (Suhrkamp, 1971), vol. 12, p. 529.
2. Karl Marx, *Marx-Engels-Werke* (Dietz, 1968), vol. 23, p. 27.
3. G. W. F. Hegel, *Phenomenology*, 105–119.
4. Georg Büchner, *Lenz*, Studienausgabe (Reclam, 1998).
5. Paul Celan, *Der Meridian*, in *Tübinger Ausgabe* (Suhrkamp, 1999), p. 7.
6. Martin Heidegger, *Einführung in die Metaphysik* (Niemeyer, 1957), p. 34. Richard Raatzsch tells me that Wittgenstein expressed similar opinions. Recently Slavoj Žižek, *Der neue Klassenkampf* (Suhrkamp, 2015), pp. 13f., has said something similar, intentionally modelling his statement on Heidegger's but substituting 'China' for 'Russia'.

7. Bertolt Brecht, *Die Gedichte in einem Band* (Suhrkamp, 1981), p. 830; see also Stephen Parker, *Bertolt Brecht: A Literary Life* (Bloomsbury, 2014), pp. 431–450.
8. One of his early plays, *Im Dickicht der Städte* (1923; Propyläen, 1927), is set in Chicago.
9. Hegel, *Rechtsphilosophie,* in *Werke* 7.386–393.
10. Hegel, *Werke* 7.27.
11. See Michael Forster, *Hegel and Skepticism* (Harvard University Press, 1989).
12. Theodor W. Adorno, *Negative Dialektik* (Suhrkamp, 1966), pp. 202–205.
13. Thomas Römer, *L'Invention de dieu* (Seuil, 2014).
14. Theodor W. Adorno *Ästhetische Theorie* (Suhrkamp, 1970), p. 56.
15. Theodor W. Adorno, et al., *The Authoritarian Personality* (Harper, 1950).
16. Hobbes, *Leviathan,* chapter 21.

## Conclusion

1. G. W. F. Hegel, *Werke in zwanzig Bänden* (Suhrkamp, 1971), vol. 13, pp. 23–26.
2. Max Weber, 'Entzauberung der Welt', in 'Wissenschaft als Beruf', in *Gesammelte Aufsätze zur Wissenschafstheorie* (Mohr, 1973), *passim.*
3. Walter Burkert, *Platon oder Pythagoras? Zum Ursprung des Wortes 'Philosophie'*, Hermes 88 (Steiner Verlag, 1960), pp. 159–177.
4. Aristophanes, *Nubes.* Also see Friedrich Nietzsche, *Kritische Studienausgabe*, edited by Mazzino Montinari and Giorgio Colli (Walter de Gruyter, 1967), vol. 7, pp. 12, 22.
5. Bee Wilson, *The Sandwich: A Global History* (Reaktion, 2010).
6. Hegel, *Werke,* vol. 12.
7. Lee Smolin, *The Trouble with Physics* (Penguin, 2008).
8. *Theaetetus,* 155d.
9. Paul Celan, *Tübinger Ausgabe* (Suhrkamp, 1999), p. 11.

# FURTHER READING

## Chapter 1. Socrates

Dewey, John. *Reconstruction in Philosophy*. Beacon, 1948.

Foucault, Michel. *Histoire de la sexualité II: L'usage des plaisirs*. Gallimard, 1984. / *History of Sexuality, Volume 2: The Use of Pleasure*. Translated by Robert Hurley. Vintage, 1990.

Foucault, Michel. *Histoire de la sexualité III: Le souci de soi*. Gallimard, 1984. / *The History of Sexuality, Vol. 3: The Care of the Self*. Translated by Robert Hurley. Vintage, 1986.

Frankfurt, Harry. *The Importance of What We Care About*. Cambridge University Press, 1988.

Hadot, Pierre. *Exercices spirituels et philosophie antique*. Études augustiniennes, 1981. / *Philosophy as a Way of Life*. Edited by Arnold Davidson and translated by Michael Chase. Blackwell, 1995.

Kierkegaard, Søren. *Concept of Irony with Constant Reference to Socrates*. Translated by Lee Cappel. Harper & Row, 1965.

Vlastos, Gregory. *Socrates: Ironist and Moral Philosopher*. Cambridge University Press, 1991.

## Chapter 2. Plato

Deleuze, Gilles, and Félix Guattari. *L'Anti-Oedipe: Capitalisme et schizophrénie.* Éditions de minuit, 1972. / *Anti-Oedipus: Capitalism and Schizophrenia.* Translated by Robert Hurley, Mark Seem, and Helen R. Lane. University of Minnesota Press, 1983.

Dostoyevski, Fyodor. *Notes from Underground.* Translated by Ronald Wilks. Penguin, 2009.

Humboldt, Wilhelm von. *Ideen zu einem Versuch, die Grenzen der Wirksamkeit des Staates.* Reclam, 1986. / *The Limits of State Action.* Edited by John Burrow. Cambridge Studies in the History and Theory of Politics. Cambridge University Press, 1969.

More, Thomas. *Utopia.* Edited by George M. Logan, Robert M. Adams, and Clarence H. Miller. [Latin and English.] Cambridge University Press, 1995.

Reeve, C. D. C. *Philosopher-Kings: The Argument of Plato's Republic.* Princeton University Press, 1989.

## Chapter 3. Lucretius

Clay, Diskin. *Lucretius and Epicurus.* Cornell University Press, 1983.

Feuerbach, Ludwig. *Das Wesen des Christentums.* Reclam, 1984. / *The Essence of Christianity.* Translated by George Eliot. Prometheus Books, 1989.

Marx, Karl. *Über die Differenz der demokritischen und der epikureischen Naturphilosophie.* In *Marx-Engels-Werke.* Supplementary vol. 1. Dietz, 1968. / *The Difference between the Democritean and the Epicurean Philosophy of Nature.* In *Marx-Engels: Collected Works.* Vol. 1. Lawrence and Wishart, 1975.

Sedley, David. *Lucretius and the Transformation of Greek Wisdom.* Cambridge University Press, 1998.

Warren, James. *Facing Death: Epicurus and His Critics.* Oxford University Press, 2006.

## Chapter 4. Augustine

Brown, Peter. *Augustine: A Biography.* University of California Press, 1967.

Flasch, Kurt. *Augustin: Einführung in sein Denken.* Reclam, 1980.

Halbertal, Moshe, and Avishai Margalit. *Idolatry.* Translated by Naomi Goldblum. Harvard University Press, 1992.

Kierkegaard, Søren. *Philosophical Fragments.* Translated by David F. Swenson. Translation revised by Howard V. Hong. Princeton University Press, 1936.

Löwith, Karl. *Meaning in History.* University of Chicago Press, 1949.

Rousseau, Jean-Jacques. *Les confessions.* In *Œuvres complètes, tome 1.* Published under the direction of Bernard Gagnebin and Marcel Raymond with the collaboration of Robert Osmont. Bibliothèque de la Pléiade. Gallimard, 1959. / *The Confessions.* Penguin, 1953.

## Chapter 5. Montaigne

La Boétie, Étienne de. *Discours de la servitude volontaire.* Gallimard, 2008. / *The Politics of Obedience: The Discourse of Voluntary Servitude.* Translated by Harry Kurz. Black Rose Books, 1997.

Laertius, Diogenes. "Life of Pyrrho." In *Lives of Eminent Philosophers.* Translated by R. D. Hicks. Vol. 2. Loeb Classical Library. Harvard University Press, 1925.

Fontana, Biancamaria. "The Political Thought of Montaigne." In *The Oxford Handbook of Montaigne,* edited by Philippe Desan. Oxford University Press, 2016.

Manent, Pierre. *Montaigne: La vie sans loi.* Flammarion, 2014.

Nietzsche, Friedrich. *Ecce homo.* In *Friedrich Nietzsche: Kritische Studien-Ausgabe.* Edited by Giorgio Colli and Mazzino Montinari. Vol. 6. De Gruyter, 1968. / *Nietzsche: The Anti-Christ, Ecce Homo, Twilight of Idols and Other Writings.* Edited by Aaron Ridley and translated by Judith Norman. Cambridge Texts in the History of Philosophy. Cambridge University Press, 2005.

Starobinski, Jean. *Montaigne en mouvement.* Gallimard, 1982.

Toulmin, Stephen. *Cosmopolis: The Hidden Agenda of Modernity*. University of Chicago Press, 1992.

## Chapter 6. Hobbes

Benjamin, Walter. "Zur Kritik der Gewalt." In *Gesammelte Schriften*. Edited by Rolf Tiedemann and Hermann Schweppenhäuser. Vol. 7. Suhrkamp, 1991. / "Critique of Violence." In *Reflections: Essays, Aphorisms, Autobiographical Writings*. Edited by Peter Demetz and translated by Edmund Jephcott. Schocken Books, 1995.

De Sade, Donatien Alfonse François. "Français, encore un effort si vous voulez être républicains." In *La Philosophie dans le boudoir* in *Œuvres*, vol. III. Edited by Michel Delon with the collaboration of Jean Depruin. Bibliothèque de la Pléiade. Gallimard, 1998. / *Justine, Philosophy in the Bedroom, and Other Writings*. Translated by Richard Seaver and Austryn Wainhouse. Grove Press, 1971.

De Sade, Donatien Alfonse François. *Justine ou les Malheurs de la vertu*. In *Œuvres*, vol. II. Edited by Michel Delon. Bibliothèque de la Pléiade. Gallimard, 1998. / *Justine, Philosophy in the Bedroom, and Other Writings*. Translated by Richard Seaver and Austryn Wainhouse. Grove Press, 1971.

Durkheim, Émile. *De la division du travail social*. Presses universitaires de France, 1991 [1893]. / *The Division of Labor in Society*. Translated by W. D. Halls. Free Press, 1984.

Grotius, Hugo. *De jure belli et pacis*. Nabu Press, 2010. / *The Rights of War and Peace*. Translated by John Morrice from the edition of Jean Barbeyrac and edited by Richard Tuck. Liberty Fund, 2005.

Kropotkin, Peter. *Mutual Aid: A Factor of Evolution*. Freedom Press, 2014.

Kropotkine, Pierre. *La Conquête du pain*. Édition du sextant, 2013. / *Conquest of Bread*. Translated by Marshall Shatz. Cambridge Texts in the History of Political Thought. Cambridge University Press, 2008.

Skinner, Quentin. *Reason and Rhetoric in the Philosophy of Hobbes*. Cambridge University Press, 1996.

Skinner, Quentin. "The State." In *Political Innovation and Conceptual Change*. Edited by Terence Ball, James Farr, and Russell L. Hanson. Cambridge University Press, 1989.

Tuck, Richard. *Hobbes*. Oxford University Press, 1989.

## Chapter 7. Hegel

Bull, Malcolm. *Seeing Things Hidden: Apocalypse, Vision and Totality.* Verso, 2000.

Fanon, Frantz. *Peau noire, masques blancs.* Seuil, 1952. / *Black Skin, White Masks.* Translated by Richard Philcox. Grove Press, 2008.

Forster, Michael. *Hegel and Skepticism.* Harvard University Press, 1989.

Fulda, Hans-Friedrich. *Das Problem einer Einleitung in Hegels Wissenschaft.* Klostermann, 1975.

Hippolyte, Jean. *Genèse et structure de la* Phénomenologie de l'esprit *de Hegel.* Aubier, 1946. / *Genesis and Structure of Hegel's* "Phenomenology of Spirit." Translated by Samuel Cherniak and John Heckman. Northwestern University Studies in Phenomenology and Existential Philosophy. Northwestern University Press, 1974.

Marx, Karl. "Ökonomisch-philosophische Manuskripte aus dem Jahre 1844." In *Marx-Engels Werke: Ergänzungsband 1.* Dietz, 1968. / "Economic and Philosophic Manuscripts of 1844." In *Collected Works.* Vol. 3. Lawrence and Wishart, 1975.

## Chapter 8. Nietzsche

Artaud, Antonin. "Pour en finire avec le jugement de dieu." In *Œuvres.* Edited by Evelyne Grossmann. Collection Quarto. Gallimard, 2004. [Audio copies of the original recording of this work in 1947 are available as a CD from Sub Rosa record company, Brussels.]

Bull, Malcolm. *Anti-Nietzsche.* Verso, 2011.

Losurdo, Domenico. *Nietzsche der aristokratische Rebell: Intellektuelle Biographie und kritische Bilanz.* Edited by Jan Rehman and translated by Erdmute Brielmeyer. 2 vols. Argument, 2009. / [The author describes the German edition as a second and corrected version of his *Nietzsche, il ribelle aristiocratico: Biografia intellettuale e bilancio critico.* Bollati Boringhieri, 2014.]

May, Simon. *Nietzsche's Ethics and His War on "Morality."* Clarendon Press, 1999.

Nehamas, Alexander. *Nietzsche: Life as Literature.* Harvard University Press, 1985.

Salomé, Lou-Andreas. *Friedrich Nietzsche in seinen Werken*. Severus, 2013.

Staten, Henry. *Nietzsche's Voice*. Cornell University Press, 1990.

## Chapter 9. Lukács

Comité invisible *L'insurrection qui vient*. La Fabrique, 2007. / *The Coming Insurrection*. Semiotext(e) Intervention Series. MIT Press, 2009.

Kierkegaard, Søren. *Concluding Unscientific Postscript*. Translated by Walter Lowrie. Princeton University Press, 1968.

Lenin, Vladimir. *What Is to Be Done?* In *Collected Works*. Translated by Joe Fineberg and George Hanna. Vol. 5. Foreign Languages Publishing House, 1961.

Luxemburg, Rosa. *Massenstreik, Partei und Gewerkschaften*. In *Gesammelte Werke*. Vol. 2. Dietz, 2000. / *The Mass Strike, the Political Party and the Trade Unions*. In *The Essential Rosa Luxemburg: Reform or Revolution and the Mass Strike*. Edited by Helen Scott and translated by Patrick Lavin. Haymarket Books, 2008.

Luxemburg, Rosa. "Sozialreform oder Revolution." In *Gesammelte Werke*. Vol. 1.1. Dietz, 1982. / "Reform or Revolution." In *The Essential Rosa Luxemburg: Reform or Revolution and the Mass Strike*. Edited by Helen Scott translated by Integer. Haymarket Books, 2008.

Merleau-Ponty, Maurice. *Humanisme et terreur: Essai sur le problème communiste*. Gallimard, 1947. / *Humanism and Terror: An Essay on the Communist Problem*. Translated by John O'Neill. Beacon Press, 1990.

Merleau-Ponty, Maurice. *Les aventures de la dialectique*. Gallimard, 1955. / *Adventures of the Dialectic*. Translated by Joseph J. Bien. Studies in Phenomenology and Existential Philosophy. Northwestern University Press, 1973.

Negt, Oskar, and Alexander Kluge. *Geschichte und Eigensinn*. Zweitausendeins, 1981. / *History and Obstinacy*. Edited by Devon Fore, Cyrus Shahan, Martin Brady, Helen Hughes, and Joel Golb, and translated by Richard Langston. MIT Press, 2014.

Weber, Max. *Die protestantische Ethik und der Geist des Kapitalismus*. In *Gesammelte Aufsätze zur Religionssoziologie*. Vol. 1. Mohr, 1921. / *The Protestant Ethic and the Spirit of Capitalism*. Translated and introduced by Stephen Kalberg. Oxford University Press, 2011.

## Chapter 10. Heidegger

Carman, Taylor. *Heidegger's Analytic: Interpretation, Discourse and Authenticity in Being and Time.* Cambridge University Press, 2003.

Marten, Rainer. "Heidegger: Die Einheit seines Denkens." In *Martin Heidegger's "Schwarze Hefte,"* edited by Marion Heinz and Sidonie Kellerer. Suhrkamp, 2016.

Meister, Eckhart. *Deutsche Predigten und Traktate.* Translated into modern German by Josef Quint. Nikol, 2007. / *The Essential Sermons, Commentaries, Treatises and Defenses.* Translated and edited by Bernard McGinn and Edmund Colledge. Paulist Press, 1981. [There is also a selection of sermons in the original Middle High German, with facing page modern German translation, published by Reclam, 2001.]

Rée, Jonathan. *Heidegger.* Phoenix, 1998.

Schneeberger, Guido. *Nachlese zu Heidegger.* Selbstverlag, 1962.

Sluga, Hans. *Heidegger's Crisis.* Harvard University Press, 1993.

## Chapter 11. Wittgenstein

Artaud, Antonin. *Le théâtre et son double.* Gallimard, 1964. / *The Theatre and Its Double.* Translated by Mary Caroline Richards. Grove Weidenfeld, 1958.

Fritz, Mauthner. *Beiträge zu einer Kritik der Sprache.* 3 vols. Cotta, 1901–1902.

Kripke, Saul. *Wittgenstein on Rules and Private Language.* Harvard University Press, 1982.

Loos, Adolf. "Ornament und Verbrechen." In *Trotzdem 1900–1930.* Edited by Adolf Opel. Brenner, 1931. / *Ornament and Crime: Selected Essays.* Translated by Michael Mitchell. Studies in Austrian Literature, Culture, and Thought. Ariadne Press, 1998.

Monk, Ray. *Ludwig Wittgenstein: The Duty of Genius.* Vintage, 1990.

Tolstoy, Leo. *A Confession and Other Religious Writings.* Translated by Jane Kentish. Penguin, 1988.

Tolstoy, Leo. *The Gospel in Brief.* Translated by Louise Maude and Aylmer Maude. Pantianos Classics, 1921.

Tolstoy, Leo. *The Kingdom of God Is Within You.* Translated by Constance Garnett. Penguin, 2010.

## Chapter 12. Adorno

Baudelaire, Charles. *"Peintre de la vie moderne."* In Œuvres complètes. Edited by Claude Pichois. Vol. 2. Bibliothèque de la Pléiade. Gallimard, 1976. / *The Painter of Modern Life and Other Essays.* Translated by Thom Mayne. Phaidon, 1995.
Benjamin, Walter. "Geschichtsphilosophische Thesen." In *Angelus Novus: Ausgewählte Schriften 2.* Suhrkamp, 1988. / "Theses on the Philosophy of History." In *Illuminations.* Translated by Harry Zohn. Schocken, 1969.
Celan, Paul. "Gespräch im Gebirg." In *Der Meridian und andere Prosa.* Suhrkamp, 1988. / "Conversation in the Mountains." In *Collected Prose.* Translated by Rosmarie Waldrop. Carcanet, 1999
Derrida, Jacques. "Les fins de l'homme." In *Marges de la philosophie.* Editions de minuit, 1972. / "The Ends of Man." In *Margins of Philosophy.* Translated by Alan Bass. University of Chicago Press, 1982.
Kürnberger, Ferdinand. *Der Amerikamüde: amerikanisches Kulturbild.* Insel, 1986.
Rimbaud, Arthur. *Une saison en enfer* in Oeuvres complètes. Edited by André Guyaux with the collaboration of Aurélia Cervoni. Bibliothèque de la Pléiade. Gallimard, 2009. / *A Season in Hell.* In Collected Works. Translated by Paul Schmidt. Harper, 2000.
Schlegel, Friedrich. *Athenäums-Fragmente.* In *Athenäums-Fragmente und andere Schriften.* Edited by Andreas Huyssen. Reclam, 1986. / "Athenaeum-Fragments." In *Friedrich Schlegel's* Lucinde *and the Fragments.* Translated by Peter Firchow. University of Minnesota Press, 1971.
Schlegel, Friedrich. "Über die Unverständlichkeit." In *Ästhetische und politische Schriften.* Hofenberg, 2014. / "On Incomprehensibility." In *Friedrich Schlegel's* Lucinde *and the Fragments.* Translated by Peter Firchow. University of Minnesota Press, 1971.

# INDEX

abstraction, 177, 202–204, 230, 237, 268, 270

account, giving an (διδόναι λόγον), 32, 35, 39, 40–41, 44, 53

action, 20–21; and authenticity, 243; cannot change our relation to being, 248; collective (as central locus of freedom), 211, 224; context of, 5, 26, 28, 171, 211; cooperative, 212; enlightened or unenlightened, 219; guide to, 18–20; habitual, 26; immediate (or unreflective), 7, 25–26, 259–260; individual, 25–26, 28; individual engaged, 245; institutionally structured, 113–114; isolation from, 291; and language, 258, 261; motivation of, 140, 144; political, 37–38, 221; and possibility, 237–238; and project, 241; reasons for, 26–30; rules for, 121; social, 255; spontaneous, 279; and the subject, 213, 217; and thought, 26, 36, 162;

traditional, 26; and underlying disposition, 50–51, 182; warrant for action, 169–171, 264

activity, 68, 71; everyday, 81–82, 238; meaningful, 294; practical, 30–31, 33; repressed, 289

advice, 49–50, 115, 117–120, 162, 246, 257, 295

affirmation, 194, 201, 278–280; resulting from rational comprehension of universal disappointment, 278; of self, 210–211; of society, 202; unconditional, 183; universal, 194, 278

afterlife, 21, 52, 55–57, 60, 91, 207

agreement, 54, 59, 61, 70, 134, 136, 147

alienation, 213, 217–219

anthropology, philosophical, 143–144, 151, 153, 254

anxiety, 226, 233–234, 239–242. *See also* fear

325

argumentation, 39, 48, 64, 116, 132–133, 171; dialectical, 53–54, 56–57, 164, 178; local form of, 171

art, 161, 164, 165, 172, 224; before and after, 294; and religion, 161, 164, 172

artificiality, 63, 126, 129, 141, 143, 150, 154, 288

atheism, 76, 81, 84–85, 89–90, 114, 232

authenticity, 191–192, 194, 204, 226, 228, 246

authority, 49–50, 117, 132–133, 168–169, 243; local, 171

being, 230; as dependent on time, 244; forgetfulness of, 231; history of, 247, 255; question of, 226, 231–233, 237, 240, 242, 244; understanding of, 240

being-in-the-world, 226, 237

belief: fixity of, 252; religious, 2, 216; self-reinforcing, 216–217, 234; valued more than life itself, 127, 152–153, 156. *See also* opinion

best, things are for the, 25, 38–39, 40, 47, 63, 66, 87, 128

capitalism, 157, 208–209, 221, 282

care, 40, 239–240, 245; relief from, 31

catastrophe: ecological, 292, 301; our world as constant, 286–288

categories, 162–165, 168; metaphysical, 229; reduction to, 196. *See also* metaphysics

certainty/uncertainty, 19–21, 61, 75, 119–120, 128, 144, 188

change: absence of, 112, 114; of human nature, 106; impossibility of, 208, 248; one's life, 294; of philosophical doctrine, 192, 250–257, 271; as

philosophical goal, 298; possibility of real, 114; prevented, 290–291; of properties, 175, 178; of self, 91, 213; social, 202, 220–221, 285; the world, 180, 298; world, self, and individual judgment as subject to, 122–123

character, 117–118, 196

choice: after death, 60; between types of life, 56; consumer, 286; economic, 209; free, 105, 238; a matter of, 24, 108; mode of, 243–244; no, 168, 223, 273, 290; rational/irrational, 223–224, 238; real, 142; the right/wrong, 52, 55, 91, 105, 110, 222

clarity, 101, 135–136, 159, 163–164, 174, 256–263, 290

coercion: individual, 146; moral, 136–137; in personal relations, 134; physical, 139–140; and religion, 80, 93; workplace, 218

command, 44, 49–52, 105, 117, 140, 154, 234, 295

common sense, 158, 160, 184, 249

competition, 154–155; economic, 209–213

concept(s) and categories, 162–169; appropriate, 107; different, 131–132, 231–236, 300; formation of, 101–102; invention of, 241–243; as mummies, 188–190; non-identity with particular, 280; origin of, 203; philosophical, 219; possibility of unitary, 54–55; as self-moving, 173–174; as 'sticky', 130; universal flux of philosophical, 169; used to grasp a historical epoch, 157, 161–162; as useless for God, 196; weight-bearing, 132

concern, 40, 238, 245

confidence, 148. *See also* diffidence

conscience: individual, 166, 223; religious, 2; social, 282

consciousness, 175–176; class, 220; forms of, 211, 213, 218–219

consensus, 70, 128, 134

consent, 136, 142–143, 148–149, 238

consistency, 7, 29, 32, 123, 125; historical dimension, 167; not viable human ideal, 123, 193

consolation, 88, 167–168

context: of action, 26, 211, 238; of desire and belief, 28; as determining meaning, 70, 124; of enquiry, 185–187; historical, 202–203, 213; and judgment, 67, 77; and language, 260–268; local, 145, 168–172; and objectivity, 68; of the problem, 206; and rules, 121; social, 280–281; and understanding, 236; variability of, 5–11, 54–55

convergence, 54, 178

conversion, 252–253

criticism: literary, 224; negative, 289, 291; social, 277, 285; subversion of, 201–202. *See also* religion: criticism of; self-criticism

culture (high), 161, 163, 224, 228; absence of, 276, 301

custom, 38, 126–131, 135, 153. *See also* nature

death: attempt to escape, 1–5, 10–12; the end of everything, 73, 91, 300; evaluating, 20–21; fear of, 39, 50, 52, 74, 75, 91, 144, 239; illusion about, 112; preferable to change of belief, 152–153; present stroke of, 142, 152, 298; and the soul, 55–57; as a way of being-in-the-world, 146, 239–244

decision, 25–27, 60, 122, 232, 289; difficult, 162; individual, 245; and meaning, 263; and rationality, 224. *See also* choice

definition, 164, 187–189, 207, 264

desire, 28, 61–63, 101, 111, 147–148, 204; ability to modify one's own desires as sign of being a subject, 213–214; of collective subject, 211; and duty, 204–205, 207–208, 219; false, 282, 288; and the good, 144, 152; opacity to others, 144, 146; as opposed to merely tolerating or enduring, 219; real, 288–289; reasonable and unreasonable, 111; satisfaction of, 60, 111–112, 287; shared, 211–212, 218; to be 'sublated', 280; to live forever, 111–113; vital, fundamental, 206–207

dialectics, 32, 36–43, 52–70, 158–165, 173, 178, 280, 289

diffidence, 148–151

disagreement, 14–16, 178, 288, 295

disappointment transformed by rational comprehension into affirmation, 278

discipline, 128–129

discussion, 51–54, 98, 158–159; idealised, 164–165, 173, 178–179; proper philosophic, 174

dominion, 141–143, 149

doubt, 118, 135, 225, 280; philosophical, 20

duty, 204–205, 207–208, 218

ecology, 249, 301. *See also* catastrophe: ecological

*s'entendre*, 133–137

environment, 53, 246, 249

epistemic opacity, 144–147, 150, 156

equality, 144, 146–147, 149–152

erotics, 48, 105, 297

ethics and action, 9; as addressed to someone, 222, 246; and biology, 246; detached from intelligence, 290; focus of, 56; as goal, 79; and the good life, 119–121; irrelevance of, 206; of letting be, 249; of masters and slaves, 195; and metaphysics, 228, 246; and other parts of philosophy, 75–76; of political choice, 222–223; role of gods in, 91; social, 83; as transcendental, 270–271; of truth, 189–191; universal, 136; Western, 193

excellence, 30–31, 33–35, 40, 46, 52, 60, 62; variety of, 124–125

experience, 133, 229; immediate/direct, 14–25, 99, 277, 281; individual, 255, 277; negative (as origin of philosophy and religion), 298; subjective, 280

explanation: as condition of knowledge, 39; good/best, 76, 86; materialist, 91–92; must stop at some point, 259; naturalistic, 41; of previous philosophical theories, 163; reasoned, 46

facts: as changeable, 250–251; historical, 105; individual, 162, 218–219; and meaning, 260–265; positivist conception of, 284–285; quasi-empirical, 29; sense for the, 187; versus interpretations, 184–187, 257; world of, 255, 265

failure (philosophically significant), 87, 165, 169, 199, 239, 298

fanaticism, 80, 153, 156

fascism, 247, 291

fear, 76, 86, 150; as origin of belief in gods, 85; as rational, 145; of the use of force, 140–143. *See also* death: fear of; gods/God: fear of

fetishism, 213, 215–216, 219

fixity and fluidity, 36, 117, 169, 178–179, 251–252, 262, 266, 269

folly/fool, 13–14, 32–33, 36, 128, 228

form of life, 262–263

freedom, 66, 142, 164–167, 204, 206–207; freedom of movement, 125; full, 210–211, 221

futility as infinite, 300

games, 1–12, 48. *See also* language-game

gods/God, 71–92, 170–171, 295; fear of, 75, 91; as good, 78, 87; indifferent to human affairs, 75, 80, 88, 91; knowledge/love of, 103–106; language inapplicable to, 230; only source of salvation, 243; origin of belief in, 85–88; real and unreal, 111; who reward, 207

good: the common, 7, 47, 146, 156, 209–212; different types of, 31; distinct from satisfying, 13–14, 186; diversity versus singularity of, 54, 58, 66–70, 144; and happiness, 66–67; highest social, 210; human, 30, 39; idea of the, 51–53, 58, 70, 159–160, 178, 239; judgment of, 109, 144–145; knowledge of the, 21, 33, 35, 40, 49–50, 70, 91; as lacking determinate content, 144; morally, 109; objective, 68–70; as object of individual desire, 144; as potentially in conflict with self-preservation, 152–153; the practical, 8; as property of an activity, 19, 33, 126–127; as property of imagined state, 286; as property of pre-existing objects,

170–171; as property of results of an activity, 30, 33, 35; as property of someone who performs an activity, 18, 33; pursuit of seeming, 144; sobriety as, 296; social definition of, 147–148. *See also* excellence; life: good (better, best)
good *as*, 67
good *at*, 31, 48, 71
good *for*, 53, 67–70, 147, 155, 186
guilt, 222–223, 226

happiness, 52, 58–60, 66, 69–70, 111–112, 297; conjoined to morality, 74; derived from understanding that our world is a catastrophe, 288
hatred, 182, 194. *See also* love
hermeneutic circle, 235–236
hero/heroism, 56, 100–101, 223
history: basic agent of, 255; as condition of possibility of experience, 281; essential, 113; happy eras as blank pages, 297; human attempt to understand, 163–168; philosophy as response to, 96–109; and the present, 279; real, 247; as story of decline, 228; and time, 247; traditional philosophy's neglect of, 188–189
hope, 39, 50, 76, 252
human being: as configuration of love, 102; as constituted by projects, 237–238; as only potentially an individual, 246; Roman difficulty in defining, 166

illusion, 9, 84–85, 88, 112, 159, 172, 198–199, 207–208, 216, 244, 260, 300
image (*Bild*), 100–101, 255, 257, 266–268, 285

imagination, 9–10, 22, 26, 56, 85–86, 97, 238–239
inadequacy, human, 87–88, 298
indeterminacy, 42–43, 256–263; made determinate, 258–259, 264–265, 290
individual: becoming or being born as, 246; elevation to universality, 279; human, 51, 57, 82, 113, 143, 149–150, 254; isolated versus socialised, 151; oppression by the universal, 279
initiative, 218
institutions, 113–114, 131, 170, 178, 277, 280; political, 165
interests, 140, 184; deepest human, 294–296
interpretation, 94, 147–148, 184–187, 226, 257–259
introspection, 103, 176, 181–183, 191
invention, 11–12, 38, 48, 85, 132, 145; of the concept, 241–243
invisible hand, 209–211, 217

judgment, 22–23, 27, 67–70, 133–136, 154–156, 166, 187; fallibility, 135–136; individual, 58, 60, 121–122, 223; opacity to others, 144–145; variability of, 123, 144
justification, as philosophically marginal concept, 168–170; local, 168–169, 173, 179–180, 264

knowledge: and advice, 162; critical potential of, 201; and doing, 32–33, 39, 237; how acquired, 13–26; of how to go on, 268–269; indispensable for politics, 65; and judgment, 136; keeps society functioning, 200; located in institutions, 178, 221–222; and love of God, 101–107; negative,

knowledge (*continued*)
291; non-verbalised, 149; and
opinion, 18–20; of the other, 51, 89,
144–148; and power, 66, 206, 214;
and projects, 238; propositional, 18,
22, 35, 118–119, 131, 134, 174,
178–179, 254–255; requires
definition, 188–189; role of
philosophical, 221; socioeconomic
limits on shared, 212; as source of
philosopher's authority, 116–119;
surviving death, 56–57; three
traditional types of, 17–18, 22; and
understanding, 157; value of,
189–190; of what one is doing,
30–49. *See also* self-knowledge

language, 16–17, 102, 131, 176–178,
230–231, 233; as form of social
action, 255–265; indeterminateness
of, 256; ordinary/everyday, 242,
249; as picture of the world, 255
language-game, 260–264, 266, 268
law, 37–38, 126, 135, 168, 200, 209;
best society lacks, 46; and its
interpretation, 148; nature has none,
120, 128
letting-go/letting-be, 125–126, 245,
249
life, 11, 22; as an activity, 30–31;
affirmers and deniers of, 194;
biological, 50, 57, 62, 67–68, 71;
coherence of, 29; different general
kinds or types of, 25–26, 29–30;
eternal, 111; everyday, 83, 267, 270,
289; good (better, best), 21, 30, 35,
46, 48, 66, 120, 182, 191, 295; how
to analyse, 133; like a game, 11; must
be considered as a whole, 24–29,
31–32, 56; must be examined, 31–36;

as necessarily incomplete, 239; not
under one's own control, 104; religion
as way of giving structure to, 183;
role of history in, 102; satisfactory,
13–14, 21–25, 59; unity of, 26, 29,
40–41, 224
live, how to, 30–40, 54, 132, 196,
233–234, 237–238, 243, 286
living, human, 67–68, 76; with other
people, 130
logic, 29, 112, 125, 146, 163, 254; as
supergame, 262
love, 101–109, 143, 177, 182–183;
possible objects of, 108–109, 111,
113; real, 108–109; universal, 183

market, 131, 170, 217, 219
martyrdom, 156
mask, 47–48, 191–193
masters, 143, 194–195
meaning, 94, 161, 165, 188, 218; of
historic events, 96–97; linguistic,
256, 263, 266; and social practices,
256, 257, 264; theory of, 161
meaningfulness, 163, 178, 278
metaphysics, 126, 175, 207, 226, 229,
232, 254; of facts, 255
mistrust: as an achievement, 149;
rationality of, 146
monotheism, 78, 86, 87, 88–89,
104–105, 108, 153, 232
morality, 69–70, 75, 77, 117, 162;
common, 83–84; conjoined to
happiness, 74; non-coercive, 90; no
pure master morality or slave
morality possible, 195; received
(religious), 81, 83–84, 88–90
motivation, 30–31, 140–141, 145,
147–148, 152, 180, 190; ethical, 75,
79, 109–110; wrong, 110

myth, 41, 48, 52, 55–56, 60, 75, 97, 106, 116, 120, 158, 163, 296

nature, 151; following or living according to, 125, 141; human, 99, 105–106, 114, 146; lacks laws, 120, 126, 128; not to be contrasted with custom, 125–135
need, 61–63, 148, 161, 184, 200–201, 260; genuine, 63; historical variability, 62–63; practical, 161–162; real, 61; social, 62; speculative, 161–162
negativism, universal, 289–290
negativity, 285–286. *See also* criticism: negative
non-individualism, 113–114, 173–175
normativity, 126–127, 130, 168, 171, 173, 177

objective, 14, 58–60, 68–70, 154–155, 174, 198, 218, 220. *See also* subjective/objective
objects and subjects, 213–218, 220–222; and understanding, 242–243. *See also* reification
opinion, 132; consistency an accident, 123; to die for, 152; difference of, 14; distinguished from 'truth', 184; fleeting or substantial, 152; giving an account of one's opinions (*see* account, giving an; knowledge: and opinion)
oppression, 279, 291
optimism, 299
orientation, 83, 97, 116, 126, 195, 218, 238, 271; derived from poetry, 255; lack of, 2, 7
origins, 182–183, 228, 247

peace, 82, 141, 143, 153, 172–173; peace of mind, 91, 97
philosopher: has no final opinions, 193; invention of term, 296–297; roles of, 118, 169, 267
philosopher-kings, 46–49, 52, 56, 70, 117, 160, 189; one or many, 65–66
philosophizing, three great established modes of, 254–255
philosophy: before and after, 295; cognitive content of, 205; as conceptual analysis of the human situation, 254; connection with periods of distress and failure, 205, 221, 285, 297–298; connection with the world, 250; as constructing new conceptual tools, 11; dispensible, 301; as essentially reenactment, 297; as extension of science, 254; as form of spirit, 161; invention of term, 296–297; as its time grasped in concept, 157, 161; and justification, 173; literary forms of, 73–74, 197–198, 265; as non-autonomous, 200, 203, 205; origins of, 116, 298–299; as a path, 248; positive role, 220; as social criticism, 285; and society, 200–205; as supergame, 262; tasks of, 98–99, 161–162, 266–267; as therapy, 267–268; as unitary configuration, 295
picture. *See* image
plans, divine, 71, 72, 80, 87; for unitary action, 211
politics, 37–38, 47, 141, 172, 177, 244, 283
possibilities, 170–171, 237–238
power(s), 102, 122, 133, 143, 147, 177; active social, 215–216; collective human, 287; exercise and development

power(s) (*continued*)
of, 210–211; falsely attributed to
objects, 215–218; increase of human,
140; overwhelming, 145, 154; pursuit
of, 144; and reputation, 154–156
practices, 133; collective, 82–83; cultic,
80; religious, 79, 82, 88; social, 256,
269; traditional, 8–9. *See also* society
principles, 121–122; best life lacks,
128; universal, 125
problem: conceptual, 207; the great
unsolved problem of modern times,
278; life, 233; philosophical, 204,
205, 219, 267–268, 272, 287;
practical, 162, 206, 257
problems and solutions, 122, 206–207,
233–234; linguistic or social, 269–270
profundity, 191, 193–194
progress, 7, 158–159, 165, 182, 228,
275, 285, 298
projects, 237–239
properties, 188, 230, 237
proposition, 260–265. *See also*
knowledge: propositional
psychology, 194; individual, 113–114,
173–177, 182
puzzles, philosophical, 207, 208, 219,
300–301

questions: ability to respond to, 36, 46;
changing the, 5; how they arise,
203–204; ignoring, 33, 116; merely
asking, 49, 115–116; philosophical,
268–269, 298; shifting, 302;
undermining assumption of,
187–188; without answers, 122

rationality, 120, 145–146, 159,
164–165, 174, 176; all forms
encompassed in system, 278–280

reason, 100–102, 110, 127–128, 146,
150, 166, 174, 204; appeal to, 64;
gives itself its own laws, 166; lacks
authority, 119; motivational force of,
74, 100; not a subjective faculty, 166,
227; as power, 106; power of, 167;
rejection of, 247; as supreme, 37; as
a whore, 228
reasons, 15, 26–28, 44, 53–55, 110,
127, 138
reconciliation, 172–173, 278, 281
reflection, 32, 56, 98, 122, 129, 228;
philosophic, 51, 166, 203, 253
reification, 213–216, 219
religion, 75–93, 181, 204, 227, 232,
271; criticism of, 76–79; not a set of
propositions, 183; three strands of,
81–85; traditional, 295; true,
109–110. *See also* monotheism
reproduction, social, 200–202, 219
resistance, 115–116, 140, 147, 289
rules, 2–11, 47–48, 119, 121, 127–128;
misplaced fixity, 168–169; stupidity
of following, 128; of thumb, 121,
125; universal (moral), non-existence
of, 120–122; usefulness of,
120–122

salvation, 283. *See also* soul: salvation of
scepticism, 118–120, 149, 278
science, 144, 184, 254, 301; as
contributing to society, 200–201;
distinguished from philosophy, 1;
natural, 190, 247, 249, 284
self, better, 177–178; real, 191, 205
self-affirmation in action, 210–211
self-criticism, 253; of society, 200–203
self-knowledge, 40–45, 100–106,
123–125, 132–133, 159, 177, 295;
social dimension of, 134

self-love, 103–105, 108, 180, 201
self-preservation, 144, 147, 151–153
sin, 103, 105–106, 232
slave-holding society, no philosophic
truth attainable in, 165–167, 179
slavery, 66, 142–143; contemporary
condemnation of, 171–172; not
theoretical issue, 206–207
slaves: ancient contrast with free men,
204; and masters, 194–195
slave trade, 279, 280
society, 28, 46–47, 51, 61, 154; civil,
156; and reason, 166; self-
justification of, 201
soul, 284; care of, 40; harmony/order
of, 51–52, 56, 60, 91, 106; as inner
state, 51, 58; salvation of, 113,
272–273; survival of, 57; tranquillity
of, 125; unity of, 40–42, 50–51, 192
sovereign, 143, 145, 147, 153–154,
258
speculation, 169, 180, 204, 242;
contrasted with knowledge, 184
spirit, 174–179, 271–273, 281, 290;
absence of, 276
state, the, 141, 146, 149–150;
rationality (and artificiality) of, 141,
143, 150
state of nature, 146, 147, 151, 153
subject, 175–176, 213–214; cognitive,
254; collective, 211; genesis of, 246;
nature of, 222, 288; and objects, 213,
221–222; self-transformation of,
213–214; unitary, 43, 221, 224–225
subjective/objective, 14, 58–60,
154–156, 174, 179
subjectivity, 95, 175–176, 218
submission to will of others, 139, 152;
by consent, 143; by force, 142–143;
by nature, 141–142

supergame, 10, 262–263
survival as human goal, 31; of societies,
200, 216, 223
system, 121, 174, 179, 196–197, 220,
265, 278; of philosophy, 158, 160,
265

teleology, 179, 201; natural, 71, 74, 80,
127, 131
theodicy, 168, 170, 172
theology, 10, 27, 80, 84–90, 108, 232;
negative, 227–228, 229–230; as
supergame, 262
thinker, types of, 270–271
thought as self-moving, 173–174, 179;
correct, 254; as perhaps futile, 288
totality, 164, 169, 219–220, 239; false,
282
transcendence, 90, 153, 229–230,
270–271
trust, 45, 145, 148–150
truth, 181, 183–194, 198, 221; final,
179; as having a temporal index,
185, 283–285; positivist conception
of, 284; power of, 166; and practice,
233–237, 243, 268–269; purportedly eternal, 117; as source of
authority, 46; theoretical and
historical, 106; understanding,
96–97, 109, 133, 139, 162; visibility
of, 163

unity of explanation, 86; of collective
subject, 211; of my projects, 239; of
subject and object, 213
utopia, 286

virtue, 30–31, 58, 60, 94, 109–110,
195, 245, 262; Christian, 84. See also
excellence

war, civil, 141, 153, 222–223
we, 160, 221, 262; a we that is an I and
  an I that is a we, 176
what is and what could be, discrepancy
  between, 287
will, the, 184, 192
wisdom, 30, 44, 46, 100, 228
world: affirmation of, 280; basic truth
  about, 74–76; changing views of,
  159–161; as composed of facts, 255,

265; external, 175, 179, 204; human,
146, 200; knowledge of the,
118–123; making sense of, 86;
natural, 189; no sharp picture of,
257; as *saeculum*, 238; social,
206–207, 219, 221–224, 281; subject
has a perspective on the, 213–214,
218; truth as structural property of,
284; as a whole, 72, 161–170, 173,
179, 196, 229–230, 240–242, 267